# Journal of a West Indian Proprietor, kept during a residence in Jamaica.

## M. G. Lewis

*Journal of a West Indian Proprietor, kept during a residence in ... Jamaica.*
Lewis, M. G.
British Library, Historical Print Editions
British Library
1834
8º.
1050.l.17.

## The BiblioLife Network

This project was made possible in part by the BiblioLife Network (BLN), a project aimed at addressing some of the huge challenges facing book preservationists around the world. The BLN includes libraries, library networks, archives, subject matter experts, online communities and library service providers. We believe every book ever published should be available as a high-quality print reproduction; printed on- demand anywhere in the world. This insures the ongoing accessibility of the content and helps generate sustainable revenue for the libraries and organizations that work to preserve these important materials.

The following book is in the "public domain" and represents an authentic reproduction of the text as printed by the original publisher. While we have attempted to accurately maintain the integrity of the original work, there are sometimes problems with the original book or micro-film from which the books were digitized. This can result in minor errors in reproduction. Possible imperfections include missing and blurred pages, poor pictures, markings and other reproduction issues beyond our control. Because this work is culturally important, we have made it available as part of our commitment to protecting, preserving, and promoting the world's literature.

## GUIDE TO FOLD-OUTS, MAPS and OVERSIZED IMAGES

In an online database, page images do not need to conform to the size restrictions found in a printed book. When converting these images back into a printed bound book, the page sizes are standardized in ways that maintain the detail of the original. For large images, such as fold-out maps, the original page image is split into two or more pages.

Guidelines used to determine the split of oversize pages:

• Some images are split vertically; large images require vertical and horizontal splits.
• For horizontal splits, the content is split left to right.
• For vertical splits, the content is split from top to bottom.
• For both vertical and horizontal splits, the image is processed from top left to bottom right.

# JOURNAL

### OF A

## WEST INDIA PROPRIETOR.

LONDON:
Printed by A. SPOTTISWOODE,
New-Street-Square.

# JOURNAL

## OF A

## WEST INDIA PROPRIETOR,

KEPT DURING A RESIDENCE IN THE ISLAND OF

## JAMAICA.

BY THE LATE

## MATTHEW GREGORY LEWIS, ESQ. M.P.

AUTHOR OF

"THE MONK," "THE CASTLE SPECTRE,"
"TALES OF WONDER," &c.

" I would give many a sugar cane,
Mat. Lewis were alive again!"
BYRON.

LONDON:

JOHN MURRAY, ALBEMARLE STREET.

MDCCCXXXIV.

## ADVERTISEMENT.

THE following Journals of two residences in Jamaica, in 1815–16, and in 1817, are now printed from the MS. of Mr. Lewis; who died at sea, on the voyage homewards from the West Indies, in the year 1818.

# JOURNAL

OF A

# WEST INDIA PROPRIETOR.

" Nunc alio patriam quæro sub sole jacentem."—Virgil.

## 1815.   November 8. (Wednesday.)

I left London, and reached Gravesend at nine in the morning, having been taught to expect our sailing in a few hours.   But although the vessel left the Docks on Saturday, she did not reach this place till three o'clock on Thursday, the 9th.   The captain now tells me, that we may expect to sail certainly in the afternoon of to-morrow, the 10th.   I expect the ship's cabin to gain greatly by my two days' residence at the " ***** ****," which nothing can exceed for noise, dirt, and dulness.   Eloisa would never have established " black melancholy" at the Paraclete as its favourite residence, if she had happened to pass three days at an inn at Gravesend : nowhere else did I ever see the sky look so dingy, and the river so dirty; to be sure, the place has all the advantages of an English November to assist it in those particulars. Just now, too, a carriage passed my windows, conveying on board a cargo of passengers, who seemed sincerely afflicted at the thoughts of leaving their dear native land! The pigs squeaked, the ducks quacked, and the fowls screamed; and all so dolefully, as clearly to prove, that *theirs* was no dissembled sorrow? And after them (more affecting than all) came a wheelbarrow, with a solitary porker tied in a basket, with his head hanging over on one side, and his legs sticking out on the other, who neither grunted nor moved, nor gave any signs of life, but seemed to be of quite the same opinion with Hannah More's heroine,

" Grief is for *little* wrongs; despair for mine !"

As Miss O'Neil is to play "Elwina" for the first time to-morrow, it is a thousand pities that she had not the previous advantage of seeing the speechless despondency of this poor pig; it might have furnished her with some valuable hints, and enabled her to convey more perfectly to the audience the " expressive silence " of irremediable distress.

## November 10.

At four o'clock in the afternoon, I embarked on board the " Sir Godfrey Webster," Captain Boyes. On approaching the vessel, we heard the loudest of all possible shrieks proceeding from a boat lying near her: and who should prove to be the complainant, but my former acquaintance, the despairing pig. He had recovered his voice to protest against entering the ship: I had already declared against climbing up the accommodation ladder; the pig had precisely the very same objection. So a *soi-disant* chair, being a broken bucket, was let down for us, and the pig and myself entered the vessel by the same conveyance; only pig had the precedence, and was hoisted up first. The ship proceeded three miles, and then the darkness obliged us to come to an anchor. There are only two other cabin passengers, a Mr. J———— and a Mr. S————; the latter is a planter in the "May-Day Mountains," Jamaica: he wonders, considering how much benefit Great Britain derives from the West Indies, that government is not careful to build more churches in them, and is of opinion, that "hedicating the negroes is the only way to make them appy; indeed, in his umble hopinion, hedication his hall in hall!"

### NOVEMBER 11.

We sailed at six o'clock, passed through "Nob's Hole," the "Girdler's Hole," and "the Pan" (all very dangerous sands, and particularly the last, where at times we had only one foot water below us), by half past four, and at five came to an anchor in the Queen's Channel. Never having seen any thing of the kind before, I was wonderfully pleased with the manœuvring of several large ships, which passed through the sands at the same time with us: their motions seemed to be effected with as much ease and dexterity as if they had been crane-necked carriages; and the effect as they pursued each other's track and windings was perfectly beautiful.

### NOVEMBER 12. (Sunday.)

The wind was contrary, and we had to beat up the whole way; we did not reach the Downs till past four o'clock, and, as there were above sixty vessels arrived before us, we had some difficulty in finding a safe berth. At length we anchored in the Lower Roads, about four miles off Deal. We can see very clearly the double lights in the vessel moored off the Goodwin sands: it is constantly inhabited by two families, who reside there alternately every fortnight, except when the weather delays the exchange. The " Sir Godfrey Webster " is a vessel of 600 tons, and was formerly in the East India service. I have a very clean cabin, a place for my books, and every thing is much more comfortable than I expected; the wind, however, is completely west, the worst that we could have, and we must not even expect a change till the full moon. The captain pointed out a man to me to-day, who had been with him in a violent storm off the Bermudas. For six hours together, the flashes of lightning were so unintermitting, that

the eye could not sustain them: at one time, the
ship seemed to be completely in a blaze; and the
man in question (who was then standing at the
wheel, near the captain) suddenly cried out, "I
don't know what has happened to me, but I can
neither see nor stand;" and he fell down upon the
deck. He was taken up and carried below; and
it appeared that the lightning had affected his eyes
and legs, in a degree to make him both blind and
lame, though the captain, who was standing by
his side, had received no injury: in three or four
days, the man was quite well again. In this storm,
no less than thirteen vessels were dismasted, or
otherwise shattered by the lightning.

Sea Terms. — *Windward, from* whence the
wind blows; *leeward, to* which it blows; *starboard,*
the *right* of the stern; *larboard,* the *left; starboard helm,* when you go to the left; but when to
the right, instead of larboard helm, *helm a-port;
luff you may,* go nearer to the wind; *theis* (*thus*)
you are near enough; *luff no near,* you are too near
the wind; the *tiller,* the handle of the rudder; the
*capstan,* the weigher of the anchor; the *buntlines,*
the ropes which move the body of the sail, the
*bunt* being the body; the *bowlines,* those which
spread out the sails, and make them swell.

## November 13.

At six this morning, came on a tremendous
gale of wind; the captain says, that he never

experienced a heavier. However, we rode it out with great success, although, at one time, it was bawled out that we were driving; and, at another, a brig which lay near us broke from her moorings, and came bearing down close upon us. The danger, indeed, from the difference of size, was all upon the side of the brig; but, luckily, the vessels cleared each other. This evening she has thought it as well to remove further from so dangerous a neighbourhood. There is a little cabin boy on board, and Mr. J———— has brought with him a black terrier; and these two at first sight swore to each other an eternal friendship, in the true German style. It is the boy's first voyage, and he is excessively sea-sick; so he has been obliged to creep into his hammock, and his friend, the little black terrier, has crept into the hammock with him. A boat came from the shore this evening, and reported that several vessels have been dismasted, lost their anchors, and injured in various ways. A brig, which was obliged to make for Ramsgate, missed the pier, and was dashed to pieces completely; the crew, however, were saved, all except the pilot; who, although he was brought on shore alive, what between bruises, drowning, and fright, had suffered so much, that he died two hours afterwards. The weather has now again become calm; but it is still full west.

## NOVEMBER 14. (Tuesday.)

### THE HOURS.

Ne'er were the zephyrs known disclosing
　　More sweets, than when in Tempe's shades
They waved the lilies, where, reposing,
　　Sat four and twenty lovely maids.

Those lovely maids were called " the Hours,"
　　The charge of Virtue's flock they kept;
And each in turn employ'd her powers
　　To guard it, while her sisters slept.

False Love, how simple souls thou cheatest!
　　In myrtle bower, that traitor near
Long watch'd an Hour, the softest, sweetest!
　　The *evening* Hour, to shepherds dear.*

In tones so bland he praised her beauty,
　　Such melting airs his pipe could play,
The thoughtless Hour forgot her duty,
　　And fled in Love's embrace away.

Meanwhile the fold was left unguarded—
　　The wolf broke in—the lambs were slain:
And now from Virtue's train discarded,
　　With tears her sisters speak their pain.

Time flies, and still they weep; for never
　　The fugitive can time restore:
An Hour once fled, has fled for ever,
　　And all the rest shall smile no more!

* L'heure du berger.

B 4

## November 15.

The wind altered sufficiently to allow us to escape from the <u>Downs</u>; and at dusk we were off <u>Beachy Head</u>. This morning, the steward left the trap-door of the store-hole open; of course, I immediately contrived to step into it, and was on the point of being precipitated to the bottom, among innumerable boxes of grocery, bags of biscuit, and porter barrels; — where a broken limb was the *least* that I could expect. Luckily, I fell across the corner of the trap, and managed to support myself, till I could effect my escape with a bruised knee, and the loss of a few inches of skin from my left arm.

## November 16.

Off the <u>Isle of Wight.</u>

## November 17.

Off the <u>St. Alban's Head</u>. <u>Sick to death</u>! My temples throbbing, my head burning, my limbs freezing, my mouth all fever, my stomach all nausea, my mind all disgust.

## November 18.

Off the <u>Lizard</u>, the last <u>point of England</u>.

## November 19. (Sunday.)

At one this morning, a violent gust of wind came on; and, at the rate of ten miles an hour, carried us through the Chops of the Channel, formed by the Scilly Rocks and the Isle of Ushant. But I thought, that the advance was dearly purchased by the terrible night which the storm made us pass. The wind roaring, the waves dashing against the stern, till at last they beat in the quarter gallery; the ship, too, rolling from side to side, as if every moment she were going to roll over and over! Mr. J——— was heaved off one of the sofas, and rolled along, till he was stopped by the table. He then took his seat upon the floor, as the more secure position; and, half an hour afterwards, another heave chucked him back again upon the sofa. The captain snuffed out one of the candles, and both being tied to the table, could not relight it with the other: so the steward came to do it; when a sudden heel of the ship made him extinguish the second candle, tumbled him upon the sofa on which I was lying, and made the candle which he had brought with him fly out of the candlestick, through a cabin window at his elbow; and thus we were all left in the dark. Then the intolerable noise! the cracking of bulkheads! the sawing of ropes! the screeching of the tiller! the trampling of the sailors! the clattering of the crockery! Every thing above deck and below deck, all in motion at once! Chairs, writing-desks, books, boxes, bundles, fire-irons and fenders, flying to one end of the room; and the next moment (as if they had made a mistake) flying back

again to the other with the same hurry and confusion! " Confusion worse confounded!" Of all
the inconveniences attached to a vessel, the incessant noise appears to me the most insupportable!
As to our live stock, they seem to have made up
their minds on the subject, and say with one of
Ariosto's knights (when he was cloven from the
head to the chine), "*or convien morire.*" Our fowls
and ducks are screaming and quacking their last
by dozens; and by Tuesday morning, it is supposed
that we shall not have an animal alive in the ship,
except the black terrier—and my friend the squeaking pig, whose vocal powers are still audible,
maugre the storm and the sailors, and who (I
verily believe) only continues to survive out of
spite, because he can join in the general chorus,
and help to increase the number of abominable
sounds.

We are now tossing about in the Bay of Biscay:
I shall remember it as long as I live. The
" beef-eater's front" could never have " beamed
more terrible " upon Don Ferolo Whiskerandos,
" in Biscay's Bay, when he took him prisoner,"
than Biscay's Bay itself will appear to *me* the next
time that I approach it.

### November 20.

Our live stock has received an increase; our
fowls and ducks are dead to be sure, but a lark
flew on board this morning, blown (as is supposed)

from the coast of France. In five minutes it
appeared to be quite at home, eat very readily
whatever was given it, and hopped about the
deck without fear of the sailors, or the more formidable black terrier, with all the ease and assurance imaginable.

I dare say, it *was* blown from the coast of
France!

### NOVEMBER 21.

The weather continues intolerable. Boisterous
waves running mountains high, with no wind, or a
foul one. Dead calms by day, which prevent our
making any progress; and violent storms by night,
which prevent our getting any sleep.

Every thing is in a state of perpetual motion. " *Nulla quies intus* (nor *outus* indeed for
the matter of that), *nulláque silentia parte.*" We
drink our tea exactly as Tantalus did in the infernal regions; we keep bobbing at the basin for half
an hour together without being able to get a drop;
and certainly nobody on ship-board can doubt the
truth of the proverb, " Many things fall out between
the cup and the lip."

### NOVEMBER 23.

#### PANDORA'S BOX.    (*Iliad* Λ.)

Prometheus once (in Tooke the tale you'll see)
  In one vast box enclosed all human evils;
But curious Woman needs the inside would see,
  And out came twenty thousand million devils.

The story's spoil'd, and Tooke should well be chid;
    The fact, sir, happen'd thus, and I've no doubt of it:
'Twas not that Woman raised the coffer's lid,
    But when the lid *was* raised, Woman popp'd out of it.

"But Hope remain'd"— true, sir, she did; but still
    All saw of what Miss Hope gave intimation;
Her right hand grasp'd an undertaker's bill,
    Her left conceal'd a deed of separation.

N. B. I was most horribly sea-sick when I took this view of the subject. Besides, grapes on ship-board, in general, are remarkably sour.

### November 24.

"Manibus date lilia plenis;
    Purpureos spargam flores!"

The squeaking pig was killed this morning.

### November 25.

Letters were sent to England by a small vessel bound for Plymouth, and laden with oranges from St. Michael's, one of the Azores.

### November 26.

A complete and most violent storm, from twelve at night till seven the next morning. The fore-top-sail, though only put up for the first time yesterday, was rent from top to bottom; and several of the other sails are torn to pieces. The

perpetual tempestuous weather which we have experienced has so shaken the planks of the vessel,
that the sea enters at all quarters. About one
o'clock in the morning I was saluted by a stream
of water, which poured down exactly upon my
face, and obliged me to shift my lodgings. The
carpenter had been made aware that there was a
leak in my cabin, and ordered to caulk the seams;
but, I suppose, he thought that during only a two
months' voyage, the rain might very possibly never
find out the hole, and that it would be quite time
enough to apply the remedy when I should have
felt the inconvenience. The best is, that the
carpenter happening to be at work in the next
cabin when the water came down upon me, I
desired him to call my servant, in order that I
might get up, on account of the leak; on which he
told me "that the leak could not be helped;"
grumbled a good deal at calling up the servant;
and seemed to think me not a little unreasonable
for not lying quietly, and suffering myself to be
pumped upon by this shower-bath of his own providing.

But if the water gets *into* the ship, on the
other hand, last night the poor old steward was
very near getting out of it. In the thick of the
storm he was carrying some grog to the mate, when
a gun, which drove against him, threw him off his
balance, and he was just passing through one of the
port-holes, when, luckily, he caught hold of a rope,

and saved himself. A screech-owl flew on board this morning: I am sure we have no need of birds of ill omen; I could supply the place of a whole aviary of them myself.

### NOVEMBER 28.

Reading Don Quixote this morning, I was greatly pleased with an instance of the hero's politeness, which had never struck me before. The Princess Micomicona having fallen into a most egregious blunder, he never so much as hints a suspicion of her not having acted precisely as she has stated, but only begs to know her reasons for taking a step so extraordinary. "But pray, madam," says he, "why *did* your ladyship land at Ossuna, seeing that it is not a seaport town?"

I was also much charmed with an instance of conjugal affection, in the same work. Sancho being just returned home, after a long absence, the first thing which his wife, Teresa, asks about, is the welfare of the ass. "I have brought him back," answers Sancho, "and in much better health and condition than I am in myself." "The Lord be praised," said Teresa, "for this his great mercy to me!"

### NOVEMBER 29.

The wind continues contrary, and the weather is as disagreeable and perverse as it can well be; indeed, I understand that in these latitudes nothing can be expected but heavy gales or dead calms, which makes them particularly pleasant for sailing, especially as the calms are by far the most disagreeable of the two: the wind steadies the ship; but when she creeps as slowly as she does at present (scarcely going a mile in four hours), she feels the whole effect of the sea breaking against her, and rolls backwards and forwards with every billow as it rises and falls. In the mean while, every thing seems to be in a state of the most active motion, except the ship; while we are carrying a spoonful of soup to our mouths, the remainder takes the " glorious golden opportunity" to empty itself into our laps, and the glasses and salt-cellars carry on a perpetual domestic warfare during the whole time of dinner, like the Guelphs and the Ghibellines. Nothing is so common as to see a roast goose suddenly jump out of its dish in the middle of dinner, and make a frisk from one end of the table to the other; and we are quite in the habit of laying wagers which of the two boiled fowls will arrive at the bottom first.

N.B. To-day the fowl without the liver wing was the favourite, but the knowing ones were taken in; the uncarved one carried it hollow.

## November 30.

" Do those I love e 'er think on me ? "
 How oft that painful doubt will start,
To blight the roseate smile of glee,
 And cloud the brow, and sink the heart !

No more can I, estranged from home,
 Their pleasures share, nor soothe their moans ;
To them I 'm dead as were the foam
 Now breaking o'er my whitening bones.

And doubtless now with newer friends,
 The tide of life content they stem ;
Nor on the sailor think, who bends
 Full many an anxious thought on them.

Should that reflection cause me pain ?
 No ease for mine their grief could bring ;
Enough if, when we meet again,
 Their answering hearts to greet me spring.

Enough, if no dull joyless eye
 Give signs of kindness quite forgot ;
Nor heartless question, cold reply,
 Speak —" all is past ; I love you not."

Too much has heav'n ordain'd of woe,
 Too much of groans on earth abounds,
For me to wish one tear to flow
 Which brings no balm for sorrow's wounds.

Love's moisten'd lid and Friendship's sigh,
 I could not see, I could not hear !
To think " they weep !" more fills mine eye,
 And smarts the more each tender tear.

Then, if there be one heart so kind,
 It mourns each hour the loss of me;
Shrinks, when it hears some gust of wind,
 And sighs — " Perhaps a storm at sea!"

Oh! if there be an heart *indeed*,
 Which beats for me, so sad, so true,
Swift to its aid, Oblivion, speed,
 And bathe it with thy poppy's dew;

My form in vapours to conceal,
 From Pleasure's wreath rich odours shake;
Nor let that heart one moment feel
 Such pangs as force my own to ache.

Demon of Memory, cherish'd grief!
 Oh, could I break thy wand in twain!
Oh, could I close thy magic leaf,
 Till those I love are mine again!

## DECEMBER 1. (Friday.)

The captain to-day pointed out to me a sailor-boy, who, about three years ago, was shaken from the mast-head, and fell through the scuttle into the hold: the distance was above eighty feet, yet the boy was taken up with only a few bruises.

## DECEMBER 3. (Sunday.)

The wind during the last two days has been more favourable; and at nine this morning we were in the latitude of Madeira.

## DECEMBER 5.

Sea Terms. — *Ratlines*, the rope ladders by which the sailors climb the shrouds; the *companion*, the

c

cabin-head ; *reefs*, the divisions by which the sails are contracted; *stunsails*, additional sails, spread for the purpose of catching all the wind possible ; the *fore-mast, main-mast, mizen-mast ; fore*, the head ; *aft*, the stern; *being pooped* (the very sound of which tells one, that it must be something very terrible), having the stern beat in by the sea ; *to belay a rope*, to fasten it.

## December 6.

I had no idea of the expense of building and preserving a ship : that in which I am at present cost 30,000*l.* at its outset. Last year the repairs amounted to 14,000*l.* ; and in a voyage to the East Indies they were more than 20,000*l.* In its return last year from Jamaica it was on the very brink of shipwreck. A storm had driven it into Bantry Bay, and there was no other refuge from the winds than Bear Haven, whose entrance was narrow and difficult ; however, a gentleman from Castletown came on board, and very obligingly offered to pilot the ship. He was one of the first people in the place, had been the owner of a vessel himself, was most thoroughly acquainted with every inch of the haven, &c. &c., and so on they went. There was but one sunken rock, and that about ten feet in diameter ; the captain knew it, and warned his gentleman-pilot to keep a little more to the eastward. " My dear friend," answered the Irishman, " now do just make yourself *asy;* I know

well enough what we are about; we are as clear of
the rock as if we were in the Red Sea, by Jasus;"
— upon which the vessel struck upon the rock, and
there she stuck. The captain fell to swearing and
tearing his hair. "God damn you, sir! didn't I tell
you to keep to eastward? Dam'me, she's on the
rock!" "Oh! well, my dear, she's now *on* the
rock, and, in a few minutes, you know, why she'll
be *off* the rock: to be sure, I'd have taken my
oath that the rock was two hundred and fifty feet
on the other side of her, but ——" — "Two hundred and fifty feet! why, the channel is not two
hundred and fifty feet wide itself! and as to getting
her off, bumping against this rock, it can only be
with a great hole in her side."—"Poh! now, bother,
my dear! why sure——"—"Leave the ship, sir;
dam'me, sir, get out of my ship this moment!"
Instead of which, with the most smiling and obliging air in the world, the Irishman turned to console
the female passengers. "Make yourselves *asy*,
ladies, pray make yourselves perfectly *asy;* but,
upon my soul, I believe your captain's mad;
no danger in life! only make yourselves *asy*, I
say; for the ship lies on the rock as safe and as
quiet, by Jasus, as if she were lying on a mud
bank!" Luckily the weather was so perfectly
calm, that the ship having once touched the rock
with her keel bumped no more. It was low water;
she wanted but five inches to float her, and when

the tide rose she drifted off, and with but little harm done. The gentleman-pilot then thought proper to return on shore, took a very polite leave of the lady-passengers, and departed with all the urbanity possible; only thinking the captain the strangest person that he had ever met with; and wondering that any man of common sense could be put out of temper by such a trifle.

## DECEMBER 7.

Yesterday we had the satisfaction of falling in with the trade wind, and now we are proceeding both rapidly and steadily. The change of climate is very perceptible; and the deep and beautiful blue which colours the sea is a certain intimation of our approach to the tropic. A few flying fish have made their appearance; and the spears are getting in order for the reception of their constant attendant, the dolphin. These spears have ropes affixed to them, and at one end of the pole are five barbs, at the other a heavy ball of lead: then, when the fish is speared, the striker lets the staff fall, on which down goes the lead into the sea, and up goes the dolphin into the air, who is in the utmost astonishment to find itself all of a sudden turned into a flying fish; so determines to cultivate the art of flying for the future, and promises itself a great many pleasant airings. The dolphin and the flying fish are beautifully coloured, and both are very good food, particularly the latter,

which move in shoals like the herring, and are
about the size of that fish. They are supposed to
feed on spawn and sea animalculæ, and will not
take the bait; but on the shores of Barbadoes,
which they frequent in great multitudes, they are
caught in wide nets, spread upon the surface of
the sea; then, upon beating the waters around, the
fish rise in clouds, and fly till, their fins getting dry,
they fall down into the nets which have been spread
to receive them. The dolphin is seldom above
three feet long; the immense strength which he
exerts in his struggles for liberty occasions the necessity of catching him in the way before described.

## December 8.

At three o'clock this afternoon we entered the
tropic of Cancer; and if our wind continues tolerably favourable, we may expect to see Antigua
on Sunday se'nnight. On crossing the line, it was
formerly usual for ships to receive a visit from
an old gentleman and his wife, Mr. and Mrs.
Cancer: the husband was, by profession, a bar-
ber; and, probably, the scullion, who insisted so
peremptorily on shaving Sancho, at the duke's
castle, had served an apprenticeship to Mr. Cancer,
for their mode of proceeding was much alike, and,
indeed, very peculiar: the old gentleman always
made a point of using a rusty iron hoop instead of
a razor, tar for soap, and an empty beef-barrel was,
in his opinion, the very best possible substitute for

a basin; in consequence of which, instead of paying him for shaving them, people of taste were
disposed to pay for not being shaved; and as Mrs.
Cancer happened to be particularly partial to gin
(when good), the gift of a few bottles was generally successful in rescuing the donor's chin from
the hands of her husband; however, to-day this
venerable pair " peradventure were sleeping, or
on a journey," for we neither saw nor heard any
thing about them.

### DECEMBER 9.

When, after his victory of the 1st of June, Lord
Howe again put to sea from Portsmouth, the number of women who were turned on shore out of the
ships (wives, sisters, &c.) amounted to above
thirty thousand!

### DECEMBER 10. (Sunday.)

What triumph moves on the billows so blue?
In his car of pellucid pearl I view,
With glorious pomp, on the dancing tide,
The tropic Genius proudly ride.

The flying fish, who trail his car,
Dazzle the eye, as they shine from afar;
Twinkling their fins in the sun, and show
All the hues which adorn the showery bow.

Of dark sea-blue is the mantle he wears;
For a sceptre a plantain branch he bears;
Pearls his sable arms surround,
And his locks of wool with coral are crown'd.

Perpetual sunbeams round him stream;
His bronzed limbs shine with golden gleam;
The spicy spray from his wheels that showers,
Makes the sense ache with its odorous powers.

Myriads of monsters, who people the caves
Of ocean, attendant plough the waves;
Sharks and crocodiles bask in his blaze,
And whales spout the waters which dance in his rays.

And as onward floats that triumph gay,
The light sea-breezes around it play;
While at his royal feet lie bound
The Ouragans, hush'd in sleep profound.

Dark Genius, hear a stranger's prayer,
Nor suffer those winds to ravage and tear
Jamaica's savannas, and loose to fly,
Mingling the earth, and the sea, and the sky.

From thy locks on my harvest of sweets diffuse,
To swell my canes, refreshing dews;
And kindly breathe, with cooling powers,
Through my coffee walks and shaddock bowers.

Let not thy strange diseases prey
On my life; but scare from my couch away
The yellow Plague's imps; and safe let me rest
From that dread black demon, who racks the breast:

Nor force my throbbing temples to know
Thy sunbeam's sudden and maddening blow;
Nor bid thy day-flood blaze too bright
On nerves so fragile, and brain so light:

And let me, returning in safety, view
Thy triumph again on the ocean blue;
And in Britain I'll oft with flowers entwine
The Tropic Sovereign's ebony shrine!

Was it but fancy? did He not frown,
And in anger shake his coral crown?
Gorgeous and slow the pomp moves on!
Low sinks the sun — and all is gone!

" And pray now do you mean to say that you really saw all this fine show?" Oh, yes, really, " in my mind's eye, Horatio," as Shakspeare says; or, if you like it better in Greek —

" Οσσομενος Πατερ' εσθλον ενι φρησιν!"    *Odyssey*, A.

### DECEMBER 11.

A dead centipes was found on the deck, supposed to have made its way on board, during the last voyage, among the logwood. This is not the only species of disagreeable passengers, who are in the habit of introducing themselves into homeward bound vessels without leave. While sleeping on deck last year, the Captain felt something run across his face; and, supposing it to be a cock-roach, he brushed off a scorpion; but not without its first biting him upon the cheek: the pain for about four hours was excessive; but although he did no more than wash the wound with spirits, he was perfectly well again in a couple of days.

### DECEMBER 12.

Since we entered the tropic, the rains have been incessant, and most violent; but the wind was brisk and favourable, and we proceeded rapidly. Now we have lost the trade-wind, and move so slowly, that it might almost be called standing still. On the other hand, the weather is now perfectly delicious; the ship makes but little way, but she moves steadily: the sun is brilliant; the sky cloudless; the sea calm, and so smooth that it looks like one extended sheet of blue glass; an awning is stretched over the deck; although there is not wind enough to fill the canvass, there is sufficient to keep the air cool, and thus, even during the day, the weather is very pleasant; but the nights are quite heavenly, and so bright, that at ten o'clock yesterday evening little Jem Parsons (the cabin boy), and his friend the black terrier, came on deck, and sat themselves down on a gun-carriage, to read by the light of the moon. I looked at the boy's book, (the terrier, I suppose, read over the other's shoulder,) and found that it was " The Sorrows of Werter." I asked who had lent him such a book, and whether it amused him? He said that it had been made a present to him, and so he had read it almost through, for he had got to Werter's dying; though, to be sure, he did not understand it all, nor like very much what he understood; for he thought the man a great fool for killing himself *for love.* I told him I thought every man a great fool who killed himself for love or for any thing else : but had he no books but " The Sorrows of Werter?"—Oh dear, yes, he said, he had a great many more; he had got " The Adventures of a Louse," which was a very curi-

ous book, indeed; and he had got besides " The
Recess," and " Valentine and Orson," and " Ros-
lin Castle," and a book of Prayers, just like the
Bible; but he could not but say that he liked
" The Adventures of a Louse" the best of any of
them.

## DECEMBER 13.

We caught a dolphin, but not with the spear:
he gorged a line which was fastened to the stern,
and baited with salt pork; but being a very large
and strong fish, his efforts to escape were so powerful, that it was feared that he would break
the line, and a *grainse* (as the dolphin-spear is
technically termed) was thrown at him: he was
struck, and three of the prongs were buried in his
side; yet, with a violent effort, he forced them out
again, and threw the lance up into the air. I am
not much used to take pleasure in the sight of
animal suffering; but if Pythagoras himself had
been present, and " of opinion that the soul of his
grandam might haply inhabit" this dolphin, I think
he must still have admired the force and agility dis-
played in his endeavours to escape. Imagination
can picture nothing more beautiful than the colours
of this fish: while covered by the waves he was
entirely green; and as the water gave him a case
of transparent crystal, he really looked like one
solid piece of living emerald; when he sprang into
the air, or swam fatigued upon the surface, his fins

alone preserved their green, and the rest of his body appeared to be of the brightest yellow, his scales shining like gold wherever they caught the sun; while the blood which, as long as he remained in the sea, continued to spout in great quantities, forced its way upwards through the water, like a wreath of crimson smoke, and then dispersed itself in separate globules among the spray. From the great loss of blood, his colours soon became paler; but when he was at length safely landed on deck, and beating himself to death against the flooring, agony renewed all the lustre of his tints: his fins were still green and his body golden, except his back, which was olive, shot with bright deep blue; his head and belly became silvery, and the spots with which the latter was mottled changed, with incessant rapidity, from deep olive to the most beautiful azure. Gradually his brilliant tints disappeared: they were succeeded by one uniform shade of slate-colour; and when he was quite dead, he exhibited nothing but dirty brown and dull dead white. As soon as all was over with him, the first thing done was to convert one of his fins into the resemblance of a flying fish, for the purpose of decoying other dolphins; and the second, to order some of the present gentleman to be got ready for dinner. He measured above four feet and a half.

## DECEMBER 14.

At noon to-day, we found ourselves in the latitude of Jamaica. We were promised the sight of <u>Antigua</u> on Sunday next, but that is now quite out of the question. We made but eight miles in the whole of yesterday; and as Jamaica is still at the distance of eighteen hundred miles, at this rate of proceeding we may expect to reach it about eight months hence. The sky this evening presented us with quite a new phenomenon, a rose-coloured moon : she is to be at her full to-morrow; and this afternoon, about half-past four, she rose like a disk of silver, perfectly white and colourless; but, as she was exactly opposite to the sun at the time of his setting, the reflection of his rays spread a kind of pale blush over her orb, which produced an effect as beautiful as singular. Indeed, the size and inconceivable brilliance of the sun, the clearness of the atmosphere, which had assumed a faint greenish hue, and was entirely without a cloud, the smoothness of the ocean, and the aforesaid rose-coloured moon, altogether rendered this sunset the most magical in effect that I ever beheld; and it was with great reluctance that I was called away from admiring it, to ascertain whether the merits of our new acquaintance, the dolphin, extended any further than his skin. Part of him, which was boiled for yesterday's dinner, was rather coarse and dry, and might have been mistaken for indifferent haddock. But his having been steeped in brine, and then broiled with a good deal of pepper and salt, had improved him wonderfully; and to-day I thought him as good as any other fish.

## DECEMBER 15.

Our wind is like Lady Townley's separate allowance : " that little has been made less ; " or, rather, it has dwindled away to nothing. We are now so absolutely becalmed, that I begin seriously to suspect all the crew of being Phæacians; and that at this identical moment Neptune is amusing himself by making the ship take root in the ocean; a trick which he played once before to a vessel (they say) in the days of Ulysses. I have got some locust plants on board in pots : if we continue to sail as slowly as we have done for the last week, before we reach Jamaica my plants will be forest trees, little Jem, the cabin-boy, will have been obliged to shave, and the black terrier will have died of old age long ago. Great numbers of porpoises were playing about to-day, and tumbling under the ship's very nose. When in their gambols they allow themselves to be seen above the surface, they are of a dirty blackish brown, and as ugly as heart can wish; but in the waves they acquire a fine sea-green cast, and their spouting up water in the sunbeams is extremely ornamental.

### THE HELMSMAN.

Hark ! the bell ! it sounds midnight !—all hail, thou new
    heav'n !
How soft sleep the stars on their bosom of night !
While o'er the full moon, as they gently are driven,
    Slowly floating the clouds bathe their fleeces in light.

The warm feeble breeze scarcely ripples the ocean,
 And all seems so hush'd, all so happy to feel!
So smooth glides the bark, I perceive not her motion,
 While low sings the sailor who watches the wheel.

That sailor I've noted — his cheek, fresh and blooming
 With health, scarcely yet twenty springs can have
  seen;
His looks they are lofty, but never presuming,
 His limbs strong, but light, and undaunted his mien.

Frank and clear is his brow, yet a thoughtful expression,
 Half tender, half mournful, oft shadows his eye;
And murmurs escape him, which make the confession,
 If not check'd by a hem, they had swell'd to a sigh.

His song is not pour'd to beguile the lone hour,
 When mid-watch on deck 'tis his duty to keep;
Nor of painful reflection to weaken the power,
 Nor chase from his eyelids the pinions of sleep.

'Tis so sad ... 'tis so sweet ... and some tones come so
  swelling,
 So right from the heart, and so pure to the ear; —
That sure at this moment his thoughts must be dwelling
 On one who is absent, most kind and most dear.

Perhaps on a mother his mind loves to linger,
 Whose wants to relieve, the rough seas hath he
  cross'd;
Who kiss'd him at parting, and vow'd he could bring her
 No jewel so dear as the one she then lost!

No, no! 'tis a sweetheart, his soul's cherish'd treasure,
 Those full melting notes ... hark! he breathes them
  again!
So mournful, and yet they're prolong'd with such plea-
  sure ......
 Oh, nothing but love could have prompted the strain.

Yet, whate'er be the cause of thy sadness, young seaman,
    That the weight be soon lighten'd, I send up my vow;
From the stings of remorse, I'll be sworn, thou'rt a
    freeman,
    No guilt ever ruffled the smooth of that brow!

That sigh which you breath'd sprang from pensive
    affection;
    That song, though so plaintive, sheds balm on the
    heart;
And the pain which you feel at each fond recollection,
    Is worth all the pleasures that vice could impart.

Oh, still may the scenes of your life, like the present,
    Shine bright to the eye, and speak calm to the breast;
May each wave flow as gentle, each breeze play as
    pleasant,
    And warm as the clime prove the friends you love best!

And may she, who now dictates that ballad so tender,
    Diffuse o'er your days the heart's solace and ease,
As yon lovely moon, with a gleam of mild splendour,
    Pure, tranquil, and bright, over-silvers the seas!

## December 16.

What little wind there is blows so perversely,
that we have been obliged to alter our course;
and instead of Antigua, we are now told that the
Summer Islands (Shakspeare's " still vexed Bermoothes") are the first land that we must expect
to see.

I am greatly disappointed at finding such a
scarcity of monsters; I had flattered myself, that
as soon as we should enter the Atlantic Ocean,

or at least the tropic, we should have seen whole shoals of sharks, whales, and dolphins wandering about as plenty as sheep upon the South Downs: instead of which, a brace of dolphins, and a few flying fish and porpoises, are the only inhabitants of the ocean who have as yet taken the trouble of paying us the common civility of a visit. However, I am promised, that as soon as we approach the islands, I shall have as many sharks as heart can wish.

As I am particularly fond of proofs of conjugal attachment between animals (in the human species they are so universal that I set no store by them), an instance of that kind which the captain related to me this morning gave me great pleasure. While lying in <u>Black River harbour,</u> Jamaica, two sharks were frequently seen playing about the ship; at length the female was killed, and the desolation of the male was excessive: —

" Che faro senz' Eurydice? "

What he did *without* her remains a secret, but what he did *with* her was clear enough; for scarce was the breath out of his Eurydice's body, when he stuck his teeth in her, and began to eat her up with all possible expedition. Even the sailors felt their sensibility excited by so peculiar a mark of posthumous attachment; and to enable him to perform this melancholy duty the more easily, they offered to be his carvers, lowered their boat, and proceeded to chop his better half in pieces with their hatchets; while the widower opened his jaws as wide as possible, and gulped down pounds upon pounds of the dear departed as fast as they were thrown to him, with the greatest delight and all the avidity imaginable. I make no doubt that all the while he was eating, he was thoroughly persuaded that every morsel which went into his stomach would make its way to his heart directly! " She was perfectly consistent," he said to himself; "she was excellent through life, and really she's extremely good now she's dead!" and then, " unable to conceal his pain,"

" He sigh'd and swallow'd, and sigh'd and swallow'd,
    And sigh'd and swallow'd again."

I doubt, whether the annals of Hymen can produce a similar instance of post-obitual affection. Certainly Calderon's " *Amor despues de la Muerte* " has nothing that is worthy to be compared to it; nor do I recollect in history any fact at all resembling it, except perhaps a circumstance which is recorded respecting Cambletes, King of Lydia, a monarch equally remarkable for his voracity and uxoriousness; and who, being one night completely overpowered by sleep, and at the same time violently tormented by hunger, eat up his queen without being conscious of it, and was mightily astonished, the next morning, to wake with her hand in his mouth, the only bit that was

D

left of her. But then, Cambletes was quite unconscious what he was doing; whereas, the shark's
mark of attachment was evidently intentional. It
may, however, be doubted, from the voracity with
which he eat, whether his conduct on this occasion
was not as much influenced by the sentiment of
hunger as of love; and if he were absolutely
on the point of starving, Tasso might have applied to this couple, with equal truth, although
with somewhat a different meaning, what he says
of his " Amanti e Sposi;" —

————— " Pende
D' un fato sol e l' una e l' altra vita:"

for if Madam Shark had not died first, Monsieur
must have died himself for want of a dinner.


## December 17. (Sunday.)

On this day, from a sense of propriety no doubt,
as well as from having nothing else to do, all the
crew in the morning betook themselves to their
studies. The carpenter was very seriously spell-
ing a comedy; Edward was engaged with " The
Six Princesses of Babylon;" a third was amusing
himself with a tract " On the Management of
Bees;" another had borrowed the cabin-boy's
" Sorrows of Werter," and was reading it aloud
to a large circle — some whistling — and others
yawning; and Werter's abrupt transitions, and

exclamations, and raptures, and refinements, read in the same loud monotonous tone, and without the slightest respect paid to stops, had the oddest effect possible. " She did not look at me; I thought my heart would burst; the coach drove off; she looked out of the window; was that look meant for me? yes it was; perhaps it might be; do not tell me that it was not meant for me. Oh, my friend, my friend, am I not a fool, a madman?" (This part is rather stupid, or so, you see, but no matter for that; where was I? oh!) " I am now sure, Charlotte loves me: I prest my hand on my heart; I said ' Klopstock;' yes, Charlotte loves me; what! does Charlotte love me? oh, rapturous thought! my brain turns round :—Immortal powers!—how! —what!—oh, my friend, my friend," &c. &c. &c. I was surprised to find that (except Edward's Fairy Tale) none of them were reading works that were at all likely to amuse them (Smollett or Fielding, for instance), or any which might interest them as relating to their profession, such as voyages and travels; much less any which had the slightest reference to the particular day. However, as most of them were reading what they could not possibly understand, they might mistake them for books of devotion, for any thing they knew to the contrary; or, perhaps, they might have so much reverence for all books in print, as to think that, provided they did but read something, it was doing a good work, and it did not much matter what. So one of Con-

greve's fine ladies swears Mrs. Mincing, the waiting maid, to secrecy, "upon an odd volume of
Messalina's Poems." Sir Dudley North, too, informs us, (or is it his brother Roger? but I mean
the Turkey merchant:) — that at Constantinople
the respect for printed books is so great, that when
people are sick, they fancy that they can be *read*
into health again ; and if the Koran should not be
in the way, they will make a shift with a few verses
of the Bible, or a chapter or two of the Talmud,
or of any other book that comes first to hand, rather
than not read something. I think Sir Dudley says,
that he himself cured an old Turk of the toothache,
by administering a few pages of " Ovid's Metamor-
phoses;" and in an old receipt-book, we are directed for the cure of a double tertian fever, " to
drink plentifully of cock-broth, and sleep with the
Second Book of the Iliad under the pillow." If,
instead of sleeping with it under the pillow, the
doctor had desired us to read the Second Book of
the Iliad in order that we *might* sleep, I should
have had some faith in his prescription myself.

### December 19.

During these last two days nothing very extraordinary, or of sufficient importance to deserve
its being handed down to the latest posterity, has
occurred ; except that this morning a swinging
rope knocked my hat into the sea, and away it
sailed upon a voyage of discovery, like poor La

Perouse, to return no more, I suppose; unless, indeed, — like Polycrates, the fortunate tyrant of Samos, who threw his favourite ring into the ocean, and found it again in the stomach of the first fish that was served up at his table, — I should have the good luck (but I by no means reckon upon it) to catch a dolphin with my hat upon his head : as to a porpoise, he never could squeeze his great num-skull into it; but our dolphin of last week was much about my own size, and I dare say such another would find my hat fit him to a miracle, and look very well in it.

## December 20.

The weather is so excessively close and sultry, that it would be allowed to be too hot to be plea-sant, even by that perfect model for all future lords of the bedchamber, who was never known to speak a word, except in praise, of any thing living or dead, through the whole course of his life : but, at last, one day he met with an acci-dent — he happened to die ; and the next day he met with another accident — he happened to be damned : and immediately upon his arrival in the infernal regions, the Devil (who was determined to be as well bred as the other could be for his ears,) came to pay his compliments to the new-comer, and very obligingly expressed his concern that his lordship was not likely to feel satisfied with his new abode; for that he must certainly find hell very hot and disagreeable. " Oh, dear, no!" exclaimed the Lord of the Bedchamber, "not at all disagreeable, by any manner of means, Mr. Devil, upon my word and honour! Rather *warm*, to be sure." In point of heat there is no difference between the days and the nights; or if there is any, it is that the nights are rather the hottest of the two. The lightning is incessant, and it does not show itself forked or in flashes, but in wide sheets of mild blue light, which spread themselves at once over the sky and sea; and, for the moment which they last, make all the objects around as distinct as in daylight. The moon now does not rise till near ten o'clock, and during her absence the size and brilliancy of the stars are admirable. In England they always seemed to me (to borrow a phrase of Shakspeare's, which, in truth, is not worth borrowing,) to " peep through the blanket of the dark ;" but here the heavens appear to be studded with them on the outside, as if they were chased with so many jewels: it is really Milton's " firmament of living sapphires ;" and what with the lightning, the stars, and the quantity of floating lights which just gleamed round the ship every moment, and then were gone again, to-night the sky had an effect so beautiful, that when at length the moon thought proper to show her great red drunken face, I thought that we did much better without her.

The above-mentioned floating lights are a kind

of sea-meteors, which, as I am told, are produced by the concussion of the waves, while eddy-
ing in whirlpools round the rudder; but still I saw
them rise sometimes at so great a distance from the
ship, and there appeared to be something so like
*Will* in the direction of their course, — sometimes
hurrying on, sometimes gliding along quite slowly;
now stopping and remaining motionless for a minute
or two, and then hurrying on again, — that I could
not be convinced of their not being Medusæ, or
some species or other of phosphoric animal: but
whatever be the cause of this appearance, the
effect is singularly beautiful. As to air, we have
not enough to bless ourselves with. I had been
led to believe, that when once we should have
fallen in with the trade winds, from that moment
we should sail into our destined port as rapidly
and as directly as Truffaldino travels in Gozzi's
farce; when, having occasion to go from Asia to
Europe, and being very much pressed for time,
he persuades a conjuror of his acquaintance to
lend him a devil, with a great pair of bellows, the
nozzle of which being directed right against his
stern, away goes the traveller before the stream
of wind, with the devil after him, and the infernal bellows never cease from working till they
have blown him out of one quarter of the globe
into another: but our trade winds must "hide
their diminished heads" before Truffaldino's bellows. It seems that like the Moors, "in Africa

the torrid," they are "of temper somewhat
mulish;" for, although, to be sure, when they *do*
blow, they will only blow in one certain direction,
yet very often they will not blow at all; which has
been our case for the last week : indeed, they seem
to be but a queerish kind of a concern at best.
About three years ago a fleet of merchantmen was
becalmed near St. Vincent's : in a few days after
their arrival, there happened a violent eruption of
a volcano in that island, nor was it long before a
favourable breeze sprang up. Unluckily, one of
the ships had anchored rather nearer to the shore
than the others, and was at the distance of about
one hundred and fifty yards from the stream of the
trade wind ; nor could any possible efforts of the
crew, by tacking, by towing, or otherwise, ever
enable the vessel to conquer that one hundred and
fifty yards : there she remained, as completely becalmed as if there were not such a thing as a
breath of wind in the universe; and on the one
hand she had the mortification to see the rest of the
merchantmen, with their convoy (for it was in the
very heat of the war), sail away with all their canvass spread and swelling ; while, on the other
hand, the sailors had the comfortable possibility of
being suffocated every moment by the clouds of
ashes which continued to fall on their deck every
moment, from the burning volcano, although they
were not nearer to St. Vincent's than eight or nine
miles; indeed that distance went for nothing, as

ashes fell upon vessels that were out at sea at least five hundred miles; and Barbadoes being to wind-ward of the volcano, such immense quantities of its contents were carried to that island as almost covered the fields; and destroying vegetation com-pletely wherever they fell, did inconceivable damage, while that which St. Vincent's itself experienced was but trifling in proportion.

Our captain is quite out of patience with the tor-toise pace of our progress; for my part I care very little about it. Whether we have sailed slowly or rapidly, when a day is once over, I am just as much nearer advanced towards April, the time fixed for my return to England; and, what is of much more consequence, whether we have sailed slowly or rapidly, when a day is once over, I am just as much nearer advanced towards "that bourne," to reach which, peaceably and harmlessly, is the only busi-ness of life, and towards which the whole of our existence forms but one continued journey.

## DECEMBER 21.

We succeeded in catching another dolphin to-day; but he had not a hat on; however, I just asked him whether he happened to have seen mine, but to little purpose; for I found that he could tell me nothing at all about it; so, instead of bothering the poor animal with any more questions, we eat him.

### DECEMBER 22.

About three years ago the Captain had the ill luck to be captured by a French frigate. As she had already made prizes of two other merchant-men, it was determined to sink his ship; which, after removing the crew and every thing in her that was valuable, was effected by firing her own guns down the hatchways. It was near three hours before she filled, then down she went with a single plunge, head foremost, with all her sails set and colours flying. This display of the ship's magnificence in her last moments reminded me of Mary Queen of Scots, arraying herself in her richest robes that she might go to the scaffold. If Yorick had fallen in with this anecdote in the course of his journey, the situation of the Captain, standing on the enemy's deck, and seeing his " brave vessel " in full and gallant trim, possessing all the abilities for a long existence, yet abandoned by every one, and sinking from the effect of her own shot, might have furnished him with a com-panion for his old commercial Marquis, lamenting over the rust of his newly recovered sword.

DECEMBER 23.

## THE DOLPHIN.

Does then the insatiate sea relent?
And hath he back those treasures sent,
  His stormy rage devoured?
All starred with gems the billows bound,
And emeralds, jacinths, sapphires round
  The bark in spray are showered.

No, no! 't is there the Dolphin plays;
His scales, enriched with sunny rays,
  Celestial tints unfold;
And as he darts, the waters blue
Are streaked with gleams of many a hue,
  Green, orange, purple, gold!

And brighter still will shine your skin,
Poor fish, more dazzling play each fin,
  On deck when dying cast;
Like good men, who, expiring, bless
The Power that calls them, all confess
  Your brightest hour your last.

And now the Spearman watchful stands!
The five-pronged *grainse*, which arms his hands,
  Your scales is doomed to gore;
The lead will sink, and soon on high,
Borne from the deep, perforce you'll fly,
  Nor e'er regain it more.

Weep, Beauty, weep! those vivid dyes,
Those splendours, but the harpooner's eyes
  To strike his victim call!
Ambition, mark the Dolphin's close —
To dangerous heights he only rose
  To find the heavier fall!

Mark, too, ye witty, rich, and gay,
How quick those sportive fins could play,
  How gay, how rich was he !
He moves no more — he's cold to touch —
He's dull—dark—dead !  The Dolphin's such,
  And such we all must be !

There is a technical fault in the above lines : the grainse, or dolphin-spear, has five barbs; but the *harpooner* never uses a lance with more than a single point.  However, the word was so agreeable to my ear, that I could not find in my heart to leave it out.

### December 24. (Sunday.)

At length we have crawled into the Caribbean Sea.  I was told that we were not to expect to see land to-day; but on shipboard our not seeing a thing *to-day* by no means implies that we shall not see it before *to-morrow ;* for the nautical day is supposed to conclude at noon, when the solar observation is taken; and, therefore, the making land *to-day,* or not, very often depends upon our making it before twelve o'clock, or after it.  This was the case in the present instance; for noon was scarcely passed when we saw Descada (a small island totally unprovided with water, and whose only produce consists in a little cotton), Guadaloupe, and Marie Galante, though the latter was at so great a distance as to be scarcely visible.  At sunset Antigua was in sight.

## DECEMBER 25.

The sun rose upon Montserrat and Nevis, with
the *Rodondo* rock between them, " apricis natio
gratissima mergis, —" for it is perpetually covered
with innumerable flocks of gulls, boobies, peli-
cans, and other sea birds. Then came St. Christopher's and St. Eustatia; and in the course of
the afternoon we passed over the *Aves* bank, a
collection of sand, rock, and mud, extending about
two hundred miles, and terminated at each end by
a small island: one of them inhabited by a few
fishermen, the other only by sea birds. Of all the
Atlantic isles the soil of St. Christopher's is by some
supposed to be the richest, the land frequently producing three hogsheads an acre. I rather think
that this was the first island discovered by Columbus, and that it took its name from his patron-saint.
Montserrat is so rocky, and the roads so steep and
difficult, that the sugar is obliged to be brought
down in bags upon the backs of mules, and not
put into casks, till its arrival on the sea shore.

The weather is now quite delicious; there is just
wind enough to send us forward and keep the air
cool: the sun is brilliant without being overpower-
ing; the swell of the waves is scarcely perceptible;
and the ship moves along so steadily, that the deck
affords almost as firm footing as if we were walking
on land. One would think that Belinda had been
smiling on the Caribbean Sea, as she once before

did on the Thames, and had "made all the world look gay." During the night we passed Santa Cruz, an island which, from the perfection to which its cultivation has been carried, is called " the Garden of the West Indies."

## DECEMBER 28.

Having left Porto Rico behind us, at noon to-day we passed the insulated rock of Alcavella, lying about six miles from St. Domingo, which is now in sight. As this part of the Caribbean Sea is much infested by pirates from the Caraccas, all our muskets have been put in repair, and to-day the guns were loaded, of which we mount eight; but as one of them, during the last voyage, went overboard in a gale of wind, its place has been supplied by a *Quaker*, i. e. a sham gun of wood, so called, I suppose, because it would not fight if it were called upon. These pirate-vessels are small schooners, armed with a single twenty-four pounder, which moves upon a swivel, and their crew is composed of negroes and outlaws of all nations, their numbers generally running from one hundred to one hundred and fifty men. To-day, for the first time, I saw some flying fish: we have also been visited by several men-of-war birds and tropic birds; the latter is a species of gull, perfectly white, and distinguished by a single very long feather in its tail: its nautical name is " the boatswain."

As we sail along, the air is absolutely loaded with "Sabean odours from the spicy shores" of St. Domingo, which we were still coasting at sunset.

## December 30.

At day-break Jamaica was in sight, or rather it would have been in sight, only that we could not see it. The weather was so gloomy, and the wind and rain were so violent, that we might have said to the Captain, as one of the two Punches who went into the ark is reported to have said to the patriarch, during the deluge, " Hazy weather, Master Noah." — I remember my good friend, Walter Scott, asserts, that at the death of a poet the groans and tears of his heroes and heroines swell the blast and increase the river; perhaps something of the same kind takes place at the arrival of a West India proprietor from Europe, and all this rain and wind proceed from the eyes and lungs of my agents and overseers, who, for the last twenty years, have been reigning in my dominions with despotic authority; but now

> " Whose groans in roaring winds complain,
>   Whose tears of rage impel the rain;"

because, on the approach of the sovereign himself, they must evacuate the palace, and resign the deputed sceptre. " Hinc illæ lachrymæ!" this is the cause of our being soaked to the skin this morning. However, about noon the weather cleared up, and allowed us to verify, with our own eyes, that we had reached " the Land of Springs," without having been invited by any Piccaroon vessel to " walk the plank" instead of the deck; which is a compliment very generally paid by those gentry, after they have taken the trouble of laying a plank over the side of a captured ship, in order that the passengers and the crew may walk overboard without any inconvenience.

We arrived at the east end of the island, passed Pedro Point and Starvegut Bay, and arrived before Black River Bay (our destined harbour) soon after two o'clock; but here we were obliged to come to a stand still: the channel is very dangerous, extremely narrow, and full of sunken rocks; so that it can only be entered by a vessel drawing so much water as ours with a particular wind, and when there is not any apprehension of a sudden squall. We were, therefore, obliged to drop anchor, and are now riding within a couple of miles of the shore, but with as utter an incapability of reaching it as if we were still at Gravesend. The north side of the island is said to be extremely beautiful and romantic; but the south, which we coasted to-day, is low, barren, and without any recommendation whatever. As yet I can only look at Jamaica as one does on a man who comes to pay money, and whom we are extremely well pleased to see, however little the fellow's appearance may be in his favour.

DECEMBER 31. (Sunday.)

We passed the whole of the day in vain endeavours to work ourselves into the bay. At one
time, indeed, we got very near the shore, but the
consequence was, that we were within an ace of
striking upon a rock, and very much obliged to
a sudden gust of wind, which, blowing right off
shore, blew us out of the channel, and left us at
night in a much more perilous situation than we
had occupied the evening before, though even that
had been by no means secure. At three o'clock,
the other passengers went on shore in the jolly-
boat, and proceeded to their destination; but as I
was still more than thirty miles distant from my
estate, I preferred waiting on board till the
Captain should have moored his vessel in safety,
and be at liberty to take me in his pinnace to
Savannah la Mar, when I should find myself
within a few miles of my own house.

In the course of the afternoon, one of the sailors
took up a fish of a very singular shape and most
brilliant colours, as it floated along upon the water.
It seemed to be gasping, and lay with its belly upwards; it was supposed to have eaten something
poisonous, as whenever it was touched it appeared
to be full of life, and squirted the water in our
faces with great spirit and dexterity. But no
sooner was he suffered to remain quiet in the tub,
than he turned upon his back and again was gasp-

ing. He had a large round transparent globule, intersected with red veins, under the belly, which some imagined to proceed from a rupture, and to be the occasion of his disease. But I could not discover any vestige of a wound; and the globule was quite solid to the touch; neither did the fish appear to be sensible when it was pressed upon. No one on board had ever seen this kind of fish till then; its name is the " Doctor Fish."

A black pilot came on board yesterday, in a canoe hollowed out of the cotton-tree; and when it returned for him this morning, it brought us a water-melon. I never met with a worse article in my life; the pulp is of a faint greenish yellow, stained here and there with spots of moist red, so that it looks exactly as if the servant in slicing it had cut his finger, and suffered it to bleed over the fruit. Then the seeds, being of a dark purple, present the happiest imitation of drops of clotted gore; and altogether (prejudiced as I was by its appearance), when I had put a single bit into my mouth, it had such a kind of Shylocky taste of raw flesh about it (not that I recollect having ever eaten a bit of raw flesh itself), that I sent away my plate, and was perfectly satisfied as to the merits of the fruit.

## 1816.—JANUARY 1.

At length the ship has squeezed herself into this champagne bottle of a bay! Perhaps, the satisfaction attendant upon our having overcome the difficulty, added something to the illusion of its effect; but the beauty of the atmosphere, the dark purple mountains, the shores covered with mangroves of the liveliest green down to the very edge of the water, and the light-coloured houses with their lattices and piazzas completely embowered in trees, altogether made the scenery of the Bay wear a very picturesque appearance. And, to complete the charm, the sudden sounds of the drum and banjee, called our attention to a procession of the *John-Canoe*, which was proceeding to celebrate the opening of the new year at the town of Black River. The John-Canoe is a Merry-Andrew dressed in a striped doublet, and bearing upon his head a kind of pasteboard house-boat, filled with puppets, representing, some sailors, others soldiers, others again slaves at work on a plantation, &c. The negroes are allowed three days for holidays at Christmas, and also New-year's day, which being the last is always reckoned by them as the festival of the greatest importance. It is for this day that they reserve their finest dresses, and lay their schemes for displaying their show and expense to the greatest advantage; and it is then that the John-Canoe is considered not merely as a person of material consequence, but one whose presence is absolutely indispensable. Nothing could look more gay than the procession which we now saw with its train of attendants, all dressed in white,

and marching two by two (except when the file
was broken here and there by a single horseman),
and its band of negro music, and its scarlet flags
fluttering about in the breeze, now disappearing
behind a projecting clump of mangrove trees, and
then again emerging into an open part of the road,
as it wound along the shore towards the town of
Black River.

> —— " Magno telluris amore
> Egressi optatâ Tröes potiuntur arenâ."

I had determined not to go on shore, till I should
land for good and all at Savannah la Mar. But
although I could resist the " telluris amor," there
was no resisting John-Canoe; so, in defiance of a
broiling afternoon's sun, about four o'clock we
left the vessel for the town.

It was, as I understand, formerly one of some
magnitude; but it now consists only of a few
houses, owing to a spark from a tobacco-pipe or
a candle having lodged upon a mosquito-net during
dry weather; and although the conflagration took
place at mid-day, the whole town was reduced to
ashes. The few streets — (I believe there were
not above two, but those were wide and regular,
and the houses looked very neat) — were now
crowded with people, and it seemed to be allowed,
upon all hands, that New-year's day had never been
celebrated there with more expense and festivity.

It seems that, many years ago, an <u>Admiral of the Red</u> was superseded on the Jamaica station by an <u>Admiral of the Blue</u>; and both of them gave balls at Kingston to the " *Brown Girls ;* " for the fair sex elsewhere are called the " Brown Girls " in Jamaica. In consequence of these balls, all Kingston was divided into parties: from thence the division spread into other districts: and ever since, the whole island, at Christmas, is separated into the rival factions of the Blues and the Reds (the Red representing also the English, the Blue the Scotch), who contend for setting forth their processions with the greatest taste and magnificence. This year, several gentlemen in the neighbourhood of Black River had subscribed very largely towards the expenses of the show; and certainly it produced the gayest and most amusing scene that I ever witnessed, to which the mutual jealousy and pique of the two parties against each other contributed in no slight degree. The champions of the rival Roses,—the Guelphs and the Ghibellines,—none of them could exceed the scornful animosity and spirit of depreciation with which the Blues and the Reds of Black River examined the efforts at display of each other. The Blues had the advantage beyond a doubt; this a Red girl told us that she could not deny; but still, " though the Reds were beaten, she would not be a Blue girl for the whole universe! " On the other hand, Miss Edwards (the mistress of the hotel from whose window we saw

the show), was rank Blue to the very tips of her
fingers, and had, indeed, contributed one of her
female slaves to sustain a very important character
in the show; for when the Blue procession was ready
to set forward, there was evidently a hitch, something was wanting; and there seemed to be no
possibility of getting on without it—when suddenly
we saw a tall woman dressed in mourning (being
Miss Edwards herself) rush out of our hotel, dragging along by the hand a strange uncouth kind
of a glittering tawdry figure, all feathers, and pitch-
fork, and painted pasteboard, who moved most
reluctantly, and turned out to be no less a personage than Britannia herself, with a pasteboard shield
covered with the arms of Great Britain, a trident
in her hand, and a helmet made of pale blue silk
and silver. The poor girl, it seems, was bashful
at appearing in this conspicuous manner before so
many spectators, and hung back when it came to
the point. But her mistress had seized hold of
her, and placed her by main force in her destined
position. The music struck up; Miss Edwards
gave the Goddess a great push forwards; the drum-
sticks and the elbows of the fiddlers attacked her
in the rear; and on went Britannia willy-nilly!

The Blue girls called themselves " the Blue girls
of Waterloo." Their motto was the more patriotic;
that of the Red was the more gallant:—" Britannia
rules the day!" streamed upon the Blue flag;
" Red girls for ever!" floated upon the Red. But,

in point of taste and invention, the former carried
it hollow. First marched Britannia; then came a
band of music; then the flag; then the Blue King
and Queen — the Queen splendidly dressed in
white and silver (in scorn of the opposite party, her
train was borne by a little girl in red); his Majesty
wore a full British Admiral's uniform, with a white
satin sash, and a huge cocked hat with a gilt paper
crown upon the top of it. These were immediately
followed by "Nelson's car," being a kind of canoe
decorated with blue and silver drapery, and with
" Trafalgar " written on the front of it ; and the
procession was closed by a long train of Blue
grandees (the women dressed in uniforms of white,
with robes of blue muslin), all Princes and Princesses, Dukes and Duchesses, every mother's child
of them.

The Red girls were also dressed very gaily
and prettily, but they had nothing in point of
invention that could vie with Nelson's Car and
Britannia ; and when the Red throne made its
appearance, language cannot express the contempt
with which our landlady eyed it. " It was neither
one thing nor t'other," Miss Edwards was of opinion. " Merely a few yards of calico stretched
over some planks — and look, look, only look at
it behind ! you may see the bare boards ! By way
of a throne, indeed ! Well, to be sure, Miss Edwards never saw a poorer thing in her life, that
she must say !" And then she told me, that some-

body had just snatched at a medal which Britannia wore round her neck, and had endeavoured to force it away. I asked her who had done so? "Oh, one of the Red party, *of course!*" The Red party was evidently Miss Edwards's Mrs. Grundy. John-Canoe made no part of the procession; but he and his rival, John-Crayfish (a personage of whom I heard, but could not obtain a sight), seemed to act upon quite an independent interest, and go about from house to house, tumbling and playing antics to pick up money for themselves.

A play was now proposed to us, and, of course, accepted. Three men and a girl accordingly made their appearance; the men dressed like the tumblers at Astley's, the lady very tastefully in white and silver, and all with their faces concealed by masks of thin blue silk; and they proceeded to perform the quarrel between Douglas and Glenalvon, and the fourth act of "The Fair Penitent." They were all quite perfect, and had no need of a prompter. As to Lothario, he was by far the most comical dog that I ever saw in my life, and his dying scene exceeded all description; Mr. Coates himself might have taken hints from him! As soon as Lothario was fairly dead, and Calista had made her exit in distraction, they all began dancing reels like so many mad people, till they were obliged to make way for the Waterloo procession, who came to collect money for the next year's festival; one of them singing, another dancing to the tune, while she presented her money-box to the spectators, and the rest of the Blue girls filling up the chorus. I cannot say much in praise of the black Catalani; but nothing could be more light, and playful, and graceful, than the extempore movements of the dancing girl. Indeed, through the whole day, I had been struck with the precision of their march, the ease and grace of their action, the elasticity of their step, and the lofty air with which they carried their heads — all, indeed, except poor Britannia, who hung down hers in the most ungoddess-like manner imaginable. The first song was the old Scotch air of "Logie of Buchan," of which the girl sang one single stanza forty times over. But the second was in praise of the Hero of Heroes; so I gave the songstress a dollar to teach it to me, and drink the Duke's health. It was not easy to make out what she said, but as well as I could understand them, the words ran as follows : —

> " Come, rise up, our gentry,
> And hear about Waterloo;
> Ladies, take your spy-glass,
> And attend to what we do;
> For one and one makes two,
> But one alone must be.
> Then singee, singee Waterloo,
> None so brave as he ! "

— and then there came something about green and white flowers, and a Duchess, and a lily-white Pig,

and going on board of a dashing man of war; but
what they all had to do with the Duke, or with
each other, I could not make even a guess. I was
going to ask for an explanation, but suddenly half
of them gave a shout loud enough " to fright the
realms of Chaos and old Night," and away they
flew, singers, dancers, and all. The cause of this
was the sudden illumination of the town with
quantities of large chandeliers and bushes, the
branches of which were stuck all over with great
blazing torches: the effect was really beautiful,
and the excessive rapture of the black multitude at
the spectacle was as well worth the witnessing as
the sight itself.

I never saw so many people who appeared to be
so unaffectedly happy. In England, at fairs and
races, half the visiters at least seem to have been
only brought there for the sake of traffic, and to
be too busy to be amused; but here nothing was
thought of but real pleasure; and that pleasure
seemed to consist in singing, dancing, and laughing, in seeing and being seen, in showing their own
fine clothes, or in admiring those of others. There
were no people selling or buying; no servants and
landladies bustling and passing about; and at eight
o'clock, as we passed through the market-place,
where was the greatest illumination, and which, of
course, was most thronged, I did not see a single
person drunk, nor had I observed a single quarrel
through the course of the day; except, indeed,

when some thoughtless fellow crossed the line of the procession, and received by the way a good box of the ear from the Queen or one of her attendant Duchesses. Every body made the same remark to me; "Well, sir, what do you think Mr. Wilberforce would think of the state of the negroes, if he could see this scene?" and certainly, to judge by this one specimen, of all beings that I have yet seen, these were the happiest. As we were passing to our boat, through the market-place, suddenly we saw Miss Edwards dart out of the crowd, and seize the Captain's arm — "Captain! Captain!" cried she, "for the love of Heaven, only look at the *Red* lights! Old iron hoops, nothing but old iron hoops, I declare! Well! for my part!" and then, with a contemptuous toss of her head, away frisked Miss Edwards triumphantly.

### JANUARY 2.

The St. Elizabeth, which sailed from England at the same time with our vessel, was attacked by a pirate from Carthagena, near the rocks of Alcavella, who attempted three times to board her, though he was at length beaten off; so that our Piccaroon preparations were by no means taken without foundation.

At four o'clock this morning I embarked in the cutter for Savannah la Mar, lighted by the most beautiful of all possible morning stars: certainly, if this star be really Lucifer, that "Son of the

Morning," the Devil must be " an extremely pretty fellow." But in spite of the fineness of the morning, our passage was a most disagreeable concern : there was a violent swell in the sea ; and a strong north wind, though it carried us forward with great rapidity, overwhelmed us with whole sheets of foam so incessantly, that I expected, as soon as the sun should have evaporated the moisture, to see the boat's crew covered with salt, and looking like so many Lot's wives after her metamorphosis.

The distance was about thirty miles, and soon after nine o'clock we reached Savannah la Mar, where I found my trustee, and a whole cavalcade, waiting to conduct me to my own estate ; for he had brought with him a curricle and pair for myself, a gig for my servant, two black boys upon mules, and a cart with eight oxen to convey my baggage. The road was excellent, and we had not above five miles to travel ; and as soon as the carriage entered my gates, the uproar and confusion which ensued sets all description at defiance. The works were instantly all abandoned ; every thing that had life came flocking to the house from all quarters ; and not only the men, and the women, and the children, but, " by a bland assimilation," the hogs, and the dogs, and the geese, and the fowls, and the turkeys, all came hurrying along by instinct, to see what could possibly be the matter, and seemed to be afraid of arriving too late. Whether the pleasure of the negroes was sincere may be doubted; but certainly it was the loudest that I ever witnessed: they all talked together, sang, danced, shouted, and, in the violence of their gesticulations, tumbled over each other, and rolled about upon the ground. Twenty voices at once enquired after uncles, and aunts, and grandfathers, and great-grandmothers of mine, who had been buried long before I was in existence, and whom, I verily believe, most of them only knew by tradition. One woman held up her little naked black child to me, grinning from ear to ear;—"Look, Massa, look here! him nice lilly neger for Massa!" Another complained, — " So long since none come see we, Massa; good Massa, come at last." As for the old people, they were all in one and the same story: now they had lived once to see Massa, they were ready for dying to-morrow, " them no care."

The shouts, the gaiety, the wild laughter, their strange and sudden bursts of singing and dancing, and several old women, wrapped up in large cloaks, their heads bound round with different-coloured handkerchiefs, leaning on a staff, and standing motionless in the middle of the hubbub, with their eyes fixed upon the portico which I occupied, formed an exact counterpart of the festivity of the witches in Macbeth. Nothing could be more odd or more novel than the whole scene; and yet there was something in it by which I could not help being affected; perhaps it was the consciousness

that all these human beings were my *slaves;*—to be
sure, I never saw people look more happy in my
life; and I believe their condition to be much
more comfortable than that of the labourers of
Great Britain; and, after all, slavery, in *their* case,
is but another name for servitude, now that no
more negroes can be forcibly carried away from
Africa, and subjected to the horrors of the voyage, and of the seasoning after their arrival: but
still I had already experienced, in the morning,
that Juliet was wrong in saying " What's in a
name?" For soon after my reaching the lodging-
house at Savannah la Mar, a remarkably clean-
looking negro lad presented himself with some
water and a towel: I concluded him to belong to
the inn; and, on my returning the towel, as he
found that I took no notice of him, he at length
ventured to introduce himself, by saying,—" Massa
not know me; *me your slave!*"—and really the
sound made me feel a pang at the heart. The
lad appeared all gaiety and good humour, and his
whole countenance expressed anxiety to recom-
mend himself to my notice; but the word "slave"
seemed to imply, that, although he did feel pleasure
then in serving me, if he had detested me he must
have served me still. I really felt quite humiliated
at the moment, and was tempted to tell him,—" Do
not say that again; say that you are my negro, but
do not call yourself my slave."

Altogether, they shouted and sang me into a

violent headach. It is now one in the morning,
and I hear them still shouting and singing. I gave
them a holiday for Saturday next, and told them
that I had brought them all presents from England;
and so, I believe, we parted very good friends.

### JANUARY 3.

I have reached Jamaica in the best season for
seeing my property in a favourable point of view;
it is crop time, when all the laborious work is
over, and the negroes are the most healthy and
merry. This morning I went to visit the hospital, and found there only eight patients out of
three hundred negroes, and not one of them a
serious case. Yesterday I had observed a remarkably handsome Creole girl, called Psyche, and she
really deserved the name. This morning a little
brown girl made her appearance at breakfast, with
an orange bough, to flap away the flies, and, on
enquiry, she proved to be an emanation of the
aforesaid Psyche. It is evident, therefore, that
Psyche has already visited the palace of Cupid; I
heartily hope that she is not now upon her road to
the infernal regions: but, as the ancients had two
Cupids, one divine and the other sensual, so am I
in possession of two Psyches; and on visiting the
hospital, *there* was poor Psyche the second. Probably this was the Psyche of the sensual Cupid.

I passed the morning in driving about the estate:
my house is frightful to look at, but very clean and

comfortable on the inside; some of the scenery is very picturesque, from the lively green of the trees and shrubs, and the hermitage-like appearance of the negro buildings, all situated in little gardens, and embosomed in sweet-smelling shrubberies. Indeed, every thing appears much better than I expected; the negroes seem healthy and contented, and so perfectly at their ease, that our English squires would be mightily astonished at being accosted so familiarly by their farmers. This delightful north wind keeps the air temperate and agreeable. I live upon shaddocks and pine-apples. The dreaded mosquitoes are not worse than gnats, nor as bad as the Sussex harvest-bugs; and, as yet, I never felt myself in more perfect health. There was a man once, who fell from the top of a steeple; and, perceiving no inconvenience in his passage through the air,—"Come," said he to himself, while in the act of falling, "really this is well enough yet if it would but last." Cubina, my young Savannah la Mar acquaintance, is appointed my black attendant; and as I had desired him to bring me any native flowers of Jamaica, this evening he brought me a very pretty one; the negroes, he said, called it " John-to-Heal," but in white language it was *hoccoco-pickang;* it proved to be the wild Ipecacuanha.

### JANUARY 4.

There were three things against which I was particularly cautioned, and which three things I was determined *not* to do: to take exercise after ten in the day; to be exposed to the dews after sun-down; and to sleep at a Jamaica lodging-house. So, yesterday, I set off for Montego Bay at eight o'clock in the morning, and travelled till three; walked home from a ball after midnight; and that home was a lodging-house at Montego Bay; but the lodging-house was such a cool clean lodging-house, and the landlady was such an obliging smiling landlady, with the whitest of all possible teeth, and the blackest of all possible eyes, that no harm could happen to me from occupying an apartment which had been prepared by *her*. She was called out of her bed to make my room ready for me; yet she did every thing with so much good-will and cordiality; no quick answers, no mutterings: inns would be bowers of Paradise, if they were all rented by mulatto landladies, like Judy James.

I was much pleased with the scenery of Montego Bay, and with the neatness and cleanliness of the town; indeed, what with the sea washing it, and the picturesque aspect of the piazzas and verandas, it is impossible for a West Indian town so situated, and in such a climate, not to present an agreeable appearance. But the first part of the road exceeds in beauty all that I have ever seen: it wound through mountain lands of my own, their summits of the boldest, and at the same time of the most beautiful shapes; their sides orna-

mented with bright green woods of bamboo, logwood, prickly-yellow, broad-leaf, and trumpet trees;
and so completely covered with the most lively
verdure, that once, when we found a piece of barren
rock, Cubina pointed it out to me as a curiosity;—
" Look, massa, rock quite naked!" The cotton-
tree presented itself on all sides ; but as this is the
season for its shedding its leaves, its wide-spreading
bare white arms contributed nothing to the beauty
of the scene, except where the wild fig and various
creeping plants had completely mantled the stems
and branches; and then its gigantic height, and
the fantastic wreathings of its limbs, from which
numberless green withes and strings of wild flowers
were streaming, rendered it exactly the very tree
for which a landscape-painter would have wished.
The air, too, was delicious ; the fragrance of the
Sweet-wood, and of several other scented trees, but
above all, of the delicious Logwood (of which most
of the fences in Westmoreland are made) composed
an atmosphere, such, that if Satan, after promising
them " a buxom air, embalmed with odours," had
transported Sin and Death thither, the charming
couple must have acknowledged their papa's promises fulfilled.

We travelled these first ten miles (Montego Bay
being about thirty from my estate of Cornwall)
without seeing a human creature, nor, indeed,
any thing that had life in it, except a black snake
basking in the sunshine, and a few John Crows

— a species of vulture, whose utility is so great
that its destruction is prohibited by law under a
heavy penalty. In a country where putrefaction
is so rapid, it is of infinite consequence to preserve
an animal which, if a bullock or horse falls dead in
the field, immediately flies to the carcass before it
has time to corrupt, and gobbles it up before you
can say " John Crow," much less Jack Robinson.
The bite of the black snake is slightly venomous,
but that is all; as to the great yellow one, it is
perfectly innoxious, and so timid that it always
runs away from you. The only dangerous species
of serpent is the Whip-snake, so called from its exactly resembling the lash of a whip, in length, thin-
ness, pliability, and whiteness; but even the bite of
this is not mortal, except from very great neglect.
The most beautiful tree, or, rather, group of trees,
all to nothing, is the Bamboo, both from its verdure
and from its elegance of form : as to the Cotton
tree, it answers no purpose, either of ornament or
utility; or, rather, it is not suffered to answer any,
since it is forbidden by law to export its down, lest
it should hurt the fur trade in the manufacture of
hats : its only present use is to furnish the negroes
with canoes, which are hollowed out of its immense
trunks. I am as yet so much enchanted with the
country, that it would require no very strong additional inducements to make me establish myself
here altogether; and in that case my first care

would be to build for myself a cottage among these mountains, in which I might pass the sultry months,

"  E bruna-si; ma il bruno il bel non toglie."

### January 5.

As I was returning this morning from Montego Bay, about a mile from my own estate, a figure presented itself before me, I really think the most picturesque that I ever beheld: it was a mulatto girl, born upon Cornwall, but whom the overseer of a neighbouring estate had obtained my permission to exchange for another slave, as well as two little children, whom she had borne to him; but, as yet, he has been unable to procure a substitute, owing to the difficulty of purchasing single negroes, and Mary Wiggins is still my slave. However, as she is considered as being manumitted, she had not dared to present herself at Cornwall on my arrival, lest she should have been considered as an intruder; but she now threw herself in my way to tell me how glad she was to see me, for that she had always thought till now (which is the general complaint) that " *she had no massa ;*" and also to obtain a regular invitation to my negro festival to-morrow. By this universal complaint, it appears that, while Mr. Wilberforce is lamenting their hard fate in being subject to a master, *their* greatest fear is the not having a master whom they know; and that to be told by the negroes of another estate that "they belong to no massa," is one of the most contemptuous reproaches that can be cast upon them. Poor creatures, when they happened to hear on Wednesday evening that my carriage was ordered for Montego Bay the next morning, they fancied that I was going away for good and all, and came up to the house in such a hubbub, that my agent was obliged to speak to them, and pacify them with the assurance that I should come back on Friday without fail.

But to return to Mary Wiggins: she was much too pretty not to obtain her invitation to Cornwall; on the contrary, I *insisted* upon her coming, and bade her tell her *husband* that I admired his taste very much for having chosen her. I really think that her form and features were the most *statue-like* that I ever met with: her complexion had no yellow in it, and yet was not brown enough to be dark — it was more of an ash-dove colour than any thing else; her teeth were admirable, both for colour and shape; her eyes equally mild and bright; and her face merely broad enough to give it all possible softness and grandness of contour: her air and countenance would have suited Yarico; but she reminded me most of Grassini in " La Vergine del Sole," only that Mary Wiggins was a thousand times more beautiful, and that, instead of a white robe, she wore a mixed dress of brown, white, and dead yellow, which harmonised excellently well with her complexion;

while one of her beautiful arms was thrown across her brow to shade her eyes, and a profusion of rings on her fingers glittered in the sunbeams. Mary Wiggins and an old Cotton-tree are the most picturesque objects that I have seen for these twenty years.

On my arrival at home, my agent made me a very elegant little present of a scorpion and a couple of centipedes : the first was given to him, but the large centipede he had shaken out of a book last night, and having immediately covered her up in a phial of rum, he found this morning that she had produced a young one, which was lying drowned by her side.

I find that my negroes were called away from their attention to the works yesterday evening (for the crop is now making with the greatest activity), and kept up all night by a fire at a neighbouring estate. On these occasions a fire-shell is blown, and all the negroes of the adjoining plantations hasten to give their assistance. On this occasion the fire was extinguished with the loss of only five negro houses; but this is a heavy concern to the poor negro proprietors, who have lost in it their whole stock of clothes, and furniture, and finery, which they had been accumulating for years, and to which their attachment is excessive.

# LANDING.

When first I gain'd the Atlantic shore,
And bade farewell to ocean's roar,
What gracious power my bosom eased,
My senses soothed, my fancy pleased,
And bade me feel, in whispers bland,
No Stranger in a Stranger-land?
'T was not at length my goal to reach,
And tread Jamaica's burning beach:
'T was not from Neptune's chains discharged,
To move, think, feel with powers enlarged:
Nor that no more my bed the wave,
Ere morning dawn'd, might prove my grave: —
A livelier chord was struck: a spell,
While heav'd my heart with gentle swell,
Crept o'er my soul with magic sweet,
And made each pulse responsive beat.
  No Sheep-bell e'er to Pilgrim's ear,
Wandering in woods unknown and drear;
No midnight lay to Spanish maid,
Conscious by whom the lute was played;
Not on the breeze the sounding wings
Of him who nurture homeward brings
To mother-bird, whose callow brood
Pain her fond heart with chirps for food, —
E'er seem'd more charming than to me,
(When two long months had past at sea,
During whose course my thirsty ear
No softer voice, no strain could hear
Nearer allied to love and pity,
Than the strong bass of seaman's ditty,)
Seem'd by the sea-gale round me flung,
Approaching sounds of female tongue!

No, Venus, no! Small right hast thou
To claim for this my grateful vow;
Nor on thine altar now bestows
My hand the gift of one poor rose!
No eager glance, no heighten'd dye
Blush'd on my cheek, nor fired mine eye;
I heard, nor felt, at each soft note,
Flutter my heart, and swell my throat.
Those sounds but spoke of bosom-balm,
Of pity prompt and kindness calm;
Of tender care, of anxious zeal;
For here were breasts whose hearts could feel!
'T was as to guest in stranger halls
If voice of friend a welcome calls:
Such pleasure soothes the starting maid,
Who finds some jewel long mislaid;
Pleasure, which blessed dew supplies,
To ease the heart, and float the eyes;
As when in pain attentions prove
A mother's care, a sister's love.
To Woman, Life its value owes!
Robb'd of her love, its dawn and close
Would find nor aid, nor soothing care;
Its middle course no joys would share.
Childhood in vain would thirst and cry,
And Age, unheeded, moan and die;
And Manhood frown to see the hours
Weave scentless wreaths unblest with flowers.
    It beam'd on cheek of sable dye;
No matter, since 't was *woman*'s eye!
Each phrase the tortured language broke;
Enough for me — 't was *woman* spoke!
    Once raven locks my temples wore;
Time has pluck'd many, sorrow more:
Through forty springs (thank God they're run!)
These weary eyes have seen the sun;

And in that space full room is found
For flowers to fade, and thorns to wound.
But now, (all fancy's freaks supprest,
Each thread-bare sneer and wanton jest,)
With hand on heart in serious tone,
With thanks, with truth, I needs must own,
Wide as I 've roam'd the world around,
Roam where I would, I ever found,
The worst of Women still possest
More virtues than of Men the best.
And, oh ! if shipwreck proves my lot,
Guide me, kind Heav'n, to some lone cot
Where *woman* dwells !   Her hand she 'll stretch
In pity to the stranger-wretch;
If virtuous want mine eye surveys,
Nor mine the power his head to raise,
I 'll pour the tale in *woman*'s ear,
She 'll aid, and, aiding, drop a tear.
And when my life-blood sickness drains,
And racks my nerves, and fires my brains,
What kinder juice, what livelier power,
Than mineral yields, or opiate flower,
Can make me e'en in pain rejoice ? —
A few sweet words in that sweet voice !

## JANUARY 6.

This was the day given to my negroes as a festival on my arrival.  A couple of heifers were slaughtered for them : they were allowed as much rum, and sugar, and noise, and dancing as they chose; and as to the two latter, certainly they profited by the permission.  About two o'clock they began to assemble round the house, all drest in their holiday clothes, which, both for men and

women, were chiefly white; only that the women
were decked out with a profusion of beads and
corals, and gold ornaments of all descriptions; and
that while the blacks wore jackets, the mulattoes
generally wore cloth coats; and inasmuch as they
were all plainly clean instead of being shabbily
fashionable, and affected to be nothing except
that which they really were, they looked twenty
times more like gentlemen than nine tenths of the
bankers' clerks who swagger up and down Bond
Street. It is a custom as to the mulatto children,
that the males born on an estate should never be
employed as field negroes, but as tradesmen; the
females are brought up as domestics about the
house. I had particularly invited " *Mr.* John-
Canoe" (which I found to be the polite manner
in which the negroes spoke of him), and there
arrived a couple of very gay and gaudy ones. I enquired whether one of them was "John-Crayfish;"
but I was told that John-Crayfish was John-Canoe's rival and enemy, and might belong to the
factions of "the Blues and the Reds;" but on
Cornwall they were all friends, and therefore there
were only the father and the son—Mr. John-Canoe,
senior, and Mr. John-Canoe, junior.

The person who gave me this information was a
young mulatto carpenter, called Nicholas, whom I
had noticed in the crowd, on my first arrival, for his
clean appearance and intelligent countenance; and
he now begged me to notice the smaller of the two

John-Canoe machines. "To be sure," he said, "it was not so large nor so showy as the other, but then it was much better *proportioned* (his own word), and altogether much prettier;" and he said so much in praise of it, that I asked him whether he knew the maker? and then out came the motive: "Oh, yes! it was made by John Fuller, who lived in the next house to him, and worked in the same shop, and indeed they were just like brothers." So I desired to see his *fidus Achates*, and he brought me as smart and intelligent a little fellow as eye ever beheld, who came grinning from ear to ear to tell me that he had made every bit of the canoe with his own hands, and had set to work upon it the moment that he knew of massa's coming to Jamaica. And indeed it was as fine as paint, pasteboard, gilt paper, and looking-glass could make it! Unluckily, the breeze being very strong blew off a fine glittering umbrella, surmounted with a plume of John Crow feathers, which crowned the top; and a little wag of a negro boy whipped it up, clapped it upon his head, and performed the part of an impromptu Mr. John-Canoe with so much fun and grotesqueness, that he fairly beat the original performers out of the pit, and carried off all the applause of the spectators, and a couple of my dollars. The John-Canoes are fitted out at the expense of the rich negroes, who afterwards share the money collected from the spectators during their performance, allotting one share to the representator himself; and it is usual for the master of the estate to give them a couple of guineas apiece.

This Nicholas, whom I mentioned, is a very interesting person, both from his good looks and gentle manners, and from his story. He is the son of a white man, who on his death-bed charged his nephew and heir to purchase the freedom of this natural child. The nephew had promised to do so; I had consented; nothing was necessary but to find the substitute (which now is no easy matter); when about six months ago the nephew broke his neck, and the property went to a distant relation. Application in behalf of poor Nicholas has been made to the heir, and I heartily hope that he will enable me to release him. I felt strongly tempted to set him at liberty at once; but if I were to begin in that way, there would be no stopping; and it would be doing a kindness to an individual at the expense of all my other negroes—others would expect the same; and then I must either contrive to cultivate my estate with fewer hands — or must cease to cultivate it altogether — and, from inability to maintain them, send my negroes to seek bread for themselves — which, as two thirds of them have been born upon the estate, and many of them are lame, dropsical, and of a great age, would, of all misfortunes that could happen to them, be the most cruel. Even when Nicholas was speaking to me about his liberty, he said, " It is not that I wish to go away, sir; it is only for the name and honour of being free: but I would always stay here and be your servant; and I had rather be an under-work-man on Cornwall, than a head carpenter any where else." Possibly, this was all palaver (in which the negroes are great dealers), but at least he *seemed* to be sincere; and I was heartily grieved that I could not allow myself to say more to him than that I sincerely wished him to get his liberty, and would receive the very lowest exchange for him that common prudence would authorize. And even for those few kind words, the poor fellow seemed to think it impossible to find means strong enough to express his gratitude.

Nor is this the only instance in which Nicholas has been unlucky. It seems that he was the first lover of the beautiful Psyche, whom I had noticed on my arrival. This evening, after the perform-ance of the John-Canoes, I desired to see some of the girls dance; and by general acclamation Psyche was brought forward to exhibit, she being avowedly the best dancer on the estate; and cer-tainly nothing could be more light, graceful, easy, and spirited, than her performance. She perfectly answered the description of Sallust's Sempronia, who was said — "Saltare elegantius, quam necesse est probæ, et cui cariora semper omnia, quam decus et pudicitia fuit." When her dance was over, I called her to me, and gave her a handful of silver. "Ah, Psyche," said Nicholas, who was standing at my elbow, " Massa no give you all that if massa know you so bad girl! she run away from me, massa!" Psyche gave him a kind of pouting look, half kind, and half reproachful, and turned away. And then he told me that Psyche had been his wife (*one* of his wives he should have said); that he had had a child by her, and then she had left him for one of my " white people" (as they call the book-keepers), because he had a good salary, and could afford to give her more presents than a slave could. " Was there not another reason for your quarrelling?" said my agent. " Was there not a shade of colour too much?"— " Oh, massa!" answered Nicholas, " the child is not my own, that is certain; it is a black man's child. But still I will always take care of the child because it have no friends, and me wish make it good neger for massa —and *she* take good care of it too," he added, throwing his arm round the waist of a sickly-looking woman rather in years; " she my wife, too, massa, long ago; old now and sick, but always good to me, so I still live with her, and will never leave her, never, massa; she Polly's mother, sir." Polly is a pretty, delicate-looking girl, nursing a young child; she belongs to the mansion-house, and seems to think it as necessary a part of her duty to nurse *me* as the child. To be sure she has not as yet insisted upon suckling me; but if I open a *jalousie* in the evening, Polly walks in and shuts it without saying aword. "Oh, don't shut the window, Polly." — "Night-air not good for massa;" and she shuts the casement without mercy. I am drinking orangeade, or some such liquid; Polly walks up to the table, and seizes it; "Leave that jug, Polly, I am dying with thirst."—"More hurt, massa;" and away go Polly and the orangeade. So that I begin to fancy myself Sancho in Barataria, and that Polly is the Señor Doctor Pedro in petticoats.

The difference of colour, which had offended Nicholas so much in Psyche's child, is a fault which no mulatto will pardon; nor can the separation of castes in India be more rigidly observed, than that of complexional shades among the Creoles. My black page, Cubina, is married: I told him that I hoped he had married a pretty woman; why had he not married Mary Wiggins? He seemed quite shocked at the very idea. "Oh, massa, me black, Mary Wiggins sambo; that not allowed."

The dances performed to-night seldom admitted more than three persons at a time: to me they appeared to be movements entirely dictated by the caprice of the moment; but I am told that there is a regular figure, and that the least mistake, or a single false step, is immediately noticed by the rest. I could indeed sometimes fancy, that one story represented an old duenna guarding a girl from a lover; and another, the pursuit of a young woman by two suitors, the one young and the other old;

but this might be only fancy. However, I am told, that they have dances which not only represent courtship and marriage, but being brought to bed. Their music consisted of nothing but Gambys (Eboe drums), Shaky-shekies, and Kitty-katties: the latter is nothing but any flat piece of board beat upon with two sticks, and the former is a bladder with a parcel of pebbles in it. But the principal part of the music to which they dance is vocal; one girl generally singing two lines by herself, and being answered by a chorus. To make out either the rhyme of the air, or meaning of the words, was out of the question. But one very long song was about the Duke of Wellington, every stanza being chorussed with,

> " Ay! hey-day! Waterloo!
> Waterloo! ho! ho! ho!"

*I* too had a great deal to do in the business, for every third word was " massa; " though how I came there, I have no more idea than the Duke.

The singing began about six o'clock, and lasted without a moment's pause till two in the morning; and such a noise never did I hear till then. The whole of the floor which was not taken up by the dancers was, through every part of the house except the bed-rooms, occupied by men, women, and children, fast asleep. But although they were allowed rum and sugar by whole pailfuls, and were most of them *merry* in consequence, there was not one of them drunk; except indeed, one person, and that was an old woman, who sang, and shouted, and tossed herself about in an elbow chair, till she tumbled it over, and rolled about the room in a manner which shocked the delicacy of even the least prudish part of the company. At twelve, my agent wanted to dismiss them; but I would not suffer them to be interrupted on the first holiday that I had given them; so they continued to dance and shout till two; when human nature could bear no more, and they left me to my bed, and a violent headache.

### JANUARY 7. (Sunday.)

In spite of their exertions of last night, the negroes were again with me by two o'clock in the day, with their drums and their chorusses. However, they found themselves unable to keep it up as they had done on the former night, and were content to withdraw to their own houses by ten in the evening. But first they requested to have to-morrow to themselves, in order that they might go to the mountains for provisions. For although their cottages are always surrounded with trees and shrubs, their provision grounds are kept quite distinct, and are at a distance among the mountains. Of course, I made no difficulty of acceding to their request, but upon condition, that they should ask for no more holidays till the crop should be completed. For the purpose of culti-

G

vating their provision-grounds, they are allowed every Saturday; but on the occasion of my arrival, they obtained permission to have the Saturday to themselves, and to fetch their week's provisions from the mountains on the following Monday. All the slaves maintain themselves in this manner by their own labour; even the domestic attendants are not exempted, but are expected to feed themselves, except stated allowances of salt fish, salt pork, &c.

### JANUARY 8.

I really believe that the negresses can produce children at pleasure; and where they are barren, it is just as hens will frequently not lay eggs on shipboard, because they do not like their situation. Cubina's wife is in a family way, and I told him that if the child should live, I would christen it for him, if he wished it. "Tank you, kind massa, me like it very much: much oblige if massa do that for *me*, too." So I promised to baptize the father and the baby on the same day, and said that I would be godfather to any children that might be born on the estate during my residence in Jamaica. This was soon spread about, and although I have not yet been here a week, two women are in the straw already, Jug Betty and Minerva: the first is wife to my head driver, the Duke of Sully; but my sense of propriety was much gratified at finding that Minerva's husband was called Captain.

I think nobody will be able to accuse me of neglecting the religious education of my negroes: for I have not only promised to baptize all the infants, but, meeting a little black boy this morning, who said that his name was Moses, I gave him a piece of silver, and told him that it was for the sake of Aaron; which, I flatter myself, was planting in his young mind the rudiments of Christianity.

In my evening's drive I met the negroes, returning from the mountains, with baskets of provisions sufficient to last them for the week. By law they are only allowed every other Saturday for the purpose of cultivating their own grounds, which, indeed, is sufficient; but by giving them every alternate Saturday into the bargain, it enables them to perform their task with so much ease as almost converts it into an amusement; and the frequent visiting their grounds makes them grow habitually as much attached to them as they are to their houses and gardens. It is also adviseable for them to bring home only a week's provisions at a time, rather than a fortnight's; for they are so thoughtless and improvident, that, when they find themselves in possession of a larger supply than is requisite for their immediate occasions, they will sell half to the wandering higglers, or at Savanna la Mar, in exchange for spirits; and then, at the end of the week, they find themselves entirely unprovided with food, and come to beg a supply from the master's storehouse.

### JANUARY 9.

The sensitive plant is a great nuisance in Jamaica: it over-runs the pastures, and, being armed with very strong sharp prickles, it wounds the mouths of the cattle, and, in some places, makes it quite impossible for them to feed. Various endeavours have been made to eradicate this inconvenient weed, but none as yet have proved effectual.

### JANUARY 10.

The houses here are generally built and arranged according to one and the same model. My own is of wood, partly raised upon pillars; it consists of a single floor: a long gallery, called a piazza, terminated at each end by a square room, runs the whole length of the house. On each side of the piazza is a range of bed-rooms, and the porticoes of the two fronts form two more rooms, with balustrades, and flights of steps descending to the lawn. The whole house is virandoed with shifting Venetian blinds to admit air; except that one of the end rooms has sash-windows on account of the rains, which, when they arrive, are so heavy, and shift with the wind so suddenly from the one side to the other, that all the blinds are obliged to be kept closed; consequently the whole house is in total darkness during their continuance, except the single sash-windowed room. There is nothing underneath except a few store-rooms and a kind of waiting-hall; but none of the domestic negroes sleep in the house, all going home at night to their respective cottages and families.

Cornwall House itself stands on a dead flat, and the works are built in its immediate neighbourhood, for the convenience of their being the more under the agent's personal inspection (a point of material consequence with them all, but more particularly for the hospital). This dead flat is only ornamented with a few scattered bread-fruit and cotton trees, a grove of mangoes, and the branch of a small river, which turns the mill. Several of these buildings are ugly enough; but the shops of the cooper, carpenter, and blacksmith, some of the trees in their vicinity, and the negro-huts, embowered in shrubberies, and groves of oranges, plantains, cocoas, and pepper-trees, would be reckoned picturesque in the most ornamented grounds. A large spreading tamarind fronts me at this moment, and overshadows the stables, which are formed of open wickerwork; and an orange-tree, loaded with fruit, grows against the window at which I am writing.

On three sides of the landscape the prospect is bounded by lofty purple mountains; and the variety of occupations going on all around me, and at the same time, give an inconceivable air of life and animation to the whole scene, especially as all those occupations look clean,—even those which in England look dirty. All the tradespeople are dressed either in white jackets and trousers, or with stripes of red and sky-blue. One band of negroes are carrying the ripe canes on their heads to the mill; another set are conveying away the *trash*, after the juice has been extracted; flocks of turkeys are sheltering from the heat under the trees; the river is filled with ducks and geese; the coopers and carpenters are employed about the puncheons; carts drawn some by six, others by eight, oxen, are bringing loads of Indian corn from the fields; the black children are employed in gathering it into the granary, and in quarrelling with pigs as black as themselves, who are equally busy in stealing the corn whenever the children are looking another way: in short, a plantation possesses all the movement and interest of a farm, without its dung, and its stench, and its dirty accompaniments.

## JANUARY 11.

I saw the whole process of sugar-making this morning. The ripe canes are brought in bundles to the mill, where the cleanest of the women are appointed, one to put them into the machine for grinding them, and another to draw them out after the juice has been extracted, when she throws them into an opening in the floor close to her; another band of negroes collects them below, when, under the name of *trash*, they are carried away to serve for fuel. The juice, which is itself at first of a pale ash-colour, gushes out in great streams, quite white

with foam, and passes through a wooden gutter
into the boiling-house, where it is received into the
siphon or " cock copper," where fire is applied to
it, and it is slaked with lime, in order to make it
granulate. The feculent parts of it rise to the top,
while the purer and more fluid flow through another
gutter into the second copper. When little but
the impure scum on the surface remains to be
drawn off, the first gutter communicating with the
copper is stopped, and the grosser parts are obliged
to find a new course through another gutter, which
conveys them to the distillery, where, being mixed
with the molasses, or treacle, they are manufactured
into rum. From the second copper they are trans-
mitted into the first, and thence into two others,
and in these four latter basins the scum is removed
with skimmers pierced with holes, till it becomes
sufficiently free from impurities to be *skipped* off,
that is, to be again ladled out of the coppers and
spread into the coolers, where it is left to granulate.
The sugar is then formed, and is removed into the
*curing-house*, where it is put into hogsheads, and
left to settle for a certain time, during which those
parts which are too poor and too liquid to granulate, drip from the casks into vessels placed beneath them: these drippings are the molasses,
which, being carried into the distillery, and mixed
with the coarser scum formerly mentioned, form
that mixture from which the spirituous liquor of
sugar is afterwards produced by fermentation:

when but once distilled, it is called "low wine;" and it is not till after it has gone through a second distillation, that it acquires the name of rum. The "trash" used for fuel consists of the empty canes, that which is employed for fodder and for thatching is furnished by the superabundant cane-tops; after so many have been set apart as are required for planting. After these original plants have been cut, their roots throw up suckers, which, in time, become canes, and are called *ratoons:* they are far inferior in juice to the planted canes; but then, on the other hand, they require much less weeding, and spare the negroes the only laborious part of the business of sugar-making, the digging holes for the plants; therefore, although an acre of ratoons will produce but one hogshead of sugar, while an acre of plants will produce two, the superiority of the ratooned piece is very great, inasmuch as the saving of time and labour will enable the proprietor to cultivate five acres of ratoons in the same time with one of plants. Unluckily, after three crops, or five at the utmost, in general the ratoons are totally exhausted, and you are obliged to have recourse to fresh plants.

Last night a poor man, named Charles, who had been coachman to my uncle ages ago, was brought into the hospital, having missed a step in the boiling-house, and plunged his foot into the siphon: fortunately, the fire had not long been kindled, and though the liquor was hot enough to scald him, it was not sufficiently so to do him any material injury. The old man had presented himself to me on Saturday's holiday (or *play-day*, in the negro dialect), and had shown me, with great exultation, the coat and waistcoat which had been the last present of his old massa. Charles is now my chief mason, .and, as one of the principal persons on the estate, was entitled, by old custom, to the compliment of a *distinguishing* dollar *on* my arrival; but at the same time that I gave him the dollar, to which his situation entitled him, I gave him another for himself, as a keepsake: he put it into the pocket of " his old massa's" waistcoat, and assured me that they should never again be separated. On hearing of his accident, I went over to the hospital to see that he was well taken care of; and immediately the poor fellow began talking to me about my grandfather, and his young massa, and the young missies, his sisters, and while I suffered him to chatter away for an hour, he totally forgot the pain of his burnt leg.

It was particularly agreeable to me to observe, on Saturday, as a proof of the good treatment which they had experienced, so many old servants of the family, many of whom had been born on the estate, and who, though turned of sixty and seventy, were still strong, healthy, and cheerful. Many manumitted negroes, also, came from other parts of the country to this festival, on hearing of my arrival, because, as they said, — "if they did not come to see massa, they were afraid that it would look ungrateful, and as if they cared no longer about him and Cornwall, now that they were free." So they stayed two or three days on the estate, coming up to the house for their dinners, and going to sleep at night among their friends in their own former habitations, the negro huts; and when they went away, they assured me, that nothing should prevent their coming back to bid me farewell, before I left the island. All this may be palaver; but certainly they at least play their parts with such an air of truth, and warmth, and enthusiasm, that, after the cold hearts and repulsive manners of England, the contrast is infinitely agreeable.

" Je ne vois que des yeux toujours prêts à sourire."

I find it quite impossible to resist the fascination of the conscious pleasure of pleasing; and my own heart, which I have so long been obliged to keep closed, seems to expand itself again in the sunshine of the kind looks and words which meet me at every turn, and seem to wait for mine as anxiously as if they were so many diamonds.

JANUARY 12.

In the year '80, this parish of Westmoreland was kept in a perpetual state of alarm by a runaway negro called *Plato*, who had established himself among the Moreland Mountains, and collected a troop of banditti, of which he was himself the chief. He robbed very often, and murdered occasionally; but gallantry was his every day occupation. Indeed, being a remarkably tall athletic young fellow, among the beauties of his own complexion he found but few Lucretias; and his retreat in the mountains was as well furnished as the haram of Constantinople. Every handsome negress who had the slightest cause of complaint against her master, took the first opportunity of eloping to join *Plato*, where she found freedom, protection, and unbounded generosity; for he spared no pains to secure their affections by gratifying their vanity. Indeed, no Creole lady could venture out on a visit, without running the risk of having her bandbox run away with by Plato for the decoration of his sultanas; and if the maid who carried the bandbox happened to be well-looking, he ran away with the maid as well as the bandbox. Every endeavour to seize this desperado was long in vain: a large reward was put upon his head, but no negro dared to approach him; for, besides his acknowledged courage, he was a professor of Obi, and had threatened that whoever dared to lay a finger upon him should suffer spiritual torments, as well as be physically shot through the head.

Unluckily for Plato, rum was an article with him of the first necessity; the look-out, which was kept for him, was too vigilant to admit of his purchasing spirituous liquors for himself; and once, when for that purpose he had ventured into the neighbourhood of Montego Bay, he was recognised by a slave, who immediately gave the alarm. Unfortunately for this poor fellow, whose name was Taffy, at that moment all his companions happened to be out of hearing; and, after the first moment's alarm, finding that no one approached, the exasperated robber rushed upon him, and lifted the bill-hook, with which he was armed, for the purpose of cleaving his skull. Taffy fled for it; but Plato was the younger, the stronger, and the swifter of the two, and gained upon him every moment. Taffy, however, on the other hand, possessed that one quality by which, according to the fable, the cat was enabled to save herself from the hounds, when the fox, with his thousand tricks, was caught by them. He was an admirable climber, an art in which Plato possessed no skill; and a bread-nut tree, which is remarkably difficult of ascent, presenting itself before him, in a few moments Taffy was bawling for help from the very top of it. To reach him was impossible for his enemy; but still his destruction was hard at hand; for Plato began to hack the tree with his bill, and it was evident that a very short space of time would be sufficient to level it with the ground. In this dilemma, Taffy had nothing for it but to break off the branches near him; and he contrived to pelt these so dexterously at the head of his assailant, that he fairly kept him at bay till his cries at length reached the ears of his companions, and their approach compelled the banditti-captain once more to seek safety among the mountains.

After this Plato no longer dared to approach Montego town; but still spirits must be had : — how was he to obtain them ? There was an old watchman on the outskirts of the estate of Canaan, with whom he had contracted an acquaintance, and frequently had passed the night in his hut; the old man having been equally induced by his presents and by dread of his corporeal strength and supposed supernatural power, to profess the warmest attachment to the interests of his terrible friend. To this man Plato at length resolved to entrust himself: he gave him money to purchase spirits, and appointed a particular day when he would come to receive them. The reward placed upon the robber's head was more than either gratitude or terror could counterbalance; and on the same day when the watchman set out to purchase the rum, he apprised two of his friends at Canaan, for whose use it was intended, and advised *them* to take the opportunity of obtaining the reward.

The two negroes posted themselves in proper time near the watchman's hut. Most unwisely, instead of sending down some of his gang, they saw Plato, in his full confidence in the friendship of his confidant, arrive himself and enter the cabin; but so great was their alarm at seeing this dreadful personage, that they remained in their concealment, nor dared to make an attempt at seizing him. The spirits were delivered to the robber: he might have retired with them unmolested; but, in his rashness and his eagerness to taste the liquor, of which he had so long been deprived, he opened the flagon, and swallowed draught after draught, till he sunk upon the ground in a state of complete insensibility. The watchman then summoned the two negroes from their concealment, who bound his arms, and conveyed him to Montego Bay, where he was immediately sentenced to execution. He died most heroically; kept up the terrors of his imposture to his last moment; told the magistrates, who condemned him, that his death should be revenged by a storm, which would lay waste the whole island, that year; and, when his negro gaoler was binding him to the stake at which he was destined to suffer, he assured him that he should not live long to triumph in his death, for that he had taken good care to Obeah him before his quitting the prison. It certainly did happen, strangely enough, that, before the year was over, the most violent storm took place ever known in Jamaica; and as to the gaoler, his imagination was so forcibly struck by the threats of the dying man, that, although every care was taken of him, the power of medicine exhausted, and even a voyage to America undertaken, in hopes that a change of scene might change the course of his ideas, still, from the moment of Plato's death, he gradually pined and withered away, and finally expired before the completion of the twelvemonth.

The belief in Obeah is now greatly weakened,

but still exists in some degree. Not above ten months ago, my agent was informed that a negro of very suspicious manners and appearance was harboured by some of my people on the mountain lands. He found means to have him surprised, and on examination there was found upon him a bag containing a great variety of strange materials for incantations; such as thunder-stones, cat's ears, the feet of various animals, human hair, fish bones, the teeth of alligators, &c.: he was conveyed to Montego Bay; and no sooner was it understood that this old African was in prison, than depositions were poured in from all quarters from negroes who deposed to having seen him exercise his magical arts, and, in particular, to his having sold such and such slaves medicines and charms to deliver them from their enemies; being, in plain English, nothing else than rank poisons. He was convicted of Obeah upon the most indubitable evidence. The good old practice of burning has fallen into disrepute; so he was sentenced to be transported, and was shipped off the island, to the great satisfaction of persons of all colours — white, black, and yellow.

### January 13.

Throughout the island many estates, formerly very flourishing and productive, have been thrown up for want of hands to cultivate them, and are now suffered to lie waste: four are in this situation in my own immediate neighbourhood. Finding their complement of negroes decrease, and having no means of recruiting them, proprietors of two estates have in numerous instances found themselves obliged to give up one of them, and draw off the negroes for the purpose of properly cultivating the other.

I have just had an instance strikingly convincing of the extreme nicety required in rearing negro children. Two have been born since my arrival. My housekeeper was hardly ever out of the lying-in apartment; I always visited it myself once a day, and sometimes twice, in order that I might be certain of the women being well taken care of; not a day passed without the inspection of a physician; nothing of indulgence, that was proper for them, was denied; and, besides their ordinary food, the mothers received every day the most nourishing and palatable dish that was brought to my own table. Add to this, that the women themselves were kind-hearted creatures, and particularly anxious to rear these children, because I had promised to be their godfather myself. Yet, in spite of all this attention and indulgence, one of the mothers, during the nurse's absence for ten minutes, grew alarmed at her infant's apparent sleepiness. To rouse it, she began dancing and shaking it till it was in a strong perspiration, and then she stood with it for some minutes at an open window, while a strong north wind was blowing. In consequence, it caught cold, and the next morning symptoms of

a locked jaw showed itself. The poor woman was
the image of grief itself: she sat on her bed,
looking at the child which lay by her side with its
little hands clasped, its teeth clenched, and its eyes
fixed, writhing in the agony of the spasm, while
she was herself quite motionless and speechless,
although the tears trickled down her cheeks incessantly. All assistance was fruitless: her thought-
lessness for five minutes had killed the infant, and,
at noon to-day it expired.

This woman was a tender mother, had borne ten
children, and yet has now but one alive: another,
at present in the hospital, has borne seven, and
but one has lived to puberty; and the instances
of those who have had four, five, six children,
without succeeding in bringing up one, in spite
of the utmost attention and indulgence, are very
numerous; so heedless and inattentive are the
best-intentioned mothers, and so subject in this
climate are infants to dangerous complaints. The
locked jaw is the common and most fatal one; so
fatal, indeed, that the midwife (the *graundee* is her
negro appellation) told me, the other day, " Oh,
massa, till nine days over, we *no hope* of them."
Certainly care and kindness are not adequate to
save the children, for the son of a sovereign could
not have been more anxiously well treated than
was the poor little negro who died this morning.

The negroes are always buried in their own gardens, and many strange and fantastical ceremonies

are observed on the occasion. If the corpse be that of a grown person, they consult it as to which way it pleases to be carried; and they make attempts upon various roads without success, before they can hit upon the right one. Till that is accomplished, they stagger under the weight of the coffin, struggle against its force, which draws them in a different direction from that in which they had settled to go; and sometimes in the contest the corpse and the coffin jump off the shoulders of the bearers. But if, as is frequently the case, any person is suspected of having hastened the catastrophe, the corpse will then refuse to go any road but the one which passes by the habitation of the suspected person, and as soon as it approaches his house, no human power is equal to persuading it to pass. As the negroes are extremely superstitious, and very much afraid of ghosts (whom they call the *duppy*), I rather wonder at their choosing to have their dead buried in their gardens; but I understand their argument to be, that they need only fear the duppies of their enemies, but have nothing to apprehend from those after death, who loved them in their lifetime; but the duppies of their adversaries are very alarming beings, equally powerful by day as by night, and who not only are spiritually terrific, but who can give very hard substantial knocks on the pate, whenever they see fit occasion, and can find a good opportunity.

Last Saturday a negro was brought into the hospital, having fallen into epileptic fits, with which till then he had never been troubled. As the faintings had seized him at the slaughter-house, and the fellow was an African, it was at first supposed by his companions, that the sight and smell of the meat had affected him; for many of the Africans cannot endure animal food of any kind, and most of the Ebres in particular are made ill by eating turtle, even although they can use any other food without injury. However, upon enquiry among his shipmates, it appeared that he had frequently eaten beef without the slightest inconvenience. For my own part, the symptoms of his complaint were such as to make me suspect him of having tasted something poisonous, especially as, just before his first fit, he had been observed in the small grove of mangoes near the house; but I was assured by the negroes, one and all, that nothing could possibly have induced him to eat an herb or fruit from that grove, as it had been used as a burying-ground for " the white people." But although my idea of the poison was scouted, still the mention of the burying-ground suggested another cause for his illness to the negroes, and they had no sort of doubt, that in passing through the burying-ground he had been struck down by the duppy of a white person not long deceased, whom he had formerly offended, and that these repeated fainting-fits were the consequence of that ghostly blow. The negroes have in various publications been accused of a total want of religion, but this appears to me quite incompatible with the ideas of spirits existing after dissolution of the body, which necessarily implies a belief in a future state; and although (as far as I can make out) they have no outward forms of religion, the most devout Christian cannot have " God bless you" oftener on his lips than the negro; nor, on the other hand, appear to feel the wish for their enemy's damnation more sincerely when he utters it.

The Africans (as is well known) generally believe, that there is a life beyond this world, and that they shall enjoy it by returning to their own country; and this idea used frequently to induce them, soon after their landing in the colonies, to commit suicide; but this was never known to take place except among fresh negroes, and since the execrable slave-trade has been abolished, such an illusion is unheard of. As to those who had once got over the dreadful period of " seasoning," they were generally soon sensible enough of the amelioration of their condition, to make the idea of returning to Africa the most painful that could be presented to them. But, to be sure, poor creatures! what with the terrors and sufferings of the voyage, and the unavoidable hardships of the seasoning, those advantages were purchased more dearly than any in this life can possibly be worth. God be thanked, all that is now at an end; and

certainly, as far as I can as yet judge, if I were
now standing on the banks of Virgil's Lethe, with a
goblet of the waters of oblivion in my hand, and
asked whether I chose to enter life anew as an
English labourer or a Jamaica negro, I should have
no hesitation in preferring the latter. For myself,
it appears to me almost worth surrendering the luxuries and pleasures of Great Britain, for the single
pleasure of being surrounded with beings who are
always laughing and singing, and who seem to perform their work with so much *nonchalance*, taking
up their baskets as if it were perfectly optional whether they took them up or left them there; saun-
tering along with their hands dangling; stopping
to chat with every one they meet; or if they meet
no one, standing still to look round, and examine
whether there is nothing to be seen that can
amuse them, so that I can hardly persuade myself
that it is really *work* that they are about. The
negro might well say, on his arrival in England
— " Massa, in England every thing work!" for
here nobody appears to work at all.

I am told that there is one part of their business
very laborious, the digging holes for receiving the
cane-plants, and which I have not as yet seen; but
this does not occupy above a month (I believe) at
the utmost, at two periods of the year; and on
my estate this service is chiefly performed by extra
negroes, hired for the purpose; which, although
equally hard on the hired negroes (called a jobbing

gang), at least relieves my own, and after all, puts
even the former on much the same footing with
English day-labourers.

But if I could be contented to *live* in Jamaica,
I am still more certain, that it is the only agreeable
place for me to die in; for I have got a family
mausoleum, which looks for all the world like the
theatrical representation of the " tomb of all the
Capulets." Its outside is most plentifully decorated
" with sculptured stones,"——

> " Arms, angels, epitaphs, and bones."

Within is a tomb of the purest white marble, raised
on a platform of ebony; the building, which is
surmounted by a statue of Time, with his scythe
and hour-glass, stands in the very heart of an
orange grove, now in full bearing; and the whole
scene this morning looked so cool, so tranquil, and
so gay, and is so perfectly divested of all vestiges
of dissolution, that the sight of it quite gave me an
appetite for being buried. It is a matter of perfect indifference to me what becomes of this little
ugly husk of mine, when once I shall have " shuffled
off this mortal coil;" or else I should certainly
follow my grandfather's example, and, die where I
might, order my body to be sent over for burial to
Cornwall; for I never yet saw a place where one
could lie down more comfortably to listen for the
last trumpet.

JANUARY 14. (Sunday.)

I gave a dinner to my " white people," as the
book-keepers, &c. are called here, and who have a
separate house and establishment for themselves;
and certainly a man must be destitute of every
spark of hospitality, and have had " Caucasus
horrens " for his great-grandmother, if he can resist
giving dinners in a country where Nature seems to
have set up a superior kind of " London Tavern "
of her own. They who are possessed by the " Ci-
borum ambitiosa fames, et lautæ gloria mensæ,"
ought to ship themselves off for Jamaica out of
hand; and even the lord mayor himself need not
blush to give his aldermen such a dinner as is
placed on my table, even when I dine alone. Land
and sea turtle, quails, snipes, plovers, and pigeons
and doves of all descriptions—of which the ring-tail
has been allowed to rank with the most exquisite
of the winged species, by epicures of such distinction, that their opinion, in matters of this nature,
almost carries with it the weight of a law, — excellent pork, barbicued pigs, pepperpots, with numberless other excellent dishes, form the ordinary
fare; while the poultry is so large and fine, that if
the Dragon of Wantley found "houses and churches
to be geese and turkies" in England, he would
mistake the geese and turkies for houses and
churches here. Then our tarts are made of pine-
apples, and pine-apples make the best tarts that I

ever tasted; there is no end of the variety of fruits, of which the shaddock is " in itself an host;" but the most singular and exquisite flavour, perhaps, is to be found in the granadillo, a fruit which grows upon a species of vine, and, in fact, appears to be a kind of cucumber. It must be suffered to hang till it is dead ripe, when it is scarcely any thing except juice and seeds, which can only be eaten with a spoon. It requires sugar, but the acid is truly delicious, and like no other separate flavour that I ever met with; what it most resembles is a *mace-doine*, as it unites the different tastes of almost all other fruits, and has, at the same time, a very strong flavour of wine.

As to fish, Savannah la Mar is reckoned the best place in the island, both for variety and *safety;* for, in many parts, the fish feed upon copperas banks, and cannot be used without much precaution: here, none is necessary, and it is only to be wished that their names equalled their flesh in taste; for it must be owned, that nothing can be less tempting than the sounds of Jew-fish, hog-fish, mud-fish, snappers, god-dammies, groupas, and grunts! Of the Sea Fish which I have hitherto met with, the Deep-water Silk appears to me the best; and of rivers, the Mountain-Mullet: but, indeed, the fish is generally so excellent, and in such profusion, that I never sit down to table without wishing for the company of Queen Atygatis of Scythia, who was so particularly fond of fish, that she prohibited all her subjects from eating it on pain of death, through fear that there might not be enough left for her majesty.

This fondness for fish seems to be a sort of royal passion: more than one of our English sovereigns died of eating too many lampreys; though, to own the truth, it was suspected that the monks, in an instance or two, improved the same by the addition of a little ratsbane; and Mirabeau assures us, that Frederick the Second of Prussia might have prolonged his existence, if he could but have resisted the fascination of an eel-pye; but the charm was too strong for him, and, like his great-grandmother of all, he ate and died—" All for eel-pye, or this world well lost!" And now, which had to resist the most difficult temptation, Frederic or Eve? *She* longed to experience pleasures yet untasted, and which she fancied to be exquisite: *he*, like Sigismunda, pined after known pleasures, and which he knew to be good; *she* was the dupe of imagination; *he* fell a victim to established habit. Which was the most deserving pardon? There is a question for the bishops: those clergymen who reside constantly on their livings (as all clergymen ought to do, or they ought not to be clergymen), I shall, in charity, believe to have something better to do with their time than to solve it.

The provision-grounds of the negroes furnish them with plantains, bananas, cocoa-nuts, and yams: of the latter there is a regular harvest once a year, and they remain in great perfection for many months, provided they are dug up carefully, but the slightest wound with the spade is sufficient to rot them. Catalue (a species of spinach) is a principal article in their pepper-pots; but in this parish their most valuable and regular supply of food arises from the cocoa-finger, or coccos, a species of the yam, but which lasts all the year round. These vegetables form the basis of negro sustenance; but the slaves also receive from their owners a regular weekly allowance of red herrings and salt meat, which serves to relish their vegetable diet; and, indeed, they are so passionately fond of salted provisions, that, instead of giving them fresh beef (as at their festival of Saturday last), I have been advised to provide some hogsheads of salt fish, as likely to afford them more gratification, at such future additional holidays as I may find it possible to allow them in this busy season of crop.

## JANUARY 15.

The offspring of a white man and black woman is a *mulatto;* the mulatto and black produce a *sambo;* from the mulatto and white comes the *quadroon;* from the quadroon and white the *mustee;* the child of a mustee by a white man is called a *musteefino;* while the children of a musteefino are free by law, and rank as white persons to all intents and purposes. I think it is Long who asserts, that two mulattoes will never have children;

but, as far as the most positive assurances can go, since my arrival in Jamaica, I have reason to believe the contrary, and that mulattoes breed together just as well as blacks and whites; but they are almost universally weak and effeminate persons, and thus their children are very difficult to rear. On a sugar estate one black is considered as more than equal to two mulattoes. Beautiful as are their forms in general, and easy and graceful as are their movements (which, indeed, appear to me so striking, that they cannot fail to excite the admiration of any one who has ever looked with delight on statues), still the women of colour are deficient in one of the most requisite points of female beauty. When Oromases was employed in the formation of woman, and said, — " Let her enchanting bosom resemble the celestial spheres," he must certainly have suffered the negress to slip out of his mind. Young or old, I have not yet seen such a thing as a *bosom*.

## JANUARY 16.

I never witnessed on the stage a scene so picturesque as a negro village. I walked through my own to-day, and visited the houses of the drivers, and other principal persons; and if I were to decide according to my own taste, I should infinitely have preferred their habitations to my own. Each house is surrounded by a separate garden, and the whole village is intersected by lanes, bordered with

all kinds of sweet-smelling and flowering plants;
but not such gardens as those belonging to our
English cottages, where a few cabbages and carrots
just peep up and grovel upon the earth between
hedges, in square narrow beds, and where the
tallest tree is a gooseberry bush: the vegetables of
the negroes are all cultivated in their provision-
grounds; these form their *kitchen*-gardens, and
these are all for ornament or luxury, and are filled
with a profusion of oranges, shaddocks, cocoa-nuts,
and peppers of all descriptions: in particular I
was shown the abba, or palm-tree, resembling the
cocoa-tree, but much more beautiful, as its leaves
are larger and more numerous, and, feathering to
the ground as they grow old, they form a kind of
natural arbour. It bears a large fruit, or rather
vegetable, towards the top of the tree, in shape
like the cone of the pine, but formed of seeds,
some scarlet and bright as coral, others of a
brownish-red or purple. The abba requires a
length of years to arrive at maturity: a very fine
one, which was shown me this morning, was supposed to be upwards of an hundred years old; and
one of a very moderate size had been planted at the
least twenty years, and had only borne fruit once.
It appears to me a strong proof of the good
treatment which the negroes on Cornwall have
been accustomed to receive, that there are many
very old people upon it; I saw to-day a woman
near a hundred years of age; and I am told that

there are several of sixty, seventy, and eighty. I was glad, also, to find, that several negroes who have obtained their freedom, and possess little pro-perties of their own in the mountains, and at Sa-vannah la Mar, look upon my estate so little as the scene of their former sufferings while slaves, that they frequently come down to pass a few days in their ancient habitations with their former com-panions, by way of relaxation. One woman in particular expressed her hopes, that I should not be offended at her still coming to Cornwall now and then, although she belonged to it no longer; and begged me to give directions before my return to England, that her visits should not be hindered on the grounds of her having no business there.

My visit to Jamaica has at least produced one advantage to myself. Several runaways, who had disappeared for some time (some even for several months), have again made their appearance in the field, and I have desired that no questions should be asked. On the other hand, after enjoying her-self during the Saturday and Sunday, which were allowed for holidays on my arrival, one of my ladies chose to *pull foot*, and did not return from her hiding-place in the mountains till this morning. Her name is Marcia; but so unlike is she to Addi-son's Marcia, that she is not only as black as Juba, (instead of being " fair, oh! how divinely fair!") but,—whereas Sempronius complains, that "Marcia, the lovely Marcia, is left behind," the complaint against my heroine is, that "Marcia, the lovely Marcia," is always running away. In excuse for her disappearance she alleged, that so far was her husband from thinking that "she towered above her sex," that he had called her "a very bad woman," which had provoked her so much, that she could not bear to stay with him; and she assured me, that he was himself "a very bad man;" which, if true, was certainly enough to justify any lady, black or white, in making a little incognito excursion for a week or so; therefore, as it appeared to be nothing more than a conjugal quarrel, and as Marcia engaged never to run away any more (at the same time allowing that she had suffered her resentment to carry her too far, when it had carried her all the way to the mountains), I desired that an act of oblivion might be passed in favour of Cato's daughter, and away she went, quite happy, to pick hog's meat.

The negro houses are composed of wattles on the outside, with rafters of sweet-wood, and are well plastered within and whitewashed; they consist of two chambers, one for cooking and the other for sleeping, and are, in general, well furnished with chairs, tables, &c., and I saw none without a four-post bedstead and plenty of bed-clothes; for, in spite of the warmth of the climate, when the sun is not above the horizon the negro always feels very chilly. I am assured that many of my slaves are very rich (and their property is inviolable), and that they are never without salt provisions, porter, and even wine, to entertain their friends and their visiters from the bay or the mountains. As I passed through their grounds, many little requests were preferred to me : one wanted an additional supply of lime for the whitewashing his house; another was building a new house for a superannuated wife (for they have all so much decency as to call their sexual attachments by a conjugal name), and wanted a little assistance towards the finishing it; a third requested a new axe to work with; and several entreated me to negotiate the purchase of some relation or friend belonging to another estate, and with whom they were anxious to be reunited : but all their requests were for additional indulgences; not one complained of ill-treatment, hunger, or over-work.

Poor Nicholas gave me a fresh instance of his being one of those whom Fortune pitches upon to show her spite : he has had four children, none of whom are alive; and the eldest of them, a fine little girl of four years old, fell into the mill-stream, and was drowned before any one was aware of her danger. His wife told me that she had had fifteen children, had taken the utmost care of them, and yet had now but two alive : she said, indeed, fifteen at the first, but she afterwards corrected herself, and explained that she had had " twelve whole children and three half ones ;" by which she meant miscarriages.

Besides the profits arising from their superabundance of provisions, which the better sort of negroes are enabled to sell regularly once a week at Savannah la Mar to a considerable amount, they keep a large stock of poultry, and pigs without number; which latter cost their owners but little, though they cost me a great deal; for they generally make their way into the cane-pieces, and sometimes eat me up an hogshead of sugar in the course of the morning: but the most expensive of the planter's enemies are the rats, whose numbers are incredible, and are so destructive that a reward is given for killing them. During the last six months my agent has paid for three thousand rats killed upon Cornwall. Nor is the sugar which they consume the worst damage which they commit; the worst mischief is, that if, through the carelessness of those whose business it is to supply the mill, one cane which has been gnawed by the rats is allowed admittance, that single damaged piece is sufficient to produce acidity enough to spoil the whole sugar.

### JANUARY 17.

In this country there is scarcely any twilight, and all nature seems to wake at the same moment. About six o'clock the darkness disperses, the sun rises, and instantly every thing is in motion: the negroes are going to the field, the cattle are driving to pasture, the pigs and the poultry are pouring out from their hutches, the old women are preparing food on the lawn for the *pickaninnies* (the very small children), whom they keep feeding at all hours of the day; and all seem to be going to their employments, none to their work, the men and the women just as quietly and leisurely as the pigs and the poultry. The sight is really quite gay and amusing, and I am generally out of bed in time to enjoy it, especially as the continuance of the cool north breezes renders the weather still delicious, though the pleasure is rather an expensive one. Not a drop of rain has fallen since the 16th of November; the young canes are burning; and the drying quality of these norths is still more detrimental than the want of rain, so that these winds may be said to blow my pockets inside out; and as every draught of air, which I inhale with so much pleasure, is estimated to cost me a guinea, I feel, while breathing it, like Miss Burney's Citizen at Vauxhall, who kept muttering to himself, with every bit of ham that he put into his mouth, "There goes sixpence, and there goes a shilling!"

## JANUARY 18.

A Galli-wasp, which was killed in the neighbouring morass, has just been brought to me. This is the Alligator in miniature, and is even more dreaded by the negroes than its great relation: it is only to be found in swamps and morasses: that which was brought to me was about eighteen inches in length, and I understand that it is sel-

I

dom longer, although, as it grows in years, its thickness and the size of its jaws and head become greatly increased. It runs away on being encountered, and conceals itself; and it is only dangerous if trampled upon by accident, or if attacked; but then its bite is a dreadful one, not only from its tongue being armed with a sting (the venom of which is very powerful, although not mortal), but from its teeth being so brittle that they generally break in the wound, and as it is hardly possible to extract the pieces entirely, the wound corrupts, and becomes an incurable sore of the most offensive nature. Luckily, these reptiles are very scarce, but nothing can exceed the terror and aversion in which they are held by the negroes. This dead one had been lying in the room for several hours, yet, on my servant's accidentally stirring the board on which the galli-wasp was stretched for my inspection, my little negro servant George darted out of the room in terror, and was at the bottom of the staircase in a moment. The skin of this animal appeared to be like shagreen in looks and strength, and was almost entirely composed of layers of very small scales; the colours were brownish-yellow and olive-green, the teeth numerous and piercing, and the claws of the feet very long and sharp: altogether it is a hideous and disgusting creature. As to the alligator of Jamaica, it is a timid animal, which never was known to attack the human species, though it frequently takes the liberty of running away with a dog or two, which appears to be their venison and turtle. There is no river on my estate large enough for their inhabiting; but, in Paradise River, which is not above four miles off, I understand that they are common.

## JANUARY 19.

A young mulatto carpenter, belonging to Horace Beckford's estate of Shrewsbury, came to beg my intercession with his overseer. He had been absent two days without leave, and on these occasions it is customary for the slaves to apply to some neighbouring gentleman for a note in their behalf, which, as I am told, never fails to obtain the pardon required, as the managers of estates are in general but too happy to find an excuse for passing over without punishment any offences which are not very heinous; indeed, what with the excellent laws already enacted for the protection of the slaves, and which every year are still further ameliorated, and what with the difficulty of procuring more negroes — (which can now only be done by purchasing them from other estates), — which makes it absolutely necessary for the managers to preserve the slaves, if they mean to preserve their own situations, — I am fully persuaded that instances of tyranny to negroes are now very rare, at least in this island. But I must still acknowledge, from my own sad experience, since my arrival, that unless a West-Indian proprietor occasionally visit his estates himself, it is utterly impossible for him to be *certain* that his deputed authority is not abused, however good may be his intentions, and however vigilant his anxiety.

My father was one of the most humane and generous persons that ever existed; there was no indulgence which he ever denied his negroes, and his letters were filled with the most absolute injunctions for their good treatment. When his estates became mine, the one upon which I am now residing was managed by an attorney, considerably advanced in years, who had been long in our employment, and who bore the highest character for probity and humanity. He was both attorney and overseer; and it was a particular recommendation to me that he lived in my own house, and therefore had my slaves so immediately under his eye, that it was impossible for any subaltern to misuse them without his knowledge. His letters to me expressed the greatest anxiety and attention respecting the welfare and comfort of the slaves;—so much so, indeed, that when I detailed his mode of management to Lord Holland, he observed, "that if he did all that was mentioned in his letters, he did as much as could possibly be expected or wished from an attorney;" and on parting with his own, Lord Holland was induced to take mine to manage his estates, which are in the immediate neighbourhood of Cornwall. This man died about two years ago, and since my arrival, I happened to hear, that during his management a remarkably fine young penn-keeper, named Richard (the brother of my intelligent carpenter, John Fuller), had run away several times to the mountains. I had taken occasion to let the brothers know, between jest and earnest, that I was aware of Richard's misconduct; and at length, one morning, John, while he blamed his brother's running away, let fall, that he had some excuse in the extreme ill-usage which he had received from one of the book-keepers, who " had had a spite against him." The hint alarmed me; I followed it, and nothing could equal my anger and surprise at learning the whole truth.

·· It seems, that while I fancied my attorney to be resident on Cornwall, he was, in fact, generally attending to a property of his own, or looking after estates of which also he had the management in distant parts of the island. During his absence, an overseer of his own appointing, without my knowledge, was left in absolute possession of his power, which he abused to such a degree, that almost every slave of respectability on the estate was compelled to become a runaway. The property was nearly ruined, and absolutely in a state of rebellion; and at length he committed an act of such severity, that the negroes, one and all, fled to Savannah la Mar, and threw themselves upon the protection of the magistrates, who immediately came over to Cornwall, investigated the complaint, and *now*, at length, the attorney, who had known frequent instances of the overseer's tyranny, had frequently rebuked him for them, and had redressed the sufferers, but who still had dared to abuse my confidence so grossly as to continue him in his situation, upon this public exposure thought proper to dismiss him.   Yet, while all this was going on—while my negroes were groaning under the iron rod of this petty tyrant—and while the public magistrature was obliged to interfere to protect them from his cruelty—my attorney had the insolence and falsehood to write me letters, filled with assurances of his perpetual vigilance for their welfare—of their perfect good treatment and satisfaction ; nor, if I had not come myself to Jamaica, in all probability should I ever have had the most distant idea how abominably the poor creatures had been misused.

I have made it my business to mix as much as possible among the negroes, and have given them every encouragement to repose confidence in me; and I have uniformly found all those, upon whom any reliance can be placed, unite in praising the humanity of their present superintendant.   Instantly on his arrival, he took the whole power of punishment into his own hands : he forbade the slightest interference in this respect of any person whatever on the estate, white or black; nor have I been able to find as yet any one negro who has any charge of harsh treatment to bring against him.

However, having been already so grossly deceived, I will never again place implicit confidence in any person whatever in a matter of such importance. Before my departure, I shall take every possible measure that may prevent any misconduct taking place without my being apprised of it as soon as possible; and I have already exhorted my negroes to apply to the magistrates on the very first instance of ill-usage, should any occur during my absence.

I am indeed assured by every one about me, that to manage a West-Indian estate without the occasional use of the cart-whip, however rarely, is impossible; and they insist upon it, that it is absurd in me to call my slaves ill-treated, because, when they act grossly wrong, they are treated like English soldiers and sailors. All this may be very true; but there is something to me so shocking in the idea of this execrable cart-whip, that I have positively forbidden the use of it on Cornwall; and if the estate must go to rack and ruin without its use, to rack and ruin the estate must go. Probably, I should care less about this punishment, if I had not been living among those on whom it may be inflicted; but now, when I am accustomed to see every face that looks upon me, grinning from ear to ear with pleasure at my notice, and hear every voice cry "God bless you, massa," as I pass, one must be an absolute brute not to feel unwilling to leave them subject to the lash; besides, they are excellent cajolers, and lay it on with a trowel. Nicholas and John Fuller came to me this morning to beg a favour, " and beg massa hard, quite hard! " It was, that when massa went away, he would leave his picture for the negroes; " that they might talk to it, all just as they did to massa." Shakspeare says —

" A little flattery does well sometimes ! "

But, although the mode of expressing it may be artifice, the sentiment of good-will may be shown. A dog grows attached to the person who feeds and makes much of him; and as they have never experienced as yet any but kind treatment from me personally, it would be against common sense and nature to suppose that my negroes do not feel kindly towards me.

## JANUARY 20.

### THE RUNAWAY.

Peter, Peter was a black boy;
   Peter, him pull foot one day :
Buckra girl, him* Peter's joy;
   Lilly white girl entice him away.
Fye, Missy Sally, fye on you !
Poor Blacky Peter why undo ?
Oh ! Peter, Peter was a bad boy;
   Peter was a runaway.

* The negroes never distinguish between " him " and " her " in their conversation.

Peter, him Massa thief — Oh ! fye !
  Missy Sally, him say him do so.
Him money spent, Sally bid him bye,
  And from Peter away him go ;
Fye, Missy Sally, fye on you !
Poor Blacky Peter what him do ?
Oh ! Peter, Peter was a sad boy ;
Peter was a runaway !

Peter, him go to him Massa back ;
  There him humbly own him crime :
" Massa, forgib one poor young Black !
  Oh ! Massa, good Massa, forgib dis time ! " —
Then in come him Missy so fine, so gay,
And to him Peter thus him say :
" Oh ! Missy, good Missy, you for me pray !
Beg Massa forgib poor runaway ! "

" Missy, you cheeks so red, so white ;
  Missy, you eyes like diamond shine !
Missy, you Massa's sole delight,
  And Lilly Sally, him was mine !
Him say — ' Come, Peter, mid me go ! ' —
Could me refuse him ?  Could me say ' no ? ' —
Poor Peter — ' no ' him could no say !
So Peter, Peter ran away ! " —

Him Missy him pray ; him Massa so kind
  Was moved by him prayer, and to Peter him say :
" Well, boy, for this once I forgive you ! — but mind !
  With the buckra girls you no more go away !
Though fair without, they 're foul within ;
Their heart is black, though white their skin.
Then Peter, Peter with me stay ;
Peter no more run away ! " —

JANUARY 21. (Sunday.)

The hospital has been crowded, since my arrival, with patients who have nothing the matter with them. On Wednesday there were about thirty invalids, of whom only four were cases at all serious; the rest had " a lilly pain here, Massa," or " a bad pain me know nowhere, Massa," and evidently only came to the hospital in order to sit idle, and chat away the time with their friends. Four of them the doctor ordered into the field peremptorily; the next day there came into the sick-house six others; upon this I resolved to try my own hand at curing them; and I directed the head-driver to announce, that the presents which I had brought from England should be distributed to-day, that the new-born children should be christened, and that the negroes might take possession of my house, and amuse themselves till twelve at night. The effect of my prescription was magical; two thirds of the sick were hale and hearty, at work in the field on Saturday morning, and to-day not a soul remained in the hospital except the four serious cases.

The christening took place about four o'clock. Sully's infant, which had been destined to perform a part on this occasion, had died in the hospital; but this morning the father came to complain of his disappointment, and to beg leave to substitute a child by *another* wife, which had been born about two months before my arrival; and as the father is a very serviceable fellow, and the mother, besides having brought up three children of her own, had the additional merit of having reared an infant whose own mother had died in child-bed, I broke through the rule of only christening those myself who should be born since my coming to Jamaica, and granted his request. By good luck, the first child to be named was the offspring of Minerva and Captain; so I told the parents that as it would be highly proper to call the boy after the greatest Captain that the world could produce, he should be named Wellington; and that I hoped that he would grow up to serve *me* in Jamaica as well as the Duke of Wellington had served his massa, the King of England, in Europe. The Duke of Sully's child I wanted to call Navarre; but the father had brought over a free negro from Savannah la Mar to stand godfather, who was his *fidus Achates*, by the name of John Davies, and I found that he had set his heart upon calling the boy John Lewis, after his friend and myself; so John Lewis he was.

There ought to have been a third child, born at seven months, whom the *graundee* had reared with great difficulty, and dismissed, quite strong, from the hospital; the mother had taken great care of it till the tenth day, when she was en- titled to an allowance of clothes, provisions, &c.; but no sooner had she received her reward, than on that very night she suffered the child to remain so

long without food, while she went herself to dance
on a neighbouring estate, that it was brought, in
an exhausted state, back to the hospital; and, in
spite of every care, it expired within four and
twenty hours after its return.

. The ceremony was performed with perfect gravity and propriety by all parties; I thought it as
well to cut the reading part of it very short; but
I read a couple of prayers, marked the foreheads
of the children with the sign of the cross, and, instead of the concluding prayer, I substituted a wish,
" that God would bless the children, and make
them live to be as good servants to me, as I prayed
him to make me a kind massa to them;" upon
which all present very gravely made me their
lowest bows and courtesies, and then gave me a
loud huzza; so unusual a mode of approbation at a
christening that it had nearly overturned my seri-
ousness; and I made haste to serve out Madeira
to the parents and assistants, that they might drink
the healths of the new Christians and of each other.
The mothers and the *graundee* were then called up
to the table, and the ladies in a family way were
arranged behind them.

. *Their* title in Jamaica is rather coarse, but very
expressive. I asked Cubina one day " who was
that woman with a basket on her head?" " Massa,"
he answered, " that one belly-woman going to sell
provisions at the Bay." As she was going to sell
*provisions*, I supposed that *belly*-woman was the

name of her trade; but it afterwards appeared that she was one of those females who had given in their names as being then labouring under

" The pleasing punishment which women bear;"

and who, in consequence, were discharged from all severe labour. I then gave the *graundee* and the mothers a dollar each, and told them, that for the future they might claim the same sum, in addition to their usual allowance of clothes and provisions, for every infant which should be brought to the overseer alive and well on the fourteenth day; and I also gave each mother a present of a scarlet girdle with a silver medal in the centre, telling her always to wear it on feasts and holidays, when it should entitle her to marks of peculiar respect and attention, such as being one of the first served, and receiving a larger portion than the rest; that the *first* fault which she might commit, should be forgiven on the production of this girdle; and that when she should have any favour to ask, she should always put it round her waist, and be assured, that on seeing it, the overseer would allow the wearer to be entitled to particular indulgence. On every additional child an additional medal is to be affixed to the belt, and precedence is to follow the greater number of medals. I expected that this notion of an order of honour would have been treated as completely fanciful and romantic; but to my great surprise, my manager told me, that " he never knew a dollar better bestowed than the one which formed the medal of the girdle, and that he thought the institution likely to have a very good effect."

Immediately after the christening the Eboe drums were produced, and in defiance of Sunday the negroes had the irreverence to be gay and happy, while the presents were getting in order for distribution. All the men got jackets, the women seven yards of stuff each for petticoats, &c., and the children as much printed cotton as would make a couple of frocks. The Creoles were delighted beyond measure when some of the African male negroes exclaimed, " Tank, massa," and made a low courtesy in the confusion of their gratitude. As they were all called to receive their presents alphabetically in pairs, some of the combinations were very amusing. We had Punch and Plato, Priam and Pam, Hemp and Hercules, and Minerva and Moll come together. By twelve they dispersed, and I went to bed, as usual on these occasions, with a violent headach.

### January 22.

While I was at dinner, a violent uproar was heard below stairs. On enquiry, it proved to be Cubina, quarrelling with his niece Phillis (a good-looking black girl employed about the house), about a broken pitcher; and as her explanation did not appear satisfactory to him, he had thought

proper to give her a few boxes on the ear. Upon
hearing this, I read him such a lecture upon the
baseness of a man's striking a woman, and told
him with so much severity that his heart must be
a bad one to commit such an offence, that poor
Cubina, having never heard a harsh word from me
before, scarcely knew whether he stood upon his
head or his heels. When he afterwards brought
my coffee, he expressed his sorrow for having
offended me, and begged my pardon in the most
humble manner. I told him, that to obtain mine,
he must first obtain that of Phillis, and he immediately declared himself ready to make her any
apology that I might dictate. So the girl was
called in; and her uncle going up to her, " I am
very sorry, Phillis," said he, " that I gave way to
high passion, and called you hard names, and
struck you: which I ought not to have done while
massa was in the house;" (here I was going to
interrupt him, but he was too clever not to perceive his blunder, and made haste to add) " nor if
he had *not* been here, nor at all; so I hope you
will have the kindness to forgive me this once, and
I never will strike you again, and so I beg your pardon." And he then put out his hand to her in the
most frank and hearty manner imaginable; and on
her accepting it, made her three or four of his very
lowest and most graceful bows. I furnished him
with a piece of money to give her as a peace-offer-
ing; they left the room thoroughly reconciled, and

in five minutes after they and the rest of the servants were all chattering, laughing, and singing
together, in the most perfect harmony and good-
humour. I suppose, if I had desired an upper
servant in England to make the same submission,
he would have preferred quitting my service to
doing what he would have called " humbling himself to an inferior;" or, if he had found himself
compelled to give way, he would have been sulky
with the girl, and found fault with every thing that
she did in the house for a twelvemonth after.

On the other hand, there are some choice ungrateful scoundrels among the negroes: on the night
of their first dance, a couple of sheep disappeared
from the pen, although they could not have been
taken from want of food, as on that very morning
there had been an ample distribution of fresh beef;
and last night another sheep and a quantity of
poultry followed them. Yesterday, too, a young
rascal of a boy called " massa Jackey," who is in
the frequent habit of running away for months at
a time, and whom I had distinguished from the
cleverness of his countenance and buffoonery of his
manners, came to beg my permission to go and
purchase food with some money which I had just
given him, " because he was almost starving; his
parents were dead, he had no provision-grounds, no
allowance, and nobody ever gave him anything."
Upon this I sent Cubina with the boy to the store-
keeper, when it appeared that he had always re-

ceived a regular allowance of provisions twice a week, which he generally sold, as well as his clothes, at the Bay, for spirits; had received an additional portion only last Friday; and, into the bargain, during the whole of that week had been fed from the house. What he could propose to himself by telling a lie which must be so soon detected, I cannot conceive; but I am assured, that unless a negro has an interest in telling the truth, he always lies — in order to keep his tongue in practice.

One species of flattery (or of *Congo-saw*, as we call it here) amused me much this morning: an old woman who is in the hospital wanted to express her gratitude for some stewed fish which I had sent her for supper, and, instead of calling me " massa," she always said — " Tank him, *my husband.*"

### JANUARY 24.

This was a day of perpetual occupation. I rose at six o'clock, and went down to the Bay to settle some business; on my return I visited the hospital while breakfast was getting ready; and as soon as it was over, I went down to the negro-houses to hear the whole body of Eboes lodge a complaint against one of the book-keepers, and appoint a day for their being heard in his presence. On my return to the house, I found two women belonging to a neighbouring estate, who came to complain of cruel treatment from their overseer, and to request

me to inform their trustee how ill they had been
used, and see their injuries redressed. They said,
that having been ill in the hospital, and ordered to
the field while they were still too weak to work, they
had been flogged with much severity (though not
beyond the limits of the law); and my head driver,
who was less scrupulously delicate than myself as
to ocular inspection of Juliet's person (which
Juliet, to do her justice, was perfectly ready to
submit to in proof of her assertions), told me, that
the woman had certainly suffered greatly; the
other, whose name was Delia, was but just recovering from a miscarriage, and declared openly that
the overseer's conduct had been such, that nothing
should have prevented her running away long ago
if she could but have had the heart to abandon a
child which she had on the estate. Both were
poor feeble-looking creatures, and seemed very
unfit subjects for any severe correction. I promised
to write to their trustee; and, as they were afraid
of being punished on their return home for having
thrown themselves on my protection, I wrote a
note to the overseer, requesting that the women
might remain quite unmolested till the trustee's
arrival, which was daily expected; and, with this
note and a present of cocoa-fingers and salt fish,
Delia and Juliet departed, apparently much com-
forted.

They were succeeded by no less a personage
than *Venus* herself — a poor, little, sickly, timid

soul, who had purchased her freedom from my
father by substituting in her place a fine stout
black wench, who, being Venus's *locum tenens*, was,
by courtesy, called Venus, too, though her right
name was " Big Joan;" but, by some neglect of
the then attorney, Venus had never received any
title, and she now came to beg " massa so good as
give paper;" otherwise she was still, to all intents
and purposes, my slave, and I might still have
compelled her to work, although, at the same
time, her substitute was on the estate. Of course,
I promised the paper required, and engaged to act
the part of a second Vulcan by releasing Venus
from my chains: but the paper was not the only
thing that Venus wanted; she also wanted a petticoat! She told me, that when the presents were
distributed on Sunday, the petticoat, which she
would otherwise have had, was, of course, " given
to the *other* Venus;" and though, to be sure, she
was free now, yet, " when she belonged to massa,
she had always worked for him well," and " she
was quite as glad to see massa as the other Venus,"
and, therefore, " ought to have quite as much
petticoat." I tried to convince her, that for Venus
to wear a petticoat of blue durant, or, indeed, any
petticoat at all, would be quite unclassical: the
goddess of beauty stuck to her point, and finally
carried off the petticoat.

Venus had scarcely evacuated the premises,
when her place was occupied by the minister of

Savannah la Mar, with proposals for instructing
the negroes in religion; and the minister, in his
turn, was replaced by one of the Sunday-night
thieves, who had been caught while in the actual
possession of one of my sheep and a great turkey-
cock; and, to make the matter worse, the de-
predator's name was Hercules! Hercules, whom
Virgil states to have exercised so much severity
on Cacus, when his own oxen were stolen, was
taken up himself for stealing my sheep in Jamaica!
The demi-god had nothing to say in his excuse:
he had just received a large allowance of beef: —
therefore, hunger had no share in his transgression;
and the committing the offence during the very time
that I was giving the negroes a festival, rendered
his ingratitude the more flagrant.

I perfectly well understood that the man was sent
to me by my agent, in order to show the absolute
necessity of sometimes employing the cart-whip, and
to see whether I would suffer the fellow to escape
unpunished. But, as this was the first offender who
had been brought before me, I took that for a
pretext to absolve him: so I lectured him for half
an hour with great severity, swore that on the very
next offence I would order him to be sold; and that if
he would not do his fair proportion of work without
being lashed, he should be sent to work somewhere
else; for I would suffer no such worthless fellows
on my estate, and would not be at the expense of
a cart-whip to correct him. He promised most

earnestly to behave better in future, and Hercules was suffered to depart: but I am told that no good can be expected of him; that he is perpetually running away; and that he had been absent for five weeks together before my arrival, and only returned home upon hearing that there was a distribution of beef, rum, and jackets going forward; in return for all which, he stole my sheep and my poor great turkey-cock.

But now came the most puzzling business of the day. About four years ago, two Eboes, called Pickle and Edward, were rivals, after being intimate friends: Pickle (who is an excellent faithful negro, but not very wise) was the successful candidate; and, of course, the friendship was interrupted, till Edward married the sister of the disputed fair one. From this time the brothers-in-law lived in perfect harmony together; but, during the first festival given on my arrival, Pickle's house was broken open, and robbed of all his clothes, &c. The thief was sought for, but in vain. On Monday last I found Pickle in the hospital, complaining of a pain in his side; and the blood, which had been taken from him, gave reason to apprehend a pleurisy arising from cold; but, as the disorder had been taken in its earliest stage, nothing dangerous was expected. The fever abated; the medicines performed their offices properly; still the man's spirits and strength appeared to decline, and he persisted in saying that he was not better,

and should never do well. At length, to-day, he
got out of his sick bed, came to the house, attended
by the whole body of drivers, and accused his
brother-in-law of having been the stealer of his
goods. I asked, " Had Edward been seen near
his house? Had any of his effects been seen in
Edward's possession? Did Edward refuse to suffer
his hut to be searched?" No. Edward, who was
present, pressed for the most strict scrutiny, and
asserted his perfect ignorance; nor could the ac-
cuser advance any grounds for the charge, except
his belief of Edward's guilt. " Why did he think
so?" After much beating about the bush, at
length out came the real *causa doloris*—" Edward
had *Obeahed* him!" He had accused Edward of
breaking open his house, and had begged him to
help him to his goods again; and " Edward had
gone at midnight into the bush" (i. e. the wood),
and " had gathered the plant whangra, which he
had boiled in an iron pot, by a fire of leaves, over
which he went puff, puffie!" and said the sautee-
sautee; and then had cut the whangra root into
four pieces, three to bury at the plantation gates,
and one to burn; and to each of these three pieces
he gave the name of a Christian, one of which was
Daniel; and Edward had said, that this would
help him to find his goods; but instead of that, he
had immediately felt this pain in his side, and
therefore he was sure that, instead of using Obeah
to find his goods, Edward had used it to kill him-

self. " And were these all his reasons ?" I enquired. " No; when he married, Edward was very
angry at the loss of his mistress, and had said that
they never would live well and happily together;
and they never *had* lived happily and well together.".

This last argument quite got the better of my
gravity. By parity of reasoning, I thought that
almost every married couple in Great Britain must
be under the influence of Obeah! I endeavoured
to convince the fellow of his folly and injustice,
especially as the person accused was the identical
man who had detected the Obeah priest harboured
in one of my negro huts last year, had seized him
with his own hands, and delivered him up to my
agent, who had prosecuted and transported him.
It was, therefore, improbable in the highest degree,
that he should be an Obeah man himself; and all
the bystanders, black and white, joined me in
ridiculing Pickle for complaints so improbable and
childish. But anger, argument, and irony were
all ineffectual. I offered to christen him, and expel
black Obeah by white, but in vain; the fellow
persisted in saying, that " he had a pain in his side,
and, *therefore*, Edward must have given it to him;"
and he went back to his hospital, shaking his head
all the way, sullen and unconvinced. He is a
young strong negro, perfectly well disposed, and
doing his due portion of work willingly; and it

will be truly provoking to lose him by the influence of this foolish prejudice.

### JANUARY 25.

I sent for Edward, had him alone with me for above two hours, and pressed him most earnestly to confide in me. I gave him a dollar to convince him of my good-will towards him; assured him that whatever he might tell me should remain a secret between us; said, that I was certain of his not having used any poison, or done any thing really mischievous; but as I suspected him of having played some monkey-tricks or other, which, however harmless in themselves, had evidently operated dangerously upon Pickle's imagination, I begged him to tell me precisely what had passed, in order that I might counteract its baleful effects. In reply, Edward swore to me most solemnly, "by the great God Almighty, who lives above the clouds," that he never had used any such practices: that he had never gone into the wood to gather whangra; and that he had considered Pickle, from the moment of his own marriage, as his brother, and had always, till then, loved him as such. His eyes filled with tears while he protested that he should be as sorry for Pickle's death as if it were himself; and he complained bitterly of having the ill name of an Obeah man given to him, which made him feared and shunned by his companions, and entirely without cause. But he said that he was certain that Pickle would never have suspected him of such a crime, if a third person had not put it into his head. There is a negro on my estate called Adam, who has been long and strongly suspected of having connections with Obeah men. When Edward was quite young, he was under this fellow's superintendence, and he now assured me, that Adam had not only endeavoured to draw him into similar practices, but had even pressed him very earnestly to lay a magical egg under the door of a book-keeper whose conduct had been obnoxious. Edward had positively refused: from that moment his superintendent, from being his protector, had become his enemy, had shown him spite upon every occasion; and he it was, he had no doubt, who, for the purpose of injuring him, had put this foolish notion into Pickle's head.

Upon enquiry it appeared, that on the very morning succeeding Pickle's entering the hospital, this suspected man had gone there also, on pretence of sickness, and had remained there to watch the invalid; although it was so evident that nothing was the matter with him, that the doctor had frequently ordered him to the field, but the man had always found means for evading the order. The first thing that we now did was to turn him out of the sick-house, neck and heels; I then took Edward with me to Pickle's bedside, where the former told his brother-in-law, that if he had ever done any thing to offend him, he heartily begged his pardon;

that he swore by the Almighty God that he had
never been in the bush to hurt him, nor any where
else; on the contrary, that he had always loved
him, and wished him well; and that he now begged
him to be friends with him again, to forget and forgive all former quarrels, and to accept the hand
which he offered him in all sincerity. The sick
man also confessed, that he had always loved Edward as his brother, had " eaten and drunk with
him for many years with perfect good-will," and that
it was his ingratitude for such affection which vexed
him more than any thing. On this I told him, that
I insisted upon their being good friends for the
future, and that I should never hear the word
Obeah, or any such nonsense, mentioned on my
estate, on pain of my extreme displeasure. I promised that, as soon as Pickle should be quite recovered, I would buy for him exactly a set of such
things as had been stolen from him; that Edward
should bring them to his house, to show that he
had rather give him things than take them away;
and I then desired to see them shake hands. They
did so, with much apparent cordiality; Edward
then went back to his work; and this evening,
when I sent him a dish from my table, Pickle desired the servant to tell me, that he had hardly any
fever, and felt " *quite so so*," which, in the negro
dialect, means " a great deal better." I begin,
therefore, to hope that we shall save the foolish fellow's life at last, which, at one time, appeared to
be in great jeopardy.

There was a great dinner and ball for the whole county given to-day at Montego Bay, to which I was invited; but I begged leave to decline this and all other invitations, being determined to give up my whole time to my negroes during my stay in Jamaica.

### JANUARY 26.

Every morning my agent regales me with some fresh instance of insubordination: he says nothing plainly, but shakes his head, and evidently gives me to understand, that the estate cannot be governed properly without the cart-whip. It seems that this morning, the women, one and all, refused to carry away the *trash* (which is one of the easiest tasks that can be set), and that without the slightest pretence: in consequence, the mill was obliged to be stopped; and when the driver on that station insisted on their doing their duty, a little fierce young devil of a Miss Whaunica flew at his throat, and endeavoured to strangle him: the agent was obliged to be called in, and, at length, this petticoat rebellion was subdued, and every thing went on as usual. I have, in consequence, assured the women, that since they will not be managed by fair treatment, I must have recourse to other measures; and that, if any similar instance of misconduct should take place, I was determined, on my return from Kingston, to sell the most refractory, ship myself immediately for England, and never return to them and Jamaica more. This threat, at the time, seemed to produce a great effect; all hands were clasped, and all voices were raised, imploring me not to leave them, and assuring me, that in future they would do their work quietly and willingly. But whether the impression will last beyond the immediate moment is a point greatly to be doubted.

## JANUARY 27.

Another morning, with the mill stopped, no liquor in the boiling-house, and no work done. The driver brought the most obstinate and insolent of the women to be lectured by me; and I bounced and stormed for half an hour with all my might and main, especially at Whaunica, whose ingratitude was peculiar; as she is the wife of Edward, the Eboe, whom I had been protecting against the charge of theft and Obeahism, and had shown him more than usual kindness. They, at last, appeared to be very penitent and ashamed of themselves, and engaged never to behave ill again, if I would but forgive them this present fault; Whaunica, in particular, assuring me very earnestly, that I never should have cause to accuse her of " bad manners " again; for, in negro dialect, ingratitude is always called " bad manners." My agent declares, that they never conducted themselves so ill before; that they worked cheerfully and properly till my arrival; but now they think that I shall protect them against all punishment, and have made regularly ten hogsheads of sugar a week less than they did before my coming upon the estate. This is the more provoking, as, by delaying the conclusion of the crop, the latter part of it may be driven into the rainy season, and then the labour is infinitely more severe both for the slaves and the cattle, and more detrimental to their health.

The minister of Savannah la Mar has shown me a plan for the religious instruction of the negroes, which was sent to him by the ecclesiastical commissaries at Kingston. It consisted but of two points: against the first (which recommended the slaves being *ordered* to go to church on a Sunday) I positively declared myself. Sunday is now the absolute property of the negroes for their relaxation, as Saturday is for the cultivation of their grounds; and I will not suffer a single hour of it to be taken from them for any purpose whatever. If my slaves choose to go to church on Sundays, so much the better; but not one of them shall be *ordered* to do one earthly thing on Sundays, but that which he chooses himself. The second article recommended occasional pastoral visits of the minister to the different estates; and in this respect I promised to give him every facility — although I greatly doubt any good effect being produced by a few short visits, at considerable intervals, on the minds of ignorant creatures, to whom no palpable and immediate benefit is offered. It appears, indeed, to me, that the only means of giving the negroes morality and religion must be through the medium of education, and their being induced to read such books in the minister's absence as may recall to their thoughts what they have heard from him; otherwise, he may talk for an hour, and they will have understood but little—and remember nothing. There is not a single negro among my whole three hundred who can read a line; and what I suppose to be wanted on West-Indian estates is not an importation of missionaries, but of schoolmasters on Dr. Bell's plan, if it could by any means be introduced here with effect. However, in the mean while I told the minister, that I was perfectly well inclined to have every measure tried that might enlighten the minds of the negroes, provided it did not interfere with their own hours of leisure, and were not compulsory. I mentioned to him a plan for commencing his instructions under the most favourable auspices, of which he seemed to approve; and he has promised to make occasional visits on my estate during my absence, which may do good and can do no harm; and, even should it fail to make the negroes religious, will, at least, add another humane inspector to my list. / Soon after the minister's departure, John Fuller came to repair one of the windows. Now John is in great disgrace with me in one respect. Instead of having a wife on the estate, he keeps one at the Bay, so that his children will not belong to me. Phillis, too, who formerly lived with John, says, that she parted with him, because he threw away all his money upon the Bay girls; though John asserts that the cause of separation was his catching the false Phillis coming out of one of the book-keepers' bedrooms.

However, it is certain, that now his connections are all at the Bay; and I have assured him, that if he does not provide himself with a wife at Cornwall, before my return from Kingston, I will put him up to auction, and call the girls together to bid for him, one offering half a dozen yams, and another a bit of salt fish; and the highest bidder shall carry him off as her property. But to-day, as he came into the room just as the minister left it, I told him that Dr. Pope was coming to give the negroes some instruction; and that he had left part of a catechism for him, which he was to get by heart against his next visit. John promised to study it diligently, and went off to get it read to him by one of the book-keepers. Several of his companions came to hear it from curiosity, and the book-keeper read aloud: —

> " John Fuller is gone to the Bay, boys,
>     On the girls to spend his cash;
>     And when John Fuller comes home, boys,
>     John Fuller deserves the lash."

So John went away shaking his head, and saying, " Massa had told him, that the minister had left that paper to make him a better Christian. But he was certain that the minister had nothing to do with that, and that massa had made it all himself about the Bay girls."

## JANUARY 28. (Sunday.)

I shall have enough to do in Jamaica if I accept all the offices that are pressed upon me. A large body of negroes, from a neighbouring estate, came over to Cornwall this morning, to complain of hard treatment, in various ways, from their overseer and drivers, and requesting me to represent their injuries to their trustee here, and their proprietor in England. The charges were so strong, that I am certain that they must be fictitious; however, I listened to their story with patience; promised that the trustee (whom I was to see in a few days) should know their complaint;—and they went away apparently satisfied. Then came a runaway negro, who wanted to return home, and requested me to write a few lines to his master, to save him from the lash. He was succeeded by a poor creature named Bessie, who, although still a young woman, is dispensed with from labour, on account of her being afflicted with the *cocoa-bay*, one of the most horrible of negro diseases. It shows itself in large blotches and swellings, and which generally, by degrees, moulder away the joints of the toes and fingers, till they rot and drop off; sometimes as much as half a foot will go at once. As the disease is communicable by contact, the person so afflicted is necessarily shunned by society; and this poor woman, who is married to John Fuller, one of the best young men on the estate, and by whom she has had four children (although they are all dead), has for some time been obliged to live separated from him, lest he should be destroyed by contracting the same complaint. She now came to tell me, that she wanted a blanket, "for that the cold killed her of nights;" cold being that which negroes dislike most, and from which most of their illnesses arise. Of course she got her blanket; then she said, that she wanted medicine for her complaint. "Had not the doctor seen her?" "Oh, yes! Dr. Goodwin; but the white doctor could do her no good. She wanted to go to a black doctor, named Ormond, who belonged to a neighbouring gentleman." I told her, that if this black doctor understood her particular disease better than others, certainly she should go to him; but that if he pretended to cure her by charms or spells, or any thing but medicine, I should desire his master to cure the black doctor by giving him the punishment proper for such an impostor. Upon this Bessie burst into tears, and said "that Ormond was not an Obeah man, and that she had suffered too much by Obeah men to wish to have any more to do with them. She had made Adam her enemy by betraying him, when he had attempted to poison the former attorney; he

L

had then cursed her, and wished that she might never be hearty again: and from that very time her complaint had declared itself; and her poor pickaninies had all died away, one after another; and she was sure that it was Adam who had done all this mischief by Obeah." Upon this, I put myself in a great rage, and asked her "how she could believe that God would suffer a low wicked fellow like Adam to make good people die, merely because he wished them dead?" "She did not know; she knew nothing about God; had never heard of any such Being, nor of any other world." I told her, that God was a great personage, "who lived up yonder above the blue, in a place full of pleasures and free from pains, where Adam and wicked people could not come; that her pickaninies were not dead for ever, but were only gone up to live with God, who was good, and would take care of them for her; and that if she were good, when she died, she too would go up to God above the blue, and see all her four pickaninies again." The idea seemed so new and so agreeable to the poor creature, that she clapped her hands together, and began laughing for joy; so I said to her every thing that I could imagine likely to remove her prejudice; told her that I should make it a crime even so much as to mention the word Obeah on the estate; and that, if any negro from that time forward should be proved to have accused another of Obeahing him, or of telling another that he had been Obeahed, he should forfeit his share of the next present of salt-fish, which I meant soon to distribute among the slaves, and should never receive any favour from me in future; so I gave Bessie a piece of money, and she seemed to go away in better spirits than she came.

This Adam, of whom she complained, is a most dangerous fellow, and the terror of all his companions, with whom he lives in a constant state of warfare. He is a creole, born on my own property, and has several sisters, who have obtained their freedom, and are in every respect creditable and praiseworthy; and to one of whom I consider myself as particularly indebted, as she was the means of saving poor Richard's life, when the tyranny of the overseer had brought him almost to the brink of the grave. But this brother is in every thing the very reverse of his sisters: there is no doubt of his having (as Bessie stated) infused poison into the water-jars through spite against the late superintendent. It was this same fellow whom Edward suspected of having put into his brother-in-law's head the idea of his having been bewitched; and it was also in his hut that the old Obeah man was found concealed, whom my attorney seized and transported last year. He is, unfortunately, clever and plausible; and I am told that the mischief which he has already done, by working upon the folly and superstition of his fellows, is incalculable; yet I cannot get rid of him: the law will not suffer any negro to be shipped off the island, until he shall have been convicted of felony at the sessions; I cannot sell him, for nobody would buy him, nor even accept him, if I would offer them so dangerous a present; if he were to go away, the law would seize him, and bring him back to me, and I should be obliged to pay heavily for his re-taking and his maintenance in the workhouse. In short, I know not what I can do with him, except indeed make a Christian of him! This might induce the negroes to believe, that he had lost his infernal power by the superior virtue of the holy water; but, perhaps he may refuse to be christened. However, I will at least ask him the question; and if he consents, I will send him — and a couple of dollars — to the clergyman — for he shall not have so great a distinction as baptism from massa's own hand — and see what effect " white Obeah" will have in removing the terrors of this professor of the black.

As to my sick Obeah patient, Pickle, from the moment of his reconciliation with his brother-in-law he began to mend, and has recovered with wonderful rapidity: the fellow seems *really* grateful for the pains which I have taken about him; and our difficulty now is to prevent his fancying himself too soon able to quit the hospital, so eager is he to return " to work for massa."

There are certainly many excellent qualities in the negro character; their worst faults appear to be, this prejudice respecting Obeah, and the facility with which they are frequently induced to poison to the right hand and to the left. A neighbouring gentleman, as I hear, has now three negroes in prison, all domestics, and one of them grown grey in his service, for poisoning him with corrosive sublimate; his brother was actually killed by similar means; yet I am assured that both of them were reckoned men of great humanity. Another agent, who appears to be in high favour with the negroes whom he now governs, was obliged to quit an estate, from the frequent attempts to poison him; and a person against whom there is no sort of charge alleged for tyranny, after being brought to the doors of death by a cup of coffee, only escaped a second time by his civility, in giving the beverage, prepared for himself, to two young book-keepers, to both of whom it proved fatal. It, indeed, came out, afterwards, that this crime was also effected by the abominable belief in Obeah: the woman, who mixed the draught, had no idea of its being poison; but she had received the deleterious ingredients from an Obeah man, as " a charm to make her massa good to her; " by which the negroes mean, the compelling a person to give another every thing for which that other may ask him.

Next to this vile trick of poisoning people (arising, doubtless, in a great measure, from their total want of religion, and their ignorance of a future state, which makes them dread no punishment hereafter for themselves, and look with but little respect on human life in others), the greatest drawback upon one's comfort in a Jamaica existence seems to me to be the being obliged to live perpetually in public. Certainly, if a man was desirous of leading a life of vice *here*, he must have set himself totally above shame, for he may depend upon every thing done by him being seen and known. The houses are absolutely transparent; the walls are nothing but windows—and all the doors stand wide open. No servants are in waiting to announce arrivals: visiters, negroes, dogs, cats, poultry, all walk in and out, and up and down your living-rooms, without the slightest ceremony.

Even the Temple of Cloacina (which, by the bye, is here very elegantly spoken of generally as "*The* Temple,") is as much latticed and as pervious to the eye as any other part of my premises; and many a time has my delicacy been put to the blush by the ill-timed civility of some old woman or other, who, wandering that way, and happening to cast her eye to the left, has stopped her course to curtsy very gravely, and pay me the passing compliment of an " Ah, massa! bless you, massa! how day ?"

#### JANUARY 29.

I find that Bessie's black doctor is really nothing more than a professor of medicine as to this par-

ticular disease ; and I have ordered her to be sent
to him in the mountains immediately. Several
gentlemen of the county dined with me to-day,
and when they left me, one of the carriages contrived to get overturned, and the right shoulder of
one of the gentlemen was dislocated. Luckily, it
happened close to the house ; and as the physician
who attends my estate had dined with me also, a
boy, on a mule, was despatched after him with all
haste. He was soon with us, the bone was replaced with perfect ease, and this morning the
patient left me with every prospect of finding no
bad effects whatever from his accident.

We had at dinner a land tortoise and a barbecued
pig, two of the best and richest dishes that I ever
tasted ; — the latter, in particular — which was
dressed in the true maroon fashion, being placed
on a barbecue (a frame of wicker-work, through
whose interstices the steam can ascend), filled with
peppers and spices of the highest flavour, wrapt in
plantain leaves, and then buried in a hole filled
with hot stones, by whose vapour it is baked, no
particle of the juice being thus suffered to evapo-
rate. I have eaten several other good Jamaica
dishes, but none so excellent as this, a large portion
of which was transferred to the most infirm patients
in the hospital. Perhaps an English physician would
have felt every hair of his wig bristle upon his head
with astonishment, at hearing me ask, this morning,
a woman in a fever, how her bark and her barbe-

cued pig had agreed with her. But, with negroes, I find that feeding the sick upon stewed fish and pork, highly seasoned, produces the very best effects possible.

Some of the fruits here are excellent, such as shaddocks, oranges, granadelloes, forbidden fruit; and one between an orange and a lemon, called " the grape or cluster fruit," appears to me quite delicious. For the vegetables, I cannot say so much, yams, plantains, cocoa poyers, yam-poys, bananas, &c. look and taste all so much alike, that I scarcely know one from the other: they are all something between bread and potatoes, not so good as either, and I am quite tired of them all. The Lima Bean is said to be more like a pea than a bean, but whatever it be like, it appeared to me very indifferent. As to peas themselves, nothing can be worse. The achie fruit is a kind of vegetable, which generally is fried in butter; many people, I am told, are fond of it, but I could find no merit in it. The palm-tree (or abba, as it is called here) produces a long scarlet or reddish brown cone, which separates into beads, each of which contains a roasting nut surrounded by a kind of stringy husk—which, being boiled in salt and water, upon being chewn has a taste of artichoke, but the consistence is very disagreeable. The only native vegetable, which I like much, is the ochra, which tastes like asparagus, though not with quite so delicate a flavour.

As to fish, the variety is endless; but I think it rather consists in variety of names than of flavour. From this, however, I must except the Silk-Fish and Mud-Fish, and above all, the Mountain-Mullet, which is almost the best fish that I ever tasted. All the shell-fish, that I have met with as yet, have been excellent; the oysters have not come in my way, but I am told that they are not only poor and insipid, but frequently are so poisonous that I had better not venture upon them; and so ends this chapter of the "Almanach des Gourmands" for Jamaica.

## JANUARY 30.

There were above twenty ladies literally at my feet this morning. I went down to the negro-village to speak to Bessie about going to her black doctor; and all the refractory females of last week heard of my being there, and came in a body to promise better conduct for the future, and implore me not to go away. The sight of my carriage getting ready to take me to Kingston, and the arrival of post-horses, had alarmed them with the idea that I was really going to put my threats into execution of leaving them for ever. They had artfully enough prevailed on the wife of Clifford (the driver whom Whannica had collared) to be their spokes-woman; and they begged, and lifted up their folded hands, and cried, and fell on the ground, and kissed my feet—and, in short, acted their part so well, that they almost made me act mine to perfection, and fall to blubbering. I told them, that I certainly should go to Kingston on Thursday; but if I had good accounts of them during my absence, I should return in a few days;— if, on the contrary, the idle negroes continued to refuse to work without compulsion, then, in justice to the good ones (who last week were obliged to do more than their share), those punishments, which I had stopped, must be resumed;—but that, as Cornwall would be unsupportable to me, if I could not live there without hearing the crack of the abominable cart-whip all day long, I would not return to it, but ship myself off for England, and never visit them or Jamaica any more. And then I talked very sternly and positively about "punishments" and "making bad negroes do their work properly," and every third word was the cart-whip, till I almost fancied myself the princess in the "Fairy Tale," who never opened her mouth, but out came two toads and three couple of serpents. However, to sweeten my oration a little at the end, I told them, that, "having enquired closely into the characters of the present book-keepers, I had found no charge against any of them except one, who was accused of having occasionally struck a negro, of using bad language to them, and of being a hasty passionate man, though in other respects very serviceable to the estate. But although these faults were but trifling,

and some of them not proved, so determined was
I to show that <u>I would suffer no white person on
the estate who maltreated the negroes, either by
word or deed,</u> that I had determined to make an
example of him for the warning of the rest; and
accordingly had dismissed him this morning."

The man in question (by his own account) had
made himself obnoxious to them; and on hearing of
his discharge, they, one and all, sprawled upon the
ground in such a rapture of joy and gratitude, that
now I may safely say with Sir Andrew Aguecheek,
" I was adored once!"

The book-keeper had denied positively the
charge of striking the negroes, and ascribed it to
the revenge of the Eboe Edward, whom he had
detected in cutting out part of a boiling-house
window, in order that he might pass out stolen
sugar unperceived; for, to do the negroes justice,
it is a doubt whether they are the greatest thieves
or liars, and the quantity of sugar which they pur-
loin during the crop, and dispose of at the Bay for
a mere trifle, is enormous. However, whether
the charge of striking were true or not, it was
sufficiently proved that this book-keeper was a
passionate man, and he said himself, " that the
negroes had conceived a spite against him," which
alone were reasons enough for removing him. Indeed, I had the less scruple from the slight nature
of his offence making it easy for him to find another
situation; and I have besides desired him to stay

out his quarter on the estate, and then receive a double salary on going away, which will free him from any charge of having been dismissed disgracefully.

JANUARY 31.

I went to enquire after my petitioners Juliet and Delia, and had the satisfaction to find that the trustee had enquired into their complaint; and, as it appeared not to be entirely unfounded, he had done every thing that was right and necessary. Aberdeen, too, the runaway cooper, who had applied to me to obtain his pardon, had been suffered to return to his work unpunished; and as it had been found that his flight had in a great measure been occasioned by his being in a bad state of health, which rendered him apprehensive of being put to labour beyond his strength, he had been permitted to select his own occupation, which, of course, was the easiest one in his trade. But I found it a more difficult matter to ascertain the truth or falsehood of the charges brought to me on Sunday last: the books positively contradicted them, but the register might have been falsely kept; and as the negroes persisted most positively in their complaint against the overseer (particularly as to his having curtailed them of the legal allowance of time for their meals, and the cultivation of their own grounds) with the concurrence of the trustee, I wrote to the magistrates of the county, desiring that they would summon the negroes in question before a

council of protection, and examine into the injuries of which they had complained to me.

#### FEBRUARY 1. (Thursday.)

I left Cornwall for Spanish Town at six in the
morning, accompanied by a young naval officer, the
son of my next neighbour, Mr. Hill of Amity, who
not only was good enough to lend me a kittereen,
with a canopy, to perform my journey, but his son
to be my *cicerone* on my tour. The road wound
through mountain passes, or else on a shelf of
rock so narrow — though without the slightest
danger — that one of the wheels was frequently
in the sea, while my other side was fenced by a
line of bold broken cliffs, clothed with trees
completely from their brows down to the very
edge of the water. Between eight and nine we
reached a solitary tavern, called Blue-fields, where
the horses rested for a couple of hours. It had a
very pretty garden on the sea-shore, which contained a picturesque cottage, exactly resembling
an ornamental Hermitage; and leaning against
one of the pillars of its porch we found a young
girl, who exactly answered George Colman's description of Yarico, " quite brown, but extremely
genteel, like a Wedgewood teapot." She told us
that she was a Spanish creole, who had fled with
her mother from the disputes between the royalists
and independents in the island of Old Providence;
and the owner of the tavern being a relation of

her mother, he had permitted the fugitives to establish themselves in his garden-cottage, till the troubles of their own country should be over. She talked perfectly good English, for she said that there were many of that nation established in Providence. Her name was Antonietta. Her figure was light and elegant; her black eyes mild and bright; her countenance intelligent and good-humoured; and her teeth beautiful to perfection: altogether, Antonietta was by far the handsomest creole that I have ever seen.

From Blue-fields we proceeded at once to Lakovia (a small village), a stage of thirty miles. Here we found a relay of horses, which conveyed us by seven o'clock to " the Gutturs ; " a house belonging to the proprietor of the post-horses, and which is situated at the very foot of the tremendous May-day Mountains. The house is an excellent one, and we found good beds, eatables, and, in short, every thing that travellers could wish. The distance from Lakovia to " the Gutturs " is sixteen miles.

## February 2.

Yesterday the only very striking point of view (although the whole of the road was picturesque) was " the Cove," situated between Blue-fields and Lakovia, and which resembled the most beautiful of the views of coves to be found in " Cook's Voyages ; " but our journey to-day was a succession of beautiful scenes, from beginning to end. Instantly on leaving " the Gutturs," we began to ascend the May-day Mountains, and it was not till after travelling for five and twenty miles, that we found ourselves at the foot of them on the other side, at a place called Williamsfield, about twelve miles from the toll-house, where we rested for the night. To be sure, the road was so rough, that it was enough to make one envy the Mahometan women, who, having no souls at all, could not possibly have them jolted out of their bodies; but the beauty of the scenery amply rewarded us for our bruised sides and battered backs. The road was, for the most part, bounded by lofty rocks on one side, and a deep precipice on the other, and bordered with a profusion of noble trees and flowering shrubs in great variety. In particular, I was struck with the picturesque appearance of some wild fig-trees of singular size and beauty. Although there were only two of us, besides servants, we found it necessary to employ seven horses and a couple of mules; and, as our cavalcade wound along through the mountains, the Spanish look of our sumpter-mules, and of our kittereens (which are precisely the vehicle in which Gil Blas is always represented when travelling with Scipio towards Lirias) gave us quite the appearance of a caravan; nor should I have been greatly surprised to see a trap-door open in the middle of the road, and Captain Rolando's whiskers make their appearance. Every one spoke

to me with contempt of this south road, in respect
of beauty, when compared with the north; however, it certainly seemed to me more beautiful than
any road which I have ever travelled as yet.

## FEBRUARY 3.

A stage of twenty miles brought us to Old Harbour, and, passing through the Dry River, twelve
more landed us at Spanish Town, otherwise called
St. Jago de la Vega, and the seat of government in
Jamaica, although Kingston is much larger and
more populous, and must be considered as the
principal town. We found very clean and comfortable lodgings at Miss Cole's. Spanish Town
has no recommendations whatever; the houses are
mostly built of wood: the streets are very irregular
and narrow; every alternate building is in a ruin-
ous state, and the whole place wears an air of gloom
and melancholy. The government house is a large
clumsy-looking brick building, with a portico the
stucco of which has suffered by the weather, and it
can advance no pretensions to architectural beauty.
On one side of the square in which it stands there
is a small temple protecting a statue of Lord Rod-
ney, executed by Bacon: some of the bas-reliefs
on the pedestal appeared to me very good; but the
old admiral is most absurdly dressed in the habit of
a Roman General, and furnished out with buskins
and a truncheon. The temple itself is quite in
opposition to good taste, with very low arches,

surmounted by heavy bas reliefs out of all proportion.

## FEBRUARY 4. (Sunday.)

We breakfasted with the Chief Justice, who is my relation, and of my own name, and then went to the church, which is a very handsome one; the walls lined with fine mahogany, and ornamented with many monuments of white marble, in memory of the former governors and other principal inhabitants. It seems that my ancestors, on both sides, have always had a taste for being well lodged after their decease; for, on admiring one of these tombs, it proved to be that of my maternal grandfather; but still this was not to be compared for a moment with my mausoleum at Cornwall. After church I went home with the Rector, who is one of the ecclesiastical commissaries, and had a long conversation with him respecting a plan which is in agitation for giving the negroes something of a religious education. We afterwards dined with the member for Westmoreland; and as every body in Jamaica is on foot by six in the morning, at ten in the evening we were quite ready to go to bed.

## FEBRUARY 5.

The Chief Justice went with me to Kingston, where I had appointed the agent for my other estate in St. Thomas's-in-the-East to meet me. The short time allotted for my stay in the island makes it impossible to attend properly both to this estate and to Cornwall at this first visit, and there-fore I determined to confine my attention to the negroes on the latter estate till my return to Jamaica. I now contented myself by impressing on the mind of my agent (whom I am certain of being a most humane and intelligent man) my extreme anxiety for the abolition of the cart-whip; and I had the satisfaction of hearing from him, that for a long time it had never been used more than perhaps twice in the year, and then only very slightly, and for some offence so flagrant that it was impossible to pass it over; and he assured me, that whenever I visit Hordley, I may depend upon its not being employed at all. On the other hand, I am told that a gentleman of the parish of Vere, who came over to Jamaica for the sole purpose of ameliorating the condition of his negroes, after abolishing the cart-whip, has at length been constrained to resume the occasional use of it, because he found it utterly impossible to keep them in any sort of subordination without it.

There is not that air of melancholy about Kingston which pervades Spanish Town; but it has no pretensions to beauty; and if any person will imagine a large town entirely composed of booths at a race-course, and the streets merely roads, without any sort of paving, he will have a perfect idea of Kingston.

FEBRUARY 6.

The Jamaica canoes are hollowed cotton-trees. We embarked in one of them at six in the morning, and visited the ruins of Port Royal, which, last year, was destroyed by fire: some of the houses were rebuilding; but it was a melancholy sight, not only from the look of the half-burnt buildings, but the dejected countenances of the ruined inhabitants. I returned to breakfast at the rectory, with two other ecclesiastical commissaries; had more conversation about their proposed plan; and became still more convinced of the difficulty of doing any thing effectual without danger to the island and to the negroes themselves, and of the extreme delicacy requisite in whatever may be attempted. We afterwards visited the school of the children of the poor, who are educating upon Dr. Bell's system; and then saw the church, a very large and handsome one on the inside, but mean enough as to its exterior. I was shown the tombstone of Admiral Benbow, who was killed in a naval engagement, and whose ship afterwards

"Bore down to Port Royal, where the people flocked very
  much
To see brave Admiral Benbow laid in Kingston Town
  Church,"

as the admiral's Homer informs us.

The church is a large one, but it is going to be still further extended; the negroes in Kingston and its neighbourhood being (as the rector assured me) so anxious to obtain religious instruction, that on Sundays not only the church but the churchyard is so completely thronged with them, as to make it difficult to traverse the crowd; and those who are fortunate enough to obtain seats for the morning service, through fear of being excluded from that of the evening, never stir out of the church during the whole day. They also flock to be baptized in great numbers, and many have lately come to be married; and their burials and christenings are performed with great pomp and solemnity.

One of the most intelligent of the negroes with whom I have yet conversed, was the coxswain of my Port Royal canoe. I asked him whether he had been christened? He answered, no; he did not yet think himself good enough, but he hoped to be so in time. Nor was he married; for he was still young, and afraid that he could not break off his bad habits, and be contented to live with no other woman than his wife; and so he thought it better not to become a Christian till he could feel certain of performing the duties of it. However, he said, he had at least cured himself of one bad custom, and never worked upon Sundays, except on some very urgent necessity. I asked what he did on Sundays instead: did he go to church?—No. Or employ himself in learning to read?—Oh, no; though he thought being able to read *was a great virtue;* (which was his constant expression for any thing right, pleasant, or profitable;) but he had no leisure to learn no week days, and as he had heard the parson say that Sunday ought to be a day of rest, he made a point of doing nothing at all on that day. He praised his former master, of whose son he was now the property, and said that neither of them had ever occasion to lay a finger on him. He worked as a waterman, and paid his master ten shillings a week, the rest of his earnings being his own profit; and when he owed wages for three months, if he brought two his master would always give him time for the remainder, and that in so kind a manner, that he always fretted himself to think that so kind a master should wait for his rights, and worked twice as hard till the debt was discharged. He said that kindness was the only way to make good negroes, and that, if *that* failed, flogging would never succeed; and he advised me, when I found my negro worthless, " to sell him at once, and not stay to flog him, and so, by spoiling his appearance, make him sell for less; for blacks must not be treated now, massa, as they used to be; they can think, and hear, and see, as well as white people: blacks are wiser, massa, than they were, and will soon be still wiser." I thought the fellow himself was a good proof of his assertion.

I left Kingston at two o'clock, in defiance of a broiling sun; reached Spanish Town in time to dine with the Attorney-General; and went afterwards to the play, where I found my acquaintance Mr. Hill of Covent Garden theatre performing Lord

William in "The Haunted Tower," and Don Juan in the pantomime which followed. The theatre is neat enough, but, I am told, very inferior in splendour to that in Kingston. As to the performance, it was about equal to any provincial theatricals that I ever saw in England; although the pieces represented were by no means well selected, being entirely musical, and the orchestra consisting of nothing more than a couple of fiddles. My stay in Spanish Town has been too short to admit of my inspecting the antiquities of it, which must be reserved for a future visit, although I never intend to make a longer than the present. The difference of climate was very sensible, both at Spanish Town and Kingston; and the suffocating closeness made me long to breathe again in the country.

The governor happened to be absent on a tour in the north; but I had an opportunity of seeing many of the principal persons of the island during my residence here; and the civilities which I received from all of them were not only more than I expected, but such as I should be unreasonable if I had desired more, and very ungrateful if I could ever forget them.

### February 7.

We were to return by the North Road, and set out at six in the morning. The first stage was to the West Tavern, nineteen miles; and nothing can be imagined at once more sublime and more beautiful than the scenery. Our road lay along the banks of the Rio Cobre, which runs up to Spanish Town, where its floods frequently commit dreadful ravages. Large masses of rock intercept its current at small intervals, which, as well as its shallowness, render it unnavigable. The cliffs and trees are of the most gigantic size, and the road goes so near the brink of a tremendous precipice, that we were obliged always to send a servant forwards to warn any other carriage of our approach, in order that it might stay in some broader part while we passed it. A bridge had been attempted to be built over the river, but a storm had demolished it before its completion, and nothing was now left standing but a single enormous arch. In like manner, " the Dry River " sets all bridges at defiance: when we crossed it between Old Harbour and Spanish Town, it was nothing but a waste of sand; but its floods frequently pour down with irresistible strength and rapidity, and sometimes render it impassable for weeks together. I was extremely delighted with the first ten miles of this stage: unluckily, a mist then arose, so thick, that it was utterly impossible even to guess at the surrounding scenery; and the morning was so cold, that I was very glad to wrap myself up in my cloak as closely as if I had been travelling in an English December.

By the time of our leaving the West Tavern the mist had dispersed, and I was able to admire the extraordinary beauty of Mount Diavolo, which we were then crossing. Though we had left the river, the road was still a narrow shelf of rock running along the edge of ravines of great depth, and filled with broken masses of stone and trees of wonderful magnitude; only that at intervals we emerged for a time into places resembling ornamental parks in England, the lawns being of the liveliest verdure, the ground rising and falling with an endless variety of surface, and enriched with a profusion of trees majestic in stature and picturesque in their shapes, many of them entirely covered with the beautiful flowers of " hogsmeat," and other creeping plants. The logwood, too, is now perfectly golden with its full bloom, and perfumes all the air; and nothing can be more gay than the quantity of wild flowers which catch the eye on all sides, particularly the wild pine, and the wild ipecacuanha. We travelled for sixteen miles, which brought us to our harbour for the night, — a solitary tavern called Blackheath, situated in the heart of the mountains of St. Anne.

## FEBRUARY 8.

The road soon brought us down to the very brink of the sea, which we continued to skirt during the whole of the stage. It then brought us to St. Anne's Bay, where we found an excellent breakfast, at an inn quite in the English fashion, — for the landlady had been long resident in Great

Britain. Every thing was clean and comfortable, and the windows looked full upon the sea. This stage was sixteen miles: the next was said to be twenty-five; but from the time which we took to travel it, I can scarcely believe it to be so much. Our road still lay by the sea-side, till we began to ascend the mountain of Rio Bueno; from which we at length perceived the river itself running into the sea. It was at Porto Bueno that Columbus is said to have made his first landing on the island. Rio Bueno is a small town with a fort, situated close to the sea. Here also we found a very good inn, kept by a Scotchman.

The present landlady (her father being from home) was a very pretty brown girl, by name Eliza Thompson. She told me that she was only residing with her parents during her *husband's* absence; for she was (it seems) the *soi-disant* wife of an English merchant in Kingston, and had a house on Tachy's Bridge. This kind of establishment is the highest object of the *brown* females of Jamaica; they seldom marry men of their own colour, but lay themselves out to captivate some white person, who takes them for mistresses, under the appellation of house-keepers.

Soon after my arrival at Cornwall, I asked my attorney whether a clever-looking brown woman, who seemed to have great authority in the house, belonged to me? — No; she was a free woman. — Was she in my service, then? — No; she was

not in my service. I began to grow impatient.
— "But what *does* she do at Cornwall? Of what
use is she in the house?" — "Why sir, as to
use .... of no great use, sir;" and then, after
a pause, he added in a lower voice, "It is the
custom, sir, in this country, for unmarried men to
have housekeepers, and Nancy is mine." But he
was unjust in saying that Nancy is of no use on
the estate; for she is perpetually in the hospital,
nurses the children, can bleed, and mix up medicines, and (as I am assured) she is of more service
to the sick than all the doctors. These brown
housekeepers generally attach themselves so sincerely to the interests of their protectors, and make
themselves so useful, that they in common retain
their situation; and their children (if slaves) are
always honoured by their fellows with the title of
Miss. My mulatto housemaid is always called
" Miss Polly," by her fellow-servant Phillis. This
kind of connection is considered by a brown girl
in the same light as marriage. They will tell you,
with an air of vanity, " I am Mr. Such-a-one's
*Love!*" and always speak of him as being her *husband;* and I am told, that, except on these terms,
it is extremely difficult to obtain the favours of a
woman of colour. To gain the situation of housekeeper to a white man, the mulatto girl

> " directs her aim;
> This makes her happiness, and this her fame."

FEBRUARY 9.

The sea-view from a bridge near Falmouth was remarkably pleasing; a stage of eighteen miles brought us to the town itself, which I understand to be in size the second in the island.

However various are the characters which actors sustain, I find their own to be the same every where. Although the Jamaica company did not consist of more than twenty persons, their green-room squabbles had divided it, and we found one half performing at Falmouth. We did not wait for the play, but proceeded for twenty-two miles to Montego Bay, where I once more found myself under the protecting roof of Miss Judy James.

On our return from dinner at Mr. Dewer's, we discovered a ball of brown ladies and gentlemen opposite to the inn. No whites nor blacks were permitted to attend this assembly; but as our landlady had two nieces there, under her auspices we were allowed to be spectators. The females chiefly consisted of the natural daughters of attorneys and overseers, and the young men were mostly clerks and book-keepers. I saw nothing at all to be compared, either for form or feature, to many of the humbler people of colour, much less to the beautiful Spaniard at Blue-fields. Long, or Bryan Edwards, asserts that mulattos never breed except with a separate black or white; but at this ball two girls were pointed out to me, the daughters of mulatto parents; and I have been assured that the assertion was a mistake, arising from such a connection being very rarely formed; the females generally preferring to live with white men, and the brown men having thus no other resource than black women. As to the above girls, the fact is certain; and the different shades of colour are distinguished by too plain a line to allow any suspicion of infidelity on the part of their parents.

## FEBRUARY 10.

We passed the day at Mr. Plummer's estate, Anchovy Bottom.

When Lord Bolingbroke was resident in America, large flocks of turkeys used to ravage his corn-fields; but, from their extreme wildness, he never could make any of them prisoners. He had a barn lighted by a large sash window, and into this he laid a train of corn, hiding some servants with guns behind the large doors, which were folded back. The turkeys picked up the corn, and gradually were enticed to enter the barn. But as soon as a dozen had passed in, the servants clapped the doors to with all possible expedition. Now they reckoned themselves secure of their game; but to their utter consternation, the turkeys in a body darted towards the light, dashed against the glass, forced out the wood-work, and away went turkeys, glass, wood-work, and all.

FEBRUARY 11. (Sunday.)

I reached Cornwall about three o'clock, after an excursion the most amusing and agreeable that I ever made in my life. Almost every step of the road presented some new and striking scene; and although we travelled at all hours, and with as little circumspection as if we had been in England, I never felt a headach except for one half hour. On my arrival, I found the satisfactory intelligence usually communicated to West Indian proprietors. My estate in the west is burnt up for want of moisture; and my estate in the east has been so completely flooded, that I have lost a whole third of my crop. At Cornwall, not a drop of rain has fallen since the 16th of November. Not a vestige of verdure is to be seen; and we begin to apprehend a famine among the negroes in consequence of the drought destroying their provision grounds. This alone is wanting to complete the dangerous state of the island; where the higher classes are all in the utmost alarm at rumours of Wilberforce's intentions to set the negroes entirely at freedom; the next step to which would be, in all probability, a general massacre of the whites, and a second part of the horrors of St. Domingo: while, on the other hand, the negroes are impatient at the delay; and such disturbances arose in St. Thomas's in the East, last Christmas, as required the interposition of the magistrates. They say

that the negroes of that parish had taken it into
their heads that *The Regent and Wilberforce* had
actually determined upon setting them all at liberty
at once on the first day of the present year, but
that the interference of the island had defeated
the plan. Their discontent was most carefully
and artfully fomented by some brown Methodists,
who held secret and nightly meetings on the different estates, and did their best to mislead and
bewilder these poor creatures with their fantastic
and absurd preaching. These fellows harp upon
sin, and the devil, and hell-fire incessantly, and
describe the Almighty and the Saviour as beings
so terrible, that many of their proselytes cannot
hear the name of Christ without shuddering. One
poor negro, on one of my own estates, told the
overseer that he knew himself to be so great a
sinner that nothing could save him from the devil's
clutches, even for a few hours, except singing
hymns; and he kept singing so incessantly day
and night, that at length terror and want of sleep
turned his brain, and the wretch died raving mad.

### FEBRUARY 12.

A Sir Charles Price, who had an estate in this
island infested by rats, imported, with much trouble, a very large and strong species for the purpose
of extirpating the others. The new-comers answered his purpose to a miracle; they attacked the
native rats with such spirit, that in a short time

they had the whole property to themselves; but no sooner had they done their duty upon the rats, than they extended their exertions to the cats, of whom their strength and size at length enabled them completely to get the better; and since that last victory, Sir Charles Price's rats, as they are called, have increased so prodigiously, that (like the man in Scripture, who got rid of one devil, and was taken possession of by seven others) this single species is now a greater nuisance to the island than all the others before them were together. The best mode of destroying rats here is with terriers; but those imported from England soon grow useless, being blinded by the sun, while their puppies, born in Jamaica, are provided by nature with a protecting film over their eyes, which effectually secures them against incurring that calamity.

## FEBRUARY 12.

Poor Philippa, the woman who used always to call me her "husband," and whom I left sick in the hospital, during my absence has gone out of her senses; and there cannot well happen any thing more distressing, as there is no separate place for her confinement, and her ravings disturb the other invalids. There is, indeed, no kind of bedlam in the whole island of Jamaica: whether this proceeds from people being so very sedate and sensible, that they never go mad, or from their all being so mad, that no one person has a right to shut up another for being out of his senses, is a point which I will not pretend to decide. One of my domestic negroes, a boy of sixteen, named Prince, was abandoned by his worthless mother in infancy, and reared by this Philippa; and since her illness he passes every moment of his leisure in her sick-room. On the other hand, there is a woman named Christian, attending two fevered children in the hospital; one her own, and the other an adopted infant, whom she reared upon the death of its mother in child-birth; and there she sits, throwing her eyes from one to the other with such unceasing solicitude, that no one could discover which was her own child and which the orphan.

### February 13.

Two Jamaica nightingales have established themselves on the orange tree which grows against my window, and their song is most beautiful. This bird is also called " the mocking-bird," from its facility of imitating, not only the notes of every other animal, but — I am told — of catching every tune that may be played or sung two or three times in the house near which it resides, after which it will go through the air with the greatest taste and precision, throwing in cadences and ornaments that Catalani herself might envy.

But by far the most curious animal that I have yet seen in Jamaica is " the soldier," a species of crab, which inhabits a shell like a snail's, so small in proportion to its limbs, that nothing can be more curious or admirable than the machinery by which it is enabled to fold them up instantly on the slightest alarm. They inhabit the mountains, but regularly once a year travel in large troops down to the sea-side to spawn and change their shells. If I recollect right, Goldsmith gives a very full and entertaining account of this animal, by the name of "the soldier crab." They are seldom used in Jamaica except for soups, which are reckoned delicious: that which was brought to me was a very small one, the shell being no bigger than a large snail's, although the animal itself, when marching with his house on his back, appears to be above thrice the size; but I am told that they are frequently as large as a man's fist. Mine was found alone in the public road: how it came to be in so solitary a state, I know not, for in general they move in armies, and march towards the sea in a straight line; I am afraid, by his being found alone, that my soldier must have been a deserter.

## FEBRUARY 14.

To-day there was a shower of rain for the first time since my arrival; indeed, not a drop has fallen since the 16th of November; and in consequence my present crop has suffered terribly, and our expectations for next season are still worse.

## February 18. (Sunday.)

The rain has brought forth the fire-flies, and in the evening the hedges are all brilliant with their numbers. In the day they seem to be torpid beetles of a dull reddish colour, but at night they become of a shining purple. The fire proceeds from two small spots in the back part of the head. It is yellow in the light, and requires motion to throw out its radiance in perfection; but as soon as it is touched, the fly struggles violently, and bends itself together with a clicking noise like the snap of a spring; and I understand that this effort is necessary to set it in motion. It is sufficiently strong to turn itself upwards with a single movement, if lying on its back: some people say that it is always obliged to throw itself upon its back in order to take wing; but this I have, again, heard others contradict. When confined in a glass, the light seems almost extinguished; nothing can be discerned but two pale yellow spots; but on being pressed by the hand it becomes more brilliant than any emerald, and when on the wing it seems entirely composed of the most beautifully coloured fire.

## February 20.

I attended the Slave Court, where a negro was tried for sheep-stealing, and a black servant girl for attempting to poison her master. The former was sentenced to be transported. The latter was a

girl of fifteen, called Minetta: she acknowledged
the having infused corrosive sublimate in some
brandy and water; but asserted that she had taken
it from the medicine chest without knowing it to
be poison, and had given it to her master at her
grandmother's desire. This account was evidently
a fabrication: there was no doubt of the grandmother's innocence, although some suspicion attached to the mother's influence; but as to the
girl herself, nothing could be more hardened than
her conduct through the whole transaction. She
stood by the bed to see her master drink the poison;
witnessed his agonies without one expression of
surprise or pity; and when she was ordered to leave
the room, she pretended to be fast asleep, and not
to hear what was said to her. Even since her imprisonment, she could never be prevailed upon to
say that she was sorry for her master's having been
poisoned; and she told the people in the gaol, that
"they could do nothing to her, for she had turned
king's evidence against her grandmother." She
was condemned to die on Thursday next, the day
after to-morrow: she heard the sentence pronounced without the least emotion; and I am told,
that when she went down the steps of the court-
house, she was seen to laugh.

The trial appeared to be conducted with all possible justice and propriety; the jury consisted of
nine respectable persons; the bench of three magistrates, and a senior one to preside. There were

no lawyers employed on either side ; consequently no appeals to the passions, no false lights thrown out, no traps, no flaws, no quibbles, no artful cross-examinings, and no brow-beating of witnesses ; and I cannot say that the trial appeared to me to go on at all the worse. Nobody appeared to be either for or against the prisoner ; the only object of all present was evidently to come at the truth, and I sincerely believe that they obtained their object. The only part of the trial of which I disapproved was the ordering the culprit to such immediate execution, that sufficient time was not allowed for the exercise of the royal prerogative, should the governor have been disposed to commute the punishment for that of transportation.

### FEBRUARY 21.

During my excursion to Spanish Town, the complaining negroes of Friendship, who had applied to me for relief, were summoned to Savannah la Mar, before the Council of Protection, and the business thoroughly investigated. Their examination has been sent to me, and they appear to have had a very fair hearing. The journals of the estate were produced ; — the book-keepers examined upon oath ; and in order to make out a case at all, the chief complainant contradicted himself so grossly, as left no doubt that the whole was a fabrication. They were, therefore, dismissed without relief, but also without punishment, in

spite of their gross falsehoods and calumnies; and
although they did not gain their object, I make no
doubt that they will go on more contentedly for
having had attention paid to their complaints. It
was indeed evident, that Nelly (the chief complainant) was actuated more by wounded pride
than any real feeling of hardship; for what she
laid the most stress upon was, the overseer's turning
his back upon her, when she stated herself to be
injured, and walking away without giving her any
answer.

There are so many pleasing and amusing parts
of the character of negroes, that it seems to me
scarcely possible not to like them. But when they
are once disposed to evil, they seem to set no
bounds to the indulgence of their bad passions. A
poor girl came into the hospital to-day, who had had
some trifling dispute with two of her companions;
on which the two friends seized her together, and
each fixing her teeth on one of the girl's hands,
bit her so severely, that we greatly fear her losing
the use of both of them. I happened also to ask,
this morning, to whom a skull had belonged,
which I had observed fixed on a pole by the road-
side, when returning last from Montego Bay. I was
told, that about five years ago a Mr. Dunbar had
given some discontent to his negroes in the article
of clothing them, although, in other respects, he
was by no means a severe master. However, this
was sufficient to induce his head driver, who had

N 3

been brought up in his own house from infancy, to
form a plot among his slaves to assassinate him;
and he was assisted in this laudable design by two
young men from a neighbouring property, who
barely knew Mr. Dunbar by sight, had no enmity
against him whatever, and only joined in the conspiracy in compliment to their worthy friend the
driver. During several months a variety of attempts were made for effecting their purpose; but
accident defeated them; till at length they were
made certain of his intention to dine out at some
distance, and of his being absolutely obliged to
return in the evening. An ambuscade was therefore
laid to intercept him; and on his passing a clump
of trees, the assassins sprang upon him, the
driver knocked him from his horse, and in a few
moments their clubs despatched him. No one
suspected the driver; but in the course of enquiry,
his house as well as the other was searched, and
not only Mr. Dunbar's watch was found concealed
there, but with it one of his ears, which the villain
had carried away, from a negro belief that, as long
as the murderer possesses one of the ears of his
victim, he will never be haunted by his spectre.
The stranger-youths, two of Dunbar's negroes,
and the driver, were tried, confessed the crime, and
were all executed; the head of the latter being
fixed upon a pole *in terrorem*. But while the
offenders were still in prison, the overseer upon a
neighbouring property had occasion to find fault

in the field with a woman belonging to a gang
hired to perform some particular work; upon
which she flew upon him with the greatest fury,
grasped him by the throat, cried to her fellows
—" Come here! come here! Let us Dunbar him!"
and through her strength and the suddenness of
her attack had nearly accomplished her purpose, before his own slaves could come to his assistance.
This woman was also executed.

This happened about five years ago, when the
mountains were in a very rebellious state. Every
thing there is at present quiet. But only last year a
book-keeper belonging to the next estate to me was
found with his skull fractured in one of my own
cane-pieces; nor have any enquiries been able to
discover the murderer.

## February 22.

During many years the Moravians have been
established upon the neighbouring estate of Mesopotamia. As the ecclesiastical commissaries had
said so much to me respecting the great appetite
of the negroes for religious instruction, I was
desirous of learning what progress had been made
in this quarter, and this morning I went over to
see one of the teachers. He told me, that he
and his wife had jointly used their best efforts to
produce a sense of religion in the minds of the
slaves; that they were all permitted to attend his
morning and evening lectures, if they chose it;

but that he could not say that they showed any
great avidity on the subject. It seems that there
are at least three hundred negroes on the estate;
the number of believers has rather increased than
diminished, to be sure, but still in a very small
proportion. When this gentleman arrived, there
were not more than forty baptised persons : he has
been here upwards of five years, and still the
number of persons " belonging to his church"
(as he expressed it) does not exceed fifty. Of these,
seldom more than ten or a dozen attend his lectures at a time. As to the remaining two hundred
and fifty, they take no more notice of his lectures
or his exhortations, than if there were no such person on the property, are only very civil to him when
they see him, and go on in their own old way,
without suffering him to interfere in any shape.
By the overseer of Greenwich's express desire,
the Moravian has, however, agreed to give up an
hour every day for the religious instruction of the
negro children on that property: and I should
certainly request him to extend his labours to
Cornwall, if I did not think it right to give the
Church of England clergymen full room for a trial
of their intended periodical visitations; which
would not be the case, if the negroes were to be
interfered with by the professors of any other
communion: otherwise I am myself ready to give
free ingress and egress upon my several estates
to the teachers of any Christian sect whatever,

the Methodists always excepted, and " Miss Peg, who faints at the sound of an organ."

For my own part, I have no hope of any material benefit arising from these religious visitations made at quarterly intervals. It seems to me as nugatory as if a man were to sow a field with horse-hair, and expect a crop of colts.

## FEBRUARY 23.

This morning my picture was drawn by a self-taught genius, a negro Apelles, belonging to Dr. Pope, the minister; and the picture was exactly such as a self-taught genius might be expected to produce. It was a straight hard outline, without shade or perspective; the hair was a large black patch, and the face covered with an uniform layer of flesh-colour, with a red spot in the centre of each cheek. As to likeness, there was not even an attempt to take any. But still, such as they were, there were eyes, nose, and mouth, to be sure. A long red nose supplied the place of my own snub; an enormous pair of whiskers stretched themselves to the very corner of my mouth; and in place of three hairs and a half, the painter, in the superabundance of his generosity, bestowed upon me a pair of eye-brows more bushy than Dr. Johnson's, and which, being formed in an exact semicircle, made the eyes beneath them stare with an expression of the utmost astonishment. The negroes, however, are in the highest admiration of the

painter's skill, and consider the portrait as a striking resemblance; for there is a very blue coat with
very yellow buttons, and white gaiters and trow-
sers, and an eye-glass so big and so blue, that it
looks as if I had hung a pewter plate about my
neck; and a bunch of watch-seals larger than those
with which Pope has decorated Belinda's great
great grandsire. John Fuller (to whom, jointly
with Nicholas, the charge of this inestimable treasure is to be entrusted) could not find words to
express his satisfaction at the performance. "Dere
massa coat! and dere him chair him sit in! and
dere massa seals, all just de very same ting! just
all as one! And-oh! ki! dere massa pye-glass!"
In the midst of his raptures he dropped the picture, and fractured the frame-glass. His despair
now equalled his former joy; — "Oh, now what for
him do? Such a pity! Just to break it after it
was all done so well! All so pretty!" However,
we stuck the broken glass together with wafers,
and he carried it off, assuring me, "that when
massa gone, he should talk to it every morning,
all one as if massa still here." Indeed, this "talking to massa" is a favourite amusement among the
negroes, and extremely inconvenient: they come
to me perpetually with complaints so frivolous,
and requests so unreasonable, that I am persuaded
they invent them only to have an excuse for
"talk to massa;" and when I have given them a
plump refusal, they go away perfectly satisfied,

and "tank massa for dis here great indulgence of talk."

There is an Eboe carpenter named Strap, who was lately sick and in great danger, and whom I nursed with particular care. The poor fellow thinks that he never can express his gratitude sufficiently; and whenever he meets me in the public road, or in the streets of Savannah la Mar, he rushes towards the carriage, roars out to the postilion to stop, and if the boy does not obey instantly, he abuses him with all his power; "for why him no stop when him want talk to massa?"—"But look, Strap, your beast is getting away!"—"Oh! damn beast, massa."—"But you should go to your mountain, or you will get no vittle."—"Oh, damn vittle, and damn mountain! me no want vittle, me want talk wid massa;" and then, all that he has got to say is, "Oh massa, massa! God bless you, massa! me quite, *quite* glad to see you come back, my own massa!" And then he bursts into a roar of laughter so wild and so loud, that the passers-by cannot help stopping to stare and laugh too.

## February 24.

On the Sunday after my first arrival, the whole body of Eboe negroes came to me to complain of the attorney, and more particularly of one of the book-keepers. I listened to them, if not with unwearied patience, at least with unsubdued fortitude, for above an hour and a half; and finding

some grounds for their complaint against the latter,
in a few days I went down to their quarter of the
village, told them that to please them I had discharged the book-keeper, named a day for examin-
ing their other grievances, and listened to them for
an hour more. When the day of trial came, they
sent me word that they were perfectly satisfied,
and had no complaint to make. I was, therefore,
much surprised to receive a visit from Edward, the
Eboe, yesterday evening, who informed me, that
during my absence his fellows had formed a plan
of making a complaint *en masse* to a neighbouring
magistrate; and that, not only against the attorney,
but against myself " for not listening to them when
they were injured;" and Edward claimed great
merit with me for having prevented their taking
this step, and convinced them, that while I was on
the estate myself, there could be no occasion for
applying to a third person. Now, having made
me aware of my great obligations to him, here
Edward meant the matter to rest; but being a
good deal incensed at their ingratitude, I instantly
sent for the Eboes, and enquired into the matter;
when it appeared, that Edward (who is a clever
fellow, and has great influence over the rest) had
first goaded them into a resolution of complaining
to a magistrate, had then stopped them from putting their plan into execution, and that the whole
was a plot of Edward's, in order to make a merit
with me for himself at the expense of his country-

men. However, as they confessed their having had the intention of applying to Mr. Hill as a magistrate, I insisted upon their executing their intention. I told them, that as Mr. Hill was the person whom they had selected for their protector, to Mr. Hill they should go; that they should either make their complaint to him against me, or confess that they had been telling lies, and had no complaint to make; and that, as the next day was to be a play-day given them by me, instead of passing it at home in singing and dancing, they should pass it at the Bay in stating their grievances.

This threw them into terrible confusion; they cried out that they wanted to make no complaint whatever, and that it was all Edward's fault, who had misled them. Three of them, one after the other, gave him the lie to his face; and each and all (Edward as well as the rest) declared that go to the Bay they absolutely would *not*. The next morning they were all at the door waiting for my coming out: they positively refused to go to Mr. Hill, and begged and prayed, and humbled themselves; now scraping and bowing to me, and then blackguarding Edward with all their might and main; and when I ordered the driver to take charge of them, and carry them to Mr. Hill, some of them fairly took to their heels, and ran away. However, the rest soon brought them back again, for they swore that if one went, all should go; and away they were marched, in a string of about twenty, with the driver at their head. When they got to the Bay, they told Mr. Hill that, as to their massa, they had no complaint to make against him, except that he had compelled them to make one; and what they said against the attorney was so trifling, that the magistrate bade the driver take them all back again. Upon which they slunk away to their houses, while the Creoles cried out " Shame ! shame !" as they passed along.

Indeed, the Creoles could not have received a greater pleasure than the mortification of the Eboes; for the two bodies hate each other as cordially as the Guelphs and Ghibellines; and after their departure for the Bay, I heard the head cook haranguing a large audience, and declaring it to be her fixed opinion, " that massa ought to sell all the Eboes, and buy Creoles instead." Probably, Mrs. Cook was not the less loud in her exclamations against the ingratitude of the Eboes, from her own loyalty having lately been questioned. She had found fault one day in the hospital with some women who feigned sickness in order to remain idle. " You no work willing for massa," said Mrs. Cook, " and him so vex, him say him go to Kingston to-morrow, and him wish him neber come back again!"—" What!" cried Philippa, the mad woman, " you wish massa neber come back from Kingston?" So she gave Mrs. Cook a box on the ear with all her might; upon which Mrs. Cook snatched up a stick and broke the mad woman's pate with it. But though she could beat a hole in her head, she never could beat out of it her having said that she wished massa might never come back. And although Philippa has recovered her senses, in her belief of Mrs. Cook's disloyalty she continues firm; and they never meet without renewing the dispute.

To-day being a play-day, the gaiety of the negroes was promoted by a distribution of an additional quantity of salt-fish (which forms a most acceptable ingredient in their pepper-pots), and as much rum and sugar as they chose to drink. But there was also a dinner prepared at the house where the " white people" reside, expressly for none but the *piccaninny-mothers;* that is, for the women who had children living. I had taken care, when this play-day was announced by the head driver, to make him inform the negroes that they were indebted for it entirely to these mothers; and to show them the more respect, I went to them after dinner myself, and drank their healths. The most respectable blacks on the estate were also assembled in the room; and I then told them that clothes would wear out, and money would be spent, and that I wished to give them something more lasting than clothes or money. The law only allows them, as a matter of right, every alternate Saturday for themselves, and holidays for three days at Christmas, which, with all Sundays, forms their whole legal time of relaxation. I therefore granted them as a matter of right, and of which no person should deprive them on any account whatever, *every* Saturday to cultivate their grounds; and in addition to their holidays at Christmas, I gave them for play-days Good-Friday, the second Friday in October, and the second Friday in July. By which means, they will in future have the same number of holidays four times a year, which hitherto they have been allowed only once, *i.e.* at Christmas. The first is to be called " the royal play-day," in honour of that excellent Princess, the Duchess of York; and the negroes are directed to give three cheers upon the head driver's announcing " The health of our good lady, H. R. H. the Duchess of York." And I told them, that before my leaving the island, I should hear them drink this health, and should not fail to let Her Royal Highness know, that the negroes of Cornwall drank her health every year. This evidently touched the right chord of their vanity, and they all bowed and courtesied down to the very ground, and said, that would do them much high honour. The ninth being my own birthday, the July play-day is to be called " the massa's;" and that in October is to be in honour of the piccaninny-mothers, from whom it is to take its name.

. . The poor creatures overflowed with gratitude; and the prospective indulgences which had just been announced, gave them such an increase of spirits, that on returning to my own residence, they fell to singing and dancing again with as much violence as if they had been a pack of French furies at the Opera. The favourite song of the night was,

" Since massa come, we very well off; "

which words they repeated in chorus, without intermission (dancing all the time), for hours together; till, at half-past three, neither my eyes nor my brain could endure it any longer, and I was obliged to send them word that I wanted to go to bed, and could not sleep till the noise should cease. The idea of my going to bed seemed never to have occurred to them till that moment. Fortunately, like Johnson's definition of wit, " the idea, although novel, was immediately acknowledged to be just." So instantly the drums and gumbies left off beating; the children left off singing; the women and men left off dancing; and they all with one accord fell to kicking, and pulling, and thumping about two dozen of their companions, who were lying fast asleep upon the floor. Some were roused, some resisted, some began fighting, some got up and lay down again; but at length, by dint of their leading some, carrying others, and rolling the remainder down the steps, I got my house clear of my black guests about four in the morning.

Another of their popular songs this evening was —

" All the stories them telling you are lies, oh ! "

which was meant as a satire upon the Eboes. My friend Strap being an Eboe, and one who had hitherto generally taken a leading part in all the discontents and squabbles of his countrymen, I was not without apprehensions of his having been concerned in the late complaint. I was, therefore, much pleased to find that he had positively refused to take any share in the business, and had been to the full as violent as any of the Creoles in reprobating the ingratitude of the Eboes. To-day he came up to the house dressed in his best clothes, to show me his seven children; and he marched at their head in all the dignity of paternal pride. He begged me particularly to notice two fine little girls, who were twins. I told him that I had seen them already. " Iss! iss!" he said; " massa see um; but massa no *admire* um enough yet." Upon which I fell to admiring them, tooth and nail, and the father went away quite proud and satisfied.

### FEBRUARY 25.

Yesterday it was observed at George's Plain, an estate about four miles off, that the water-mill did not work properly, and it was concluded that the grating was clogged up with rubbish. To clear it away, a negro immediately jumped down into the trench upon a log of wood; when he felt the log move under him, and of course jumped out again with all possible expedition. It was then discovered that the impediment in question proceeded from a large alligator which had wandered from the morass, and, in the hope of finding his way to the river, had swam up the mill-trench till he found himself stopped by the grating; and the banks being too high for him to gain them by leaping upwards, and the place of his confinement too narrow to admit of his turning round to go back again, his escape was impossible, and a ball, lodged near his eye, soon put an end to him. I went over to see him this morning; but I was not contented with merely seeing him, so I begged to have a steak cut off for me, brought it home, and ordered it to be broiled for dinner. One of the negroes happened to see it in the kitchen; the news spread through the estate like wildfire; and I had immediately half a dozen different deputations, all hoping that massa would not think of eating the alligator, for it was poisonous. However, I was obstinate, and found the taste of the flesh, when broiled with pepper and salt, and assisted by an onion sauce, by no means to be despised; but the consistence of the meat was disagreeable, being as tough as a piece of eel-skin. Perhaps any body who wishes to eat alligator steaks in perfection, ought to keep them for two or three days before dressing them; or the animal's age might be in fault, for the fellow was so old that he had scarcely a tooth in his head; I therefore contented myself with two or three morsels; but a person who was dining

with me ate a whole steak, and pronounced the
dish to be a very good one. The eggs are said to
be very palatable; nor have the negroes who live
near morasses, the same objection with those of
Cornwall to eating the flesh; it is, however, true
that the gall of the alligator, if not extracted carefully, will render the whole animal unfit for food;
and when this gall is reduced to powder, it forms a
poison of the most dangerous nature, as the negroes
know but too well.

## February 26.

I had given the most positive orders that no
person whatever should presume to strike a negro,
or give him abusive language, or, however great
the offence might be, should inflict any punishment,
except by the sole direction of the trustee himself.
Yet, although I had already discharged one book-
keeper on this account, this evening another of
them had a dispute in the boiling-house with an
African named Frank, because a pool of water was
not removed fast enough; upon which he called him
a rascal, sluiced him with the dirty water, and
finally knocked him down with the broom. The
African came to me instantly; four eye-witnesses,
who were examined separately, proved the truth of
his ill-usage; and I immediately discharged the
book-keeper, who had contented himself with
simply denying the blow having been given by
him: but I told him that I could not possibly allow

his single unsupported denial to outweigh five con-
cordant witnesses to the assertion; and that, if he
grounded his claim to being believed merely upon
his having a white skin, he would find that, on
Cornwall estate at least, that claim would not be
admitted. The fact was established as evident as
the sun; and nothing should induce me to retain
him on my property, except his finding some means
of appeasing the injured negro, and prevailing on
him to intercede in his behalf. This was an humi-
liation to which he could not bring himself to
stoop; and, accordingly, the man has left the
estate. Probably, indeed, the attempt at reconciliation would have been unsuccessful; for when one
of his companions asked Frank whether, if Mr.
Barker would make him a present, he had not
better take it, and beg massa to let him stay, he
exclaimed, in the true spirit of a Zanga, — " No,
no, no! me no want present! me no want noting!
Me no beg for Mr. Barker! him go away!" — I
was kept awake the greatest part of the night by
the songs and rejoicings of the negroes, at their
triumph over the offending book-keeper.

## February 27.

The only horned cattle said to be fit for Jamaica
work, are those which have a great deal of black
in them. The white are terribly tormented by the
insects, and they are weak and sluggish in propor-

tion to their quantity of white. On the contrary I am told that such a thing as a black horse is not to be found in the island; those which may be imported black soon change their colour into a bay; and colts are said to have been dropped perfectly black, which afterwards grew lighter and lighter till they arrived at being perfectly white.

## FEBRUARY 28.

Hearing that a manati (the sea-cow) had been taken at the mouth of the Cabrita River, and was kept alive at the Hope Wharf, I got a sailing-boat, and went about eight miles to see the animal. It was suffered to live in the sea, a rope being fastened round it, by which it could be landed at pleasure. It was a male, and a very young one, not exceeding nine feet in length, whereas they have frequently been found on the outside of eighteen. The females yield a quart of milk at a time: a gentleman told me that he had tasted it, and could not have distinguished it from the sweetest cow's milk. Unlike the seal, it never comes on shore, although it ventures up rivers in the night, to feed on the grass of their banks; but during the day it constantly inhabits the ocean, where its chief enemy is the shark, whose attacks it beats off with its tail, the strength of which is prodigious. It was killed this morning, and the gentleman to whom it belonged was obliging enough to send me part of it; we roasted it for dinner, and, except that its consistence was rather firmer, I should not have known it from veal.

## FEBRUARY 29.

The wife of an old negro on the neighbouring estate of Anchovy had lately forsaken him for a younger lover. One night, when she happened to be alone, the incensed husband entered her hut unexpectedly, abused her with all the rage of jealousy, and demanded the clothes to be restored, which he had formerly given her. On her refusal he drew a knife, and threatened to cut them off her back; nor could she persuade him to depart, till she had received a severe beating. He had but just left the hut, when he encountered his successful rival, who was returning home: a quarrel instantly ensued; and the husband, having the knife still unsheathed in his hand, plunged it into the neck of his antagonist. It pierced the jugular vein; of course the man fell dead on the spot; and the murderer has been sent to Montego Bay, to take his trial.

## MARCH 1. (Friday.)

One of my house-boys, named Prince, is son to the Duke of Sully; and to-day his Grace came to beg that, when I should leave Jamaica, I would direct the boy to be made a tradesman, instead of being sent back to be a common field-negro: but my own shops are not only full at present, but

loaded with future engagements. Sully then requested that I would send his son to learn some
other trade (a tailor's, for instance) at Savannah la
Mar, as had been frequently done in former times;
but this, also, I was obliged to refuse. I told him,
that formerly a master could pay for the apprenticeship of a clever negro boy, and, instead of employing him afterwards on the estate, could content
himself with being repaid by a share of the profits;
but that, since The Abolition had made it impossible
for the proprietor of an estate to supply the place
of one negro by the purchase of another, it would
be unjust to his companions to suffer any one in
particular to be withdrawn from service; as in that
case two hundred and ninety-nine would have to
do the work, which was now performed by three
hundred; and, therefore, I could allow my negroes
to apply themselves to no trades but such as related to the business of the property, such as carpenters, coopers, smiths, &c. " All true, massa,"
said Sully; " all fair and just; and, to be sure, a
tailor or a saddler would be of no great use towards
your planting and getting in your crop; nor——"
He hesitated for a moment, and then added, with
a look of doubt, and in a lower voice, — " Nor —
nor a fiddler either, I suppose, massa?" I began
to laugh. " No, indeed, Sully; nor a fiddler
either!" It seems the lad, who is about sixteen,
very thoughtless, and *un tantino* stupid, has a
passion for playing the fiddle, and, among other

trades, had suggested this to his father, as one which would be extremely to his taste. We finally settled, that when the plough should be introduced on my estate (which I am very anxious to accomplish, and substitute the labour of oxen for that of negroes, wherever it can possibly be done), Prince should be instructed in farming business, and in the mean while should officiate as a pen-keeper to look after the cattle.

Just now Prince came to me with a request of his own. " Massa, please, me want one little coat." — "A little coat! For what?" — " Massa, please, for wear when me go down to the Bay." — " And why should you wear a little coat when you go to the Bay?"—" Massa, please, make me look eerie (buckish) when me go abroad." So I assured him that he looked quite *eerie* enough already; and that, as I was going away too soon to admit of my seeing him in his little coat, there could not be the slightest occasion for his being a bit *eerier* than he was. A master in England would probably have been not a little astonished at receiving such a request from one of his groom-boys; but here one gets quite accustomed to them; and when they are refused, the petitioners frequently laugh themselves at their own unreasonableness.

## MARCH 2.

Most of those negroes who are tolerably industrious, breed cattle on my estate, which are their own peculiar property, and by the sale of which they obtain considerable sums. The pasturage of a steer would amount, in this country, to 12*l.* a year; but the negro cattle get their grass from me without its costing them a farthing; and as they were very desirous that I should be their general purchaser, I ordered them to agree among themselves as to what the price should be. It was, therefore, settled that I should take their whole stock, good and bad indifferently, at the rate of 15*l.* a head for every three-year-old beast; and they expressed themselves not only satisfied, but very grateful for my acceptance of their proposal. John Fuller and the beautiful Psyche had each a steer to sell (how Psyche came to be so rich, I had too much discretion to enquire), and they were paid down their 15*l.* a piece instantly, which they carried off with much glee.

### March 3. (Sunday.)

In this country it may be truly said that "it never rains but it pours." After a drought of three months, it began to rain on Thursday morning, and has never stopped raining since, with thunder all the day, and lightning all the night; one consequence of which incessant showers is, that it has brought out all sorts of insects and reptiles in crowds: the ground is covered with lizards; the air is filled with mosquitoes, and their bite is infinitely more envenomed than on my first arrival. A

centipes was found squeezed to death under the
door of my bed-room this morning. As to the
cock-roaches, they are absolutely in legions; every
evening my negro boys are set to hunt them, and
they kill them by dozens on the chairs and sofas, in
the covers of my books, and among the leaves in
my fruit-baskets. Yesterday I wanted to send
away a note in a great hurry, snatched up a wafer,
and was on the point of putting it into my mouth,
when I felt it move, and found it to be a cock-
roach, which had worked its way into the wafer-
box.

### MARCH 4. (Monday.)

Since my arrival in Jamaica, I am not conscious
of having omitted any means of satisfying my
negroes, and rendering them happy and secure
from oppression. I have suffered no person to be
punished, except the two female demons who
almost bit a girl's hands off (for which they received a slight switching), and the most worthless
rascal on the estate, whom for manifold offences I
was compelled, for the sake of discipline, to allow
to pass two days in the bilboes. I have never refused a favour that I could possibly grant. I have
listened patiently to all complaints. I have increased the number of negro holidays, and have
given away money and presents of all kinds incessantly. Now for my reward. On Saturday morning there were no fewer than forty-five persons (not
including children) in the hospital; which makes

nearly a fifth of my whole gang. Of these, the medical people assured me that not above seven had any thing whatever the matter with them; the rest were only feigning sickness out of mere idleness, and in order to sit doing nothing, while their companions were forced to perform their part of the estate-duty. And sure enough, on Sunday morning they all walked away from the hospital to amuse themselves, except about seven or eight: they will, perhaps, go to the field for a couple of days; and on Wednesday we may expect to have them all back again, complaining of pains, which (not existing) it is not possible to remove. Jenny (the girl whose hands were bitten) was told by the doctoress, that having been in the hospital all the week, she ought not, for very shame, to go out on Sunday. She answered, " She wanted to go to the mountains, and go she would." " Then," said the doctoress, " you must not come back again on Monday at least." " Yes," Jenny said, " she *should* come back ;" and back this morning Jenny came. But as her wounds were almost completely well, she had tied packthread round them so as to cut deep into the flesh, had rubbed dirt into them, and, in short, had played such tricks as nearly to produce a mortification in one of her fingers.

The most worthless fellow on the whole property is one Nato, — a thief, a liar, a runaway, and one who has never been two days together out of the hospital since my arrival, although he has nothing the matter with him; indeed, when the other negroes abused him for his laziness, and leaving them to do his work for him, he told them plainly that he did not mean to work, and that nobody should make him. The only real illness which brought him to the hospital, within my knowledge, was the consequence of a beating received from his own father, who had caught him in the act of robbing his house by the help of a false key. In the hospital he found his wife, Philippa, the mad woman, with whom he instantly quarrelled, and she cut his head open with a plate; and as she might have served one of the children in the same way, we were obliged to confine her. Her husband was thought to be the fittest person to guard her; and accordingly they were locked up together in a separate room from the other invalids, till a straight waistcoat could be made. The husband was then restored to freedom, and desired to go to work, which he declared to be impossible from illness; yet he disappeared the whole of the next day; and on his return on the following morning, he had the impudence to assert that he had never been out of the hospital for an hour. For this runaway offence, and for endeavouring to exasperate his wife's phrensy, he was put into the bilboes for two days: on the third he was released; when he came to me with tears in his eyes, implored me most earnestly to forgive what had past, and promised to behave better for the future, " to so good a massa." It appeared afterwards, that he had employed his absence in complaining to Mr. Williams, a neighbouring magistrate, that, " having a spite against them, although neither he nor his wife had committed any fault, I had punished them both by locking them up for several days in a solitary prison, under pretence of his wife's insanity, when, in fact, she was perfectly in her senses." Unluckily, one of my physicians had told Mr. Williams, that very morning, how much he had been alarmed at Cornwall, when, upon going into a mad woman's room, her husband had fastened the door, and he had found himself shut up between them; the woman really mad, and the man pretending to be so too. The moment that Nato mentioned the mad woman as his wife, " What then," said Mr. Williams, " you are the fellow who alarmed the doctor so much two days ago?" Upon which Nato had the impudence to burst into a fit of laughter, —" Oh, ki, massa, doctor no need be fright; we no want to hurt him; only make lilly bit fun wid him, massa, that all." On which he was ordered to get out of Mr. Williams's house, slunk back into the Cornwall hospital, and in a few days came to me with such a long story of penitence, and " so good massa," that he induced me to forgive him.

To sum up the whole, about three this morning an alarm was given that the pen-keeper had suffered the cattle to get among the canes, where they might do infinite mischief; the trustee was roused out of his bed; the drivers blew their shells to summon the negroes to their assistance; when it appeared, that there was not a single watchman at his post; the watch-fires had all been suffered to expire; not a single domestic was to be found, nor a horse to be procured; even the little servant boys, whom the trustee had locked up in his own house, and had left fast asleep when he went to bed, had got up again, and made their escape to pass the night in play and rioting; and although they were perfectly aware of the detriment which the cattle were doing to my interests, not a negro could be prevailed upon to rouse himself and help to drive them out, till at length Cubina (who had run down from his own house to mine on the first alarm) with difficulty collected about half a dozen to assist him: but long before this, one of my best cane-pieces was trampled to pieces, and the produce of this year's crop considerably diminished.—And so much for negro gratitude! However, they still continue their eternal song of "Now massa come, we very well off;" but their satisfaction evidently begins and ends with themselves. They rejoice sincerely at being very well off, but think it unnecessary to make the slightest return to massa for making them so.

## March 5.

The worst of negro diseases is " the cocoa-bag:" it is both hereditary and contagious, and will lurk in the blood of persons apparently the most healthy and of regular habits, till a certain age; when it declares itself in the form of offensive sores, attended with extreme debility. No cure for it has yet been discovered : there are negro doctors, who understand how to prepare diet drinks from simples of the island, which moderate its virulence for a time; but the disease itself is never entirely subdued. On the contrary, " the yaws," although it defies the power of medicine, ultimately cures itself. This, also, is communicated by contact, and that of so slight a nature, that a fly, which had touched an ulcer produced by the yaws, has been known to convey the infection by merely alighting on the wound of a cut finger. It generally shows itself by a slight pimple, which is soon converted into a sore ; and this spreads itself gradually over the invalid's whole body, till having made its progress through the system completely, its virulence gradually abates, and at length the disease disappears all together. As " the yaws " can only be taken once, inoculation has been tried upon the most hopeful subjects; but the disease showed itself with as much violence as when contracted in the natural way.

## March 6.

Nato has kept his promise as yet, and has actually past a whole week in the field; a thing which he was never known to do before within the memory of man. So I sent him a piece of money to encourage him; and told him, that I sent him a *maccarony* for behaving well, and wished to know whether any one had ever given him a maccarony for behaving ill. I hear that he was highly delighted at my thinking him worthy to receive a present from me, and sent me in return the most positive assurances of perseverance in good conduct. On the other hand, Mackaroo has not only run away himself, but has carried his wife away with him. This is improving upon the profligacy of British manners with a vengeance. In England, a man only runs away with another person's wife: but to run away with his own—what depravity!— As to my ungrateful demigod of a sheep-stealer, Hercules, the poor wretch has brought down upon himself a full punishment for all his misdeeds. By running away, and sleeping in the woods, exposed to all the fury of the late heavy rains, he has been struck by the palsy. Yesterday some of my negroes found him in the mountains, unable to raise himself from the ground, and brought him in a cart to the hospital; where he now lies, having quite lost the use of one side, and without any hopes of recovery. He is still a young man, and in every

P

other respect strong and healthy; so that he may look forward to a long and miserable existence.

## March 8.

### THE HUMMING BIRD.

Deck'd with all that youth and beauty
   E'er bestow'd on sable maid,
Gathering bloom her fragrant duty,
   Down the lime-walk Zoè stray'd.

Many a logwood brake was ringing
   With the chicka-chinky's cry;
Many a mock-bird loudly singing
   Bless'd the groves with melody.

Fly-birds, on whose plumage showers
   Nature's hand her wealth profuse,
Humming round, from banks of flowers
   Suck'd the rich ambrosial juice.

There an orange-plant, perfuming
   All the air with blossoms white,
Near a bush of roses blooming,
   Charm'd at once the scent and sight.

Of that plant the loveliest daughter,
   One sweet bloom-bough all preferr'd;
When his glittering eye had caught her,
   Oh, how joy'd the Humming Bird!

Here the fairest blossoms thinking,
   Swift he flies, nor loads the stem;
Poised in air, and odour drinking,
   Fluttering hangs the feather'd Gem.

Sure, he deems, these cups untasted,
   Many a honied drop allow!
Soon he finds his labour wasted;
   Bees have robb'd that orange bough.

Wandering bees, at blush of morning,
   Drain'd of all their sweets the bells;
Then the rifled beauty scorning,
   How his angry throat he swells!

See his bill the blossoms rending;
   Round their leaves in wrath he throws;
Then, once more his wings extending,
   Flies to woo the opening rose.

" Mark, my Zoè," said her mother,
   " Mark that bough, so lovely late!
Thou in bloom art such another —
   Such, perhaps, may be thy fate.

" Some wild youth may charm and cheat thee,
   Sip thy sweets, and break his vow;
Then the world will scorn and treat thee
   As the Fly-Bird did just now."

British mothers thus impress on
   Virgin minds some maxim true;
Zoè heard and used the lesson
   Just as British daughters do.

## March 9.

The shaddock contains generally thirty-two seeds, two of which only will reproduce shaddocks; and these two it is impossible to distinguish: the rest will yield, some sweet oranges, others bitter ones, others again forbidden fruit, and, in short, all the varieties of the orange; but until the trees actually are in bearing, no one can guess what the fruit is likely to prove; and even then, the seeds which produce shaddocks, although taken from a tree remarkable for the excellence of its fruit, will frequently yield only such as are scarcely eatable. So also the varieties of the mango are infinite: the fruit of no two trees resembling each other; and the seeds of the very finest mango (although sown and cultivated with the utmost care) seldom affording any thing at all like the parent stock. The two first mangoes which I tasted were nothing but turpentine and sugar; the third was very delicious; and yet I was told that it was by no means of a superior quality. The *sweet* cassava requires no preparation; the *bitter* cassava, unless the juice is carefully pressed out of it, is a deadly poison; there is a third kind, called the *sweet-and-bitter* cassava, which is perfectly wholesome till a certain age, when it acquires its deleterious qualities. Many persons have been poisoned by mistaking these various kinds of cassava for each other. As soon as the plantain has done bearing, it is cut down; when four or five suckers spring from each root, which become plants themselves in their turn. Ratoons are suckers of the sugar-cane: they are far preferable to the original plants, where the soil is rich enough to support them; but they are much better adapted to some estates than to

others. Thus, on my estate in St. Thomas's in the
East, they can allow of ten ratoons from the
same plant, and only dig cane-holes every eleventh
year; while, at Cornwall, the strength of the cane
is exhausted in the fourth ratoon, or the fifth at
furthest. The fresh plants are cane-tops; but
those canes which bear *flags* or feathers at their
extremities will not answer the purpose, as dry
weather easily burns up the slight arrows to which
the flags adhere, and destroys them before they
can acquire sufficient vigour to resist the climate.

### MARCH 10. (Sunday.)·

I find that I have not done justice to the cotton
tree, and, on the other hand, have given too much
praise to the Jamaica kitchen. The first cotton
trees which I saw, were either withered by age, or
struck by lightning, or happened to be ill-shaped
of their kind; but I have since met with others,
than which nothing could be more noble or picturesque, from their gigantic height, the immense
spread of their arms, the colour of their stems and
leaves, and the wild fantastic wreathings of their
roots and branches. As to the kitchen, nothing
can be larger and finer in appearance than the
poultry of all kinds, but nothing can be uniformly
more tough and tasteless; and the same is the case
with all butcher's meat, pork excepted, which is
much better here than in Europe. The fault is in
the climate, which prevents any animal food from

being kept sufficiently long to become tender; so
that when a man sits down to a Jamaica dinner, he
might almost fancy himself a guest at Macbeth's
Covent-Garden banquet, where the fowls, hams,
and legs of mutton are all made of deal boards.    I
ordered a duck to be kept for two days; but it was
so completely spoiled, that there was no bearing it
upon the table.    Then I tried the expedient of
boiling a fowl till it absolutely fell to pieces; but
even this violent process had not the power of
rendering it tender.    The only effect produced by
it was, that instead of being helped to a wing of
solid wood, I got a plateful of splinters.    Perhaps,
my having totally lost my appetite (probably from
my not being able to take, in this climate, sufficient
of my usual exercise) makes the meat appear to me
less palatable than it may to others; but I have
observed, that most people here prefer living upon
soups, stews, and salted provisions.    For my own
part, I have for the last few weeks eaten nothing
except black crabs, than which I never met with a
more delicious article for the table.    I have also
tried the *soldier* soup, which is in great estimation
in this island; but although it greatly resembled
the very richest cray-fish soup, it seemed to be
composed of cray-fish which had been kept too
long.    The *soldiers* themselves were perfectly fresh,
for they were brought to the kitchen quite alive
and merry; but I was told that this taste of
staleness is their peculiar flavour, as well as their

peculiar scent even when alive, and is precisely the quality which forms their recommendation. It was quite enough to fix my opinion of the soup: I ate two spoonfuls, and never mean to venture on a third.

## MARCH 12.

The most general of negro infirmities appears to be that of lameness. It is chiefly occasioned by the *chiga,* a diminutive fly which works itself into the feet to lay its eggs, and, if it be not carefully extracted in time, the flesh around it corrupts, and a sore ensues not easily to be cured. No vigilance can prevent the attacks of the chiga; and not only soldiers, but the very cleanest persons of the highest rank in society, are obliged to have their feet examined regularly. The negroes are all provided with small knives for the purpose of extracting them: but as no pain is felt till the sore is produced, their extreme laziness frequently makes them neglect that precaution, till all kinds of dirt getting into the wound, increases the difficulty of a cure; and sometimes the consequence is lameness for life.

There is another disease which commits great ravages among them; for although in this climate its quality is far from virulent, and it is easy to be cured in its beginning, the negro will most carefully conceal his having such a complaint, till it has made so great a progress that its effects are perceived by others. Even then, they will never acknowledge the way in which they have contracted it; but men and women, whose noses almost shake while speaking to you, will still insist upon it that their illness arises from catching cold, or from a strain in lifting a weight, or, in short, from any cause except the true one. Yet why they act thus it is difficult to imagine; for certainly it does not arise from shame.

Indeed, it is one of their singular obstinacies, that, however ill they may be, they scarcely ever will confess to the physician what is really the matter with them on their first coming into the hospital, but will rather assign some other cause for their being unwell than the true one; and it is only by cross-questioning, that their superintendents are able to understand the true nature of their case. Perhaps this duplicity is occasioned by fear; for in any bodily pain it is not possible to be more cowardly than the negro; and I have heard strong young men, while the tears were running down their cheeks, scream and roar as if a limb was amputating, although the doctoress was only applying a poultice to a whitlow on the finger. I suppose, therefore, that dread of the pain of some unknown mode of treatment makes them conceal their real disease, and name some other, of which they know the cure to be unattended with bodily suffering or long restraint. In the disease I allude to, such a motive would operate with peculiar force, as one of their chief aversions is the necessarily being long confined to one certainly not fragrant room.

## MARCH 13.

The Reporter of the African Institution asserts, in a late pamphlet, that in the West Indies the breeding system is to this day discouraged, and that the planters are still indifferent to the preservation of their present stock of negroes, from their confidence of getting fresh supplies from Africa. Certainly the negroes in Jamaica are by no means of this Reporter's opinion, but are thoroughly sensible of their intrinsic value in the eyes of the proprietor. On my arrival, every woman who had a child held it up to show to me, exclaiming,—"See massa, see! here nice new neger me bring for work for massa;" and those who had more than one did not fail to boast of the number, and make it a claim to the greater merit with me. Last week, an old watchman was brought home from the mountains almost dead with fever; he would neither move, nor speak, nor notice any one, for several days. For two nights I sent him soup from my own table; but he could not even taste it, and always gave it to his daughter. On the third evening, there happened to be no soup at dinner, and I sent other food instead; but old Cudjoe had been accustomed to see the soup arrive, and the disappointment made him fancy himself hungry, and that he could have eaten the soup if

it had been brought as usual : accordingly, when I
visited him the next morning, he bade the doctoress
tell me that massa had send him no soup the
night before. This was the first notice that he
had ever taken of me. I promised that some
soup should be ordered for him on purpose that
evening. Could he fancy any thing to eat *then?*—
" Milk ! milk !" So milk was sent to him, and he
drank two full calabashes of it. I then tried him
with an egg, which he also got down ; and at night,
by spoonfuls at a time, he finished the whole bason
of soup ; but when I next came to see him, and he
wished to thank me, the words in which he thought
he could comprise most gratitude were bidding the
doctoress tell me he would do his best not to die
yet ; he promised to *fight hard* for it. He is now
quite out of danger, and seems really to be grateful.
When he was sometimes too weak to speak, on my
leaving the room he would drag his hand to his
mouth with difficulty, and kiss it three or four
times to bid me farewell ; and once, when the doctoress mentioned his having charged her to tell me
that he owed his recovery to the good food that I
had sent him, he added, " And him kind words too,
massa ; kind words do neger much good, much as
good food." In my visits to the old man, I observed a young woman nursing him with an infant
in her arms, which (as they told me) was her own,
by Cudjoe. I therefore supposed her to be his
wife : but I found that she belonged to a *brown*

man in the mountains; and that Cudjoe hired her from her master, at the rate of thirty pounds a year!

I hope this fact will convince the African *Reporter*, that it is possible for some of this "oppressed race of human beings" — "of these our most unfortunate fellow-creatures," — to enjoy at least *some* of the luxuries of civilised society; and I doubt, whether even Mr. Wilberforce himself, with all his benevolence, would not allow a negro to be quite rich enough, who can afford to pay thirty pounds a year for the hire of a kept mistress.

## MARCH 14.

Poor Nato's stock of goodness is quite exhausted; and the day before yesterday he returned to the hospital with most piteous complaints of pains and aches, whose existence he could persuade no person to credit. His pulse was regular, his skin cool, his tongue red and moist, and the doctor declared nothing whatever to be the matter with him. However, on my arrival, he began to moan, and groan, and grunt, and all so lamentably, that every soul in the hospital, sick or well, burst into a fit of laughter. For my part, I told him that I really believed him to be very bad; and that, as he met with no sympathy in the hospital, I should remove him from such unfeeling companions. Accordingly I had a comfortable bed made for him in a separate house. Here he was plentifully supplied with provisions: but, in order that he might enjoy perfect repose during his illness, the doors were kept locked, and no person allowed to disturb him with their conversation; while, by the doctor's orders, he was obliged to take frequent doses of Bitter-Wood and Assafœtida. Shame would not suffer him to get well all at once; so yesterday he still complained of a pain in his chest, and begged to be blooded. His request was granted; and the blood proved to be so pure and well-coloured, that every one exclaimed, that for a man who had such good blood to part with it so wantonly was a shame and a folly. The fellow was at length convinced that his tricks would serve no object; and this morning he begged me to suffer him to return to his duty, and promised that I should have no more cause to complain of him. So I consented to consider his cure as completed, and he set off for the field perfectly satisfied with his release.

## MARCH 15.

On opening the Assize-court for the county of Cornwall on March 4., Mr. Stewart, the Custos of Trelawny, and Presiding Judge, said, in his charge to the jury, he wished to direct their attention in a peculiar manner to the infringement of slave-laws in the island, in consequence of charges having been brought forward in England of slave laws not being enforced in this country, and being in fact perfect dead letters. The charge was unfounded;

but it became proper, in consequence, for the bench to call in a strong manner on the grand jury to be particularly vigilant and attentive to the discharge of this part of their duty. The bench at the same time adverted to another subject connected with the above. Many out of the country, and *some in it*, had thought proper to interfere with our system, and by their insidious practices and dangerous doctrines to call the peace of the island into question, and to promote disorder and confusion. The jury were therefore enjoined, in every such case, to investigate it thoroughly, and to bring the parties concerned before the country, and not to suffer the systems of the island, as established by the laws of the land, to be overset or endangered. It was their bounden duty to watch over and support the established laws, and to act against those who dared to infringe them ; and that, otherwise, it was imperiously called for on the principle of self-preservation. Every country had its peculiar laws, on the due maintenance of which depended the public safety and welfare. I read all this with the most perfect unconsciousness ; when, lo and behold! I have been assured, from a variety of quarters, that all this was levelled at myself! It is I (it seems) who am " calling the peace of the island in question ; " who am " promoting disorder and confusion ; " and who am " infringing the established laws!" I should never have guessed it! By " insidious practices" is meant (as I am told) my over-indulgence to my negroes; and my endeavouring to obtain either redress or pardon for those belonging to other estates, who occasionally appeal to me for protection: while " dangerous doctrines " alludes to my being of opinion, that the evidence of negroes ought at least to be *heard* against white persons; the jury always making proportionable abatements of belief, from bearing in mind the bad habits of most negroes, their general want of probity and good faith in every respect, and their total ignorance of the nature of religious obligations. At the same time, these defects may be counterbalanced by the respectable character of the particular negro; by the strength of corroborating circumstances; and, finally, by the irresistible conviction which his evidence may leave upon the minds of the jury. They are not obliged to *believe* a negro witness, but I maintain that he ought to be *heard*, and then let the jury give their verdict according to their conscience. But this, in the opinion of the bench at Montego Bay, it seems, is " dangerous doctrine!" At least, the venom of my doctrines is circumscribed within very narrow limits; for as I have made a point of never stirring off my own estate, nobody could possibly be corrupted by them, except those who were at the trouble of walking into my house for the express purpose of being corrupted.

At all events, if I *really* am the person to whom Mr. Stewart alluded, I must consider his speech as the most flattering compliment that I ever received. If my presence in the island has made the bench of a whole country think it necessary to exact from the jury a more severe vigilance than usual in all causes relating to the protection of negroes, I cannot but own myself most richly rewarded for all my pains and expense in coming hither, for every risk of the voyage, and for every possible sacrifice of my pleasures. There is nothing earthly that is too much to give for the power of producing an effect so beneficial; and I would set off for Constantinople to-morrow, could I only be convinced that my arrival would make the Mufti redress the complaints of the lower orders of Turks with more scrupulous justice, and the Bashaws relax the fetters of their slaves as much as their safety would permit. But I cannot flatter myself with having done either the one or the other in Jamaica; and if Mr. Stewart *really* alluded to me in his charge, I am certainly greatly obliged to him; but he has paid me much too high a compliment; —God grant that I may live to deserve it!

## MARCH 16.

Hercules, the poor paralytic runaway, has neither moved nor spoken since his being brought into the hospital. For the two last days he refused all sustenance; blisters, rubbing with mustard, &c. were tried without producing the least sensation; and in the course of last night he expired without a groan.

Another offender, by name Charles Fox, is also under the doctor's hands, suffering under the effects of his own transgressions. Having been Pickle's shipmate, he professed the strongest attachment to him, and was perpetually at his house; till Pickle's wife made her husband aware that love for herself was the real object of his shipmate's visits. Finding her story disbelieved, she hid Pickle behind the bed, when he had an opportunity of hearing the solicitations of his perfidious Pylades; and, rushing from his concealment, he gave Fox so complete a thrashing, that he was obliged to come to the hospital. Here is another proof that negroes, " our unfortunate fellow-creatures," are not without some of the luxuries of civilised life; old men of sixty keeping mistresses, and young ones seducing their friends' wives; why, what would the Reporter of the African Institution have?

It is only to be wished, that the negroes would content themselves with these fashionable peccadilloes; but, unluckily, there are some palates among them which require higher seasoned vices; and besides their occasional amusements of poisoning, stabbing, thieving, &c., a plan has just been discovered in the adjoining parish of St. Elizabeth's, for giving themselves a grand fête by murdering all the whites in the island. The focus of this meditated insurrection was on Martin's Penn, the property of Lord Balcarras, where the overseer is an old man of the mildest character, and the negroes had always been treated with peculiar indulgence. Above a thousand persons were engaged in the plot, three hundred of whom had been regularly sworn to assist in it with all the usual accompanying ceremonies of drinking human blood, eating earth from graves, &c. Luckily, the plot was discovered time enough to prevent any mischief; and yesterday the ringleaders were to be tried at Black River.

### March 17. (Sunday.)

The Cornwall Chronicle informs us, that, at the Montego Bay assizes, a man was tried on the Monday, for assaulting, while drunk, an officer who had served with great distinction, and calling him a coward; for which offence he was sentenced to a month's imprisonment and fine of 100*l.*; and on the Tuesday the same man brought an action against another person for calling him a "drunken liar," for which he was awarded 1000*l.* for damages! A plain man would have supposed two such verdicts to be rather incompatible; but one lives to learn.

I remember to have read the case of a French nobleman, who was accused of impotence by his wife before the Parliament of Paris, and by a farmer's daughter for seduction and getting her with child before the Parliament of Rouen; he thought himself perfectly sure of gaining either

Q

the one cause or the other : but, however, he was condemned in both. Certainly the poor Frenchman had no luck in matters of justice.

To make the matter better, in the present instance, the man was a clergyman; and his cause of quarrel against the officer was the latter's refusal to give him a puncheon of rum to christen all his negroes in a lump.

## MARCH 22.

Mr. Plummer came over from St. James's to-day, and told me, that the "insidious practices and dangerous doctrines" in Mr. Stewart's speech were intended for the Methodists, and that only the charge to the grand jury respecting " additional vigilance" was in allusion to myself; but he added that it was the report at Montego Bay, that, in consequence of my over-indulgence to my negroes, a song had been made at Cornwall, declaring that -I was come over to set them all free, and that this was now circulating through the neighbouring parishes. If there be any such song (which I do not believe), I certainly never heard it. However, my agent here says, that he has reason to believe that my negroes really have spread the report that I intend to set *them* free in a few years; and this merely out of vanity, in order to give themselves and their master the greater credit upon other estates. As to the truth of an assertion, that is a point which never enters into negro consideration.

The two ringleaders of the proposed rebellion have been condemned at Black River, the one to be hanged, the other to transportation. The plot was discovered by the overseer of Lyndhurst Penn (a Frenchman from St. Domingo) observing an uncommon concourse of stranger negroes to a child's funeral, on which occasion a hog was roasted by the father. He stole softly down to the feasting hut, and listened behind a hedge to the conversation of the supposed mourners; when he heard the whole conspiracy detailed. It appears that above two hundred and fifty had been sworn in regularly, all of them Africans; not a Creole was among them. But there was a *black* ascertained to have stolen over into the island from St. Domingo, and a *brown* Anabaptist missionary, both of whom had been very active in promoting the plot. They had elected a King of the Eboes, who had two Captains under him; and their intention was to effect a complete massacre of all the whites on the island; for which laudable design His Majesty thought Christmas the very fittest season in the year, but his Captains were more impatient, and were for striking the blow immediately. The next morning information was given against them: one of the Captains escaped to the woods; but the other, and the King of the Eboes, were seized and brought to justice. On their trial they were perfectly cool and unconcerned, and did not even profess to deny the facts with which they were charged.

Indeed, proofs were too strong to admit of denial; among others, a copy of the following song was found upon the King, which the overseer had heard him sing at the funeral feast, while the other negroes joined in the chorus : —

### SONG OF THE KING OF THE EBOES.

Oh me good friend, Mr. Wilberforce, make we free !
God Almighty thank ye ! God Almighty thank ye !
   God Almighty, make we free !
Buckra in this country no make we free :
What Negro for to do?   What Negro for to do?
   Take force by force !   Take force by force !

**CHORUS.**

To be sure ! to be sure ! to be sure !

The Eboe King said, that he certainly had made use of this song, and what harm was there in his doing so? He had sung no songs but such as his brown priest had assured him were approved of by John the Baptist. "And who, then, was John the Baptist?" He did not very well know; only he had been told by his brown priest, that John the Baptist was a friend to the negroes, and had got his head in a pan!

As to the Captain, he only said in his defence, that if the court would forgive him this once, he would not do so again, " as he found the whites did not like their plans;" which, it seems, till that moment they had never suspected! They had all along imagined, no doubt, that the whites would find as much amusement in having their throats cut, as the blacks would find in cutting them. I remember hearing a sportsman, who was defending the humanity of hunting, maintain, that it being as much the nature of a hare to run away as of a dog to run after her, consequently the hare must receive as much pleasure from being coursed, as the dog from coursing.

## MARCH 23.

Two negroes upon Amity estate quarrelled the other day about some trifle, when the one bit the other's nose off completely. Soon after his accident, the overseer meeting the sufferer — "Why, Sambo," he exclaimed, "where's your nose?" "I can't tell, massa," answered Sambo; "I looked every where about, but I could not find it."

## MARCH 24. (Sunday.)

Every Sunday since my return from Kingston I have read prayers to such of the negroes as chose to attend, preparatory to the intended visitations of the minister, Dr. Pope. About twenty or thirty of the most respectable among them generally attended, and behaved with great attention and propriety. I read the Litany, and made them repeat the responses. I explained the Commandments and the Lord's Prayer to them, teaching them to say each sentence of the latter after me, as I read it slowly, in hopes of impressing it upon their memory. Then came "the good Samaritan," or some such apologue; and, lastly, I related to them a portion of the life of Christ, and explained to them the object of his death and sufferings. The latter part of my service always seemed to interest them greatly; but, indeed, they behaved throughout with much attention. Unluckily, the head driver, who was one of the most zealous of my disciples, never could repeat the responses of the Litany without an appeal to myself, and always made a point of saying — "Good Lord, deliver us; yes, sir!" and made me a low bow: and one day when I was describing the wonderful precocity of Christ's understanding, as evidenced by his interview with the doctors in the temple, while but a child, the head driver thought fit to interrupt me with — "Beg massa pardon, but want know one ting as puzzle me. Massa say 'the child,' and me want know, massa, one ting much; was Jesus Christ a boy or a girl?" Like my friend the Moravian, at Mesopotamia, I cannot boast of any increased audience; and if the negroes will not come to hear massa, I have little hope of their giving up their time to hear Dr. Pope, who inspires them with no interest, and can exert no authority. Indeed, I am afraid that I am indebted for the chief part of my present auditory to my quality of massa rather than that of priest; and when I ask any of them why they did not come to prayers on the preceding Sunday, their excuse is always coupled with an assurance, that they wished very much to come,

" because they wish to do *any thing* to oblige massa."

MARCH 25.

The negroes certainly are perverse beings. They had been praying for a sight of their master year after year; they were in raptures at my arrival; I have suffered no one to be punished, and shown them every possible indulgence during my residence amongst them; and one and all they declare themselves perfectly happy and well treated. Yet, previous to my arrival, they made thirty-three hogsheads a week; in a fortnight after my landing, their product dwindled to twenty-three; during this last week they have managed to make but thirteen. Still they are not ungrateful; they are only selfish: they love me very well, but they love themselves a great deal better; and, to do them justice, I verily believe that every negro on the estate is extremely anxious that all should do their full duty, except himself. My censure, although accompanied with the certainty of their not being punished, is by no means a matter of indifference. If I express myself to be displeased, the whole property is in an uproar; every body is finding fault with every body; nobody that does not represent the shame of neglecting my work, and the ingratitude of vexing me by their ill-conduct; and then each individual — having said so much, and said it so strongly, that he is convinced of its having its ful. effect in making the others do their duty — thinks himself quite safe and snug in skulking away from his own.

MARCH 26.

Young Hill was told at the Bay this morning, that I make a part of the Eboe King's song! According to this report, " good King George and good Mr. Wilberforce" are stated to have " given me a paper" to set the negroes free (i. e. an order), but that the white people of Jamaica will not suffer me to show the paper, and I am now going home to say so, and " to resume my chair, which I have left during my absence to be filled by the Regent."

Since I heard the report of a rebellious song issuing from Cornwall, I have listened more attentively to the negro chaunts; but they seem, as far as I can make out, to relate entirely to their own private situation, and to have nothing to do with the negro state in general. Their favourite, " We varry well off," is still screamed about the estate by the children; but among the grown people its nose has been put out of joint by the following stanzas, which were explained to me this morning. For several days past they had been dinned into my ears so incessantly, that at length I became quite curious to know their import, which I learned from Phillis, who is the family minstrel. It will be evident from this specimen, that the Cornwall bards are greatly inferior to those of Black River, who have actually advanced so far as to make an attempt at rhyme and metre.

### NEGRO SONG AT CORNWALL.

Hey-ho-day ! me no care a dammee ! (i. e. a damn,)
Me acquire a house, (i. e. I have a solid foundation to
    build on,)
Since massa come see we — oh !

Hey-ho-day ! neger now quite eerie, (i. e. hearty,)
For once me see massa — hey-ho-day !
When massa go, me no care a dammee,
For how them usy we — hey-ho-day !

\*   \*   \*   \*   \*   \*   \*

An Alligator, crossing the morass at Bellisle, an
estate but a few miles distant from Cornwall, fell
into a water-trench, from which he struggled in
vain to extricate himself, and was taken alive; so
that, according to the vulgar expression, he may
literally be said to "have put his foot in it." Fon-
tenelle says, that when Copernicus published his
system, he foresaw the contradictions which he
should have to undergo — " Et il se tira d'affaire
très-habilement. Le jour qu'on lui présentoit le
premier exemplaire, scavez-vous ce qu'il fit? Il
mourut;" which was precisely the resource resorted
to by the alligator. He died on the second morning of his captivity, and his proprietor, Mr. Storer,
was obliging enough to order the skin to be stuffed,
and to make me a present of him. Neptune was
despatched to bring him (or rather her, for nineteen eggs were found within her) over to Cornwall; and at dinner to-day we were alarmed with a

general hubbub. It proved to be occasioned by Neptune's arrival (if Thames or Achelous had been despatched on this errand, it would have been more appropriate) with the alligator on his head. In a few minutes every thing on the estate that was alive, without feathers, and with only two legs, flocked into the room, and requested to take a bird's-eye view of the monster; for as to coming near her, *that* they were much too cowardly to venture. It was in vain that I represented to them, that being dead it was utterly impossible that the animal could hurt them: they allowed the impossibility, but still kept at a respectful distance; and when at length I succeeded in persuading them to approach it, upon some one accidentally moving the alligator's tail, they all, with one accord, set up a loud scream, and men, women, and children tumbled out of the room over one another, to the irreparable ruin of some of my glasses and decanters, and the extreme trepidation of the whole side-board.

\* \* \* \* \* \* \* \*

The negro-husband, who stabbed his rival in a fit of jealousy, has been tried at Montego Bay, and acquitted. On the other hand, the King of the Eboes has been hung at Black River, and died, declaring that he left enough of his countrymen to prosecute the design in hand, and revenge his death upon the whites. Such threats of a rescue were held out, that it was judged advisable to put the militia under arms, till the execution should have taken place; and also to remove the King's Captain to the gaol at Savannah la Mar, till means can be found for transporting him from the island.

## MARCH 27.

The Eboe Captain has effected his escape by burning down the prison door. It is supposed that he has fled towards the fastnesses in the interior of the mountains, where I am assured that many settlements of run-away slaves have been formed, and with which the inhabited part of the island has no communication. However, the chief of the Accompong Maroons, Captain Roe, is gone in pursuit of him, and has promised to bring him in, alive or dead. The latter is the only reasonable expectation, as the fugitive is represented as a complete desperado.

\* \* \* \* \* \* \* \* \* \*

The negroes have at least given me one proof of their not being entirely selfish. When they heard that the boat was come to convey my baggage to the ship at Black River, they collected all their poultry, and brought it to my agent, desiring him to add it to my sea-stores. Of course I refused to let them be received, and they were evidently much disappointed, till I consented to accept the fowls and ducks, and then gave them back to them again, telling them to consider them as a present from my own hen-house, and to distinguish them by the name of " massa's poultry."

## MARCH 28.

I have been positively assured, that an attempt was made to persuade the grand jury at Montego Bay, to present me for over-indulgence to my own negroes! It is a great pity that so reasonable an attempt should not have succeeded. — The rebel captain who broke out of prison, has been found concealed in the hut of a notorious Obeah-man, and has been lodged a second time in the gaol of Savannah la Mar.

## MARCH 29.

About two months ago, a runaway cooper, belonging to Shrewsbury estate, by name Edward, applied to me to intercede for his not being punished on his return home. As soon as he got the paper requested, he gave up all idea of returning to the estate, and instead of it went about the country stealing every thing upon which he could lay his hands; and whenever his proceedings were enquired into by the magistrates, he stated himself to be on the road to his trustee, and produced my letter as a proof of it. At length some one had the curiosity to open the letter, and found that it had been written two months before.

MARCH 30.

This was the day appointed for the first " Royal play-day," when I bade farewell to my negroes. I expected to be besieged with petitions and complaints, as they must either make them on this occasion or not at all. I was, therefore, most agreeably surprised to find, that although they had opportunities of addressing me from nine in the morning till twelve at night, the only favours asked me were by a poor old man, who wanted an iron cooking pot, and by Adam, who begged me to order a little daughter of his to be instructed in needle-work: and as to complaints, not a murmur of such a thing was heard; they all expressed themselves to be quite satisfied, and seemed to think that they could never say enough to mark their gratitude for my kindness, and their anxiety for my getting safe to England. We began our festival by the head driver's drinking the health of H. R. H. the Duchess of York, whom the negroes cheered with such a shout as might have " rent hell's concave."

Then we had a christening of such persons as had been absent on the former occasion, one of whom was Adam, the reputed Obeah-man. In the number was a new-born child, whom we called Shakspeare, and whom Afra, the Eboe mother, had very earnestly begged me to make a Christian, as well as a daughter of hers, about four or five years old; at the same time that she declined being christened herself! In the same manner Cubina's wife, although her father and husband were both baptised on the former occasion, objected to going through the ceremony herself; and the reason which she gave was, that "she did not like being christened while she was with child, as she did not know what change it might not produce upon herself and the infant."

After the christening there was a general distribution of salt-fish by the trustee; and I also gave every man and woman half a dollar each, and every child a maccarony (fifteen pence) as a parting present, to show them that I parted with them in good-humour. While the money was distributing, young Hill arrived, and finding the house completely crowded, he enquired what was the matter. "Oh, massa," said an old woman, "it is only *my son*, who is giving the negroes all something."

I also read to them a new code of laws, which I had ordered to be put in force at Cornwall, for the better security of the negroes. The principal were, that "a new hospital for the lying-in women, and for those who might be seriously ill, should be built, and made as comfortable as possible; while the present one should be reserved for those whom the physicians might declare to be very slightly indisposed, or not ill at all; the doors being kept constantly locked, and the sexes placed in separate chambers, to prevent its being made a place of amuse-

ment by the lazy and lying, as is the case at present."
—" A book register of punishments to be kept, in
which the name, offence, and nature and quantity
of punishment inflicted must be carefully put
down; and also a note of the same given to the
negro, in order that if he should think himself
unjustly, or too severely punished, he may show
his note to my other attorney on his next visit, or
to myself on my return to Jamaica, and thus get
redress if he has been wronged."—" No negro is
to be struck, or punished in any way, without the
trustee's express orders : the black driver so offending to be immediately degraded, and sent to
work in the field ; and the white person, for such a
breach of my orders, to be discharged upon the
spot."—" No negro is to be punished till twenty-
four hours shall have elapsed between his committing the fault and suffering for it, in order that
nothing should be done in the heat of passion,
but that the trustee should have time to consider
the matter coolly. But to prevent a guilty person
from avoiding punishment by running away, he is
to pass those twenty-four hours in such confinement as the trustee may think most fitting."—
" Any white person, who can be proved to have
had an improper connection with a woman known
publicly to be living as the wife of one of my
negroes, is to be discharged immediately upon
complaint being made." I also gave the head
driver a complete list of the allowances of clothing,

food, &c. to which the negroes were entitled, in order that they might apply to it if they should have any doubts as to their having received their full proportion; and my new rules seemed to add greatly to the satisfaction of the negroes, who were profuse in their expressions of gratitude.

The festival concluded with a grander ball than usual, as I sent for music from Savanna la Mar to play country dances to them; and at twelve o'clock at night they left me apparently much pleased, only I heard some of them saying to each other, " When shall we have such a day of pleasure again, since massa goes to-morrow?"

### MARCH 31. (Sunday.)

With their usual levity, the negroes were laughing and talking as gaily as ever till the very moment of my departure; but when they saw my curricle actually at the door to convey me away, then their faces grew very long indeed. In particular, the women called me by every endearing name they could think of. " My son! my love! my husband! my father!" " You no my massa, you my tata!" said one old woman (upon which another wishing to go a step beyond her, added, " Iss, massa, iss! It was you"); * * * * * * * and when I came down the steps to depart, they crowded about me, kissing my feet, and clasping my knees, so that it was with difficulty that I could get into the carriage. And this was done with such marks of truth and feeling, that I cannot believe the whole to be mere acting and mummery.

I dined with Mr. Allwood at Shaftstone, his pen near Blue-fields, and at half past seven found myself once more on board the Sir Godfrey Webster.

To fill up my list of Jamaica delicacies, I must not forget to mention, that I did my best to procure a Cane-piece Cat roasted in the true African fashion. The Creole negroes, however, greatly disapproved of my venturing upon this dish, which they positively denied having tasted themselves; and when, at length, the Cat was procured, last Saturday, instead of plainly boiling it with negro-pepper and salt, they made into a high seasoned stew, which rendered it impossible to judge of its real flavour. However, I tasted it, as did also several other people, and we were unanimous in opinion, that it might have been mistaken for a very good game-soup, and that, when properly dressed, a Cane-piece Cat must be excellent food.

One of the best vegetable productions of the island is esteemed to be the Avogada pear, sometimes called "the vegetable marrow." It was not the proper season for them, and with great difficulty I procured a couple, which were said to be by no means in a state of perfection. Such as they were, I could find no great merit in them; they were to be eaten cold with pepper and salt, and seemed to be an insipid kind of melon, with no other resemblance to marrow than their softness.

## APRIL 1. (Monday.)

At eight this morning we weighed anchor on our return to England.

### YARRA.

Poor Yarra comes to bid farewell,
But Yarra's lips can never say it!
Her swimming eyes — her bosom's swell —
The debt she owes you, these must pay it.
She ne'er can speak, though tears can start,
Her grief, that fate so soon removes you;
But One there is, who reads the heart,
And well He knows how Yarra loves you!

See, massa, see this sable boy!
When chill disease had nipp'd his flower,
You came and spoke the word of joy,
And poured the juice of healing power.
To visit far Jamaica's shore
Had no kind angel deign'd to move you,
These laughing eyes had laugh'd no more,
Nor Yarra lived to thank and love you.

Then grieve not, massa, that to view
Our isle you left your British pleasures:
One tear, which falls in grateful dew,
Is worth the best of Britain's treasures.
And sure, the thought will bring relief,
What e'er your fate, wherever rove you,
Your wealth 's not given by pain and grief,
But hands that know, and hearts that love you.

May He, who bade you cross the wave,
   Through care for Afric's sons and daughters;
When round your bark the billows rave,
   In safety guide you through the waters!
By all you love with smiles be met;
   Through life each good man's tongue approve you:
And though far distant, don't forget,
   While Yarra lives, she'll live to love you!

### April 3.

The trade-winds which facilitate the passage to Jamaica, effectually prevent the return of vessels by the same road. The common passage is through the Gulf of Florida, but there is another between Cuba and St. Domingo, which is at least 1000 miles nearer. The first, however, affords almost a certainty of reaching Europe in a given time; while you may keep tacking in the attempt to make the windward passage (as it is called) for months together. Last night the wind was so favourable for this attempt, that the captain determined upon risking it. Accordingly he altered his course; and had not done so for more than a few hours, when the wind changed, and became as direct for the Gulf, as till then it had been contrary. The consequence was, that the Gulf passage was fixed once for all, and we are now steering towards it with all our might and main. Besides the distance saved, there was another reason for preferring the windward passage, if it could have been effected. The Gulf of Florida has for some time past been infested by a pirate called Captain Mitchell, who, by all accounts, seems to be of the very worst description. It is not long ago, since, in company with another vessel of his own stamp, he landed on the small settlement of St. Andrews, plundered it completely, and on his departure carried off the governor, whom he kept on board for more than fourteen days, and then hung him at the yard-arm out of mere wanton devilry; and indeed he is said to show no more mercy to any of his prisoners than he did to the poor governor. His companion has been captured and brought into Kingston, and the conquering vessel is gone in search of Captain Mitchell. If it does not fall in with him, and *we* do, I fear that we shall stand but a bad chance; for he has one hundred men on board according to report, while we have not above thirty. However, the captain has harangued them, represented the necessity of their fighting if attacked, as Captain Mitchell is known to spare no one, high or low, and has engaged to give every man five guineas apiece, if a gun should be fired. The sailors promise bravery; whether their promises will prove to be pie-crust, we must leave to be decided by time and Captain Mitchell. In the mean while, every sail that appears on the horizon is concluded to be this terrible pirate, and every thing is immediately put in readiness for action.

### April 4.

This day we passed the Caymana islands; but owing to our having always either a contrary wind, or no wind at all, it was not till the 12th that Cuba was visible, nor till the 14th that we reached Cape Florida.

### April 15.

At noon this day we found ourselves once more sailing on the Atlantic, and bade farewell to the Gulf of Florida without having heard any news of the dreaded Commodore Mitchell. The narrow and dangerous part of this Gulf is about two hundred miles in length, and fifty in breadth, bordered on one side by the coast of Florida, and on the other, first by Cuba, and then by the Bahama Islands, of which the Manilla reef forms the extremity, and which reef also terminates the Gulf. But on both sides of these two hundred miles, at the distance of about four or five miles from the main land, there extends a reef which renders the navigation extremely dangerous. The reef is broken at intervals by large inlets; and the sudden and violent squalls of wind to which the Gulf is subject, so frequently drive vessels into these perilous openings, that it is worth the while of many of the poorer inhabitants of Florida to establish their habitations within the reef, and devote themselves and their small vessels entirely to the occupation of assisting vessels in distress. They are known by the general name of "wreckers," and are allowed a certain salvage upon such ships as they may rescue. As a proof of the violence of the gales which are occasionally experienced in this Gulf, our captain, about nine years ago, saw the wind suddenly take a vessel (which had unwisely suffered her canvass to stand, while the rest of the ships under convoy had taken theirs down,) and turn her completely over, the sails in the water and the keel uppermost. It happened about four o'clock in the afternoon: the captain and the passengers were at dinner in the cabin; but as she went over very leisurely, they and the crew had time allowed them to escape out of the windows and port-holes, and sustain themselves upon the rigging, till boats from the ships near them could arrive to take them off. As she filled, she gradually sunk, and in a quarter of an hour she had disappeared totally.

## APRIL 17.

## THE FLYING FISH.

Bright ocean-bird, alike who sharing
Both elements, could sport the air in,
Or swim the sea, your winged fins wearing
    The rainbow's hues,
Your fate this day full long shall bear in
    Her mind the muse.

In vain for you had nature blended
Two regions, and your powers extended;
Now high you rose, now low descended;
      But folly marred
Those gifts, the bounteous dame intended
       To prove your guard.

A flying fish, could bounds include her?
She winged the deep, if birds pursued her;
She swam the sky, if dolphins viewed her;
      But now what wish
Tempts you to watch yon bright deluder,
       Unthinking fish?

Alas! — a fly above you viewing,
Gay tints his gilded wings imbuing,
You mount; and ah! too far pursuing
      At fancy's call,
Heedless you strike the sails, where ruin
       Awaits your fall.

Your fins, too dry, no longer play you,
And soon those fins no more upstay you;
You drop; and now on deck survey you
      Jack, Tom, and Bill,
Who up may take, and down may lay you,
       As suits their will.

Oh! list my tale, fair maids of Britain!
This subject fain I'd try my wit on,
And show the rock you 're apt to split on:
      Then cry not — " Pish!" —
You 're all (I 'm glad the thought I hit on)
       Just flying fish!

Beauty, does nature's hand bestow it?
It swells your pride, and plain you show it;

Though wealthy cit, and airy poet
    Your charms pursue,
Church — physic — law — you 're fair, you know it,
    You 'll none, not you !

Age looks too dry, and youth too blooming :
The scholar's face there 's too much gloom in ;
*This* man 's too dull, *that* too presuming ;
    *His* mouth 's too wide ! —
For mending, Lord ! you think there's room in
    The best, when tried.

In each you find some fault to snarl at,
And wilful seek the sun by starlight ;
Till some gay glittering rogue in scarlet,
    Who lures the eye,
Dazzles poor miss, and then the varlet
    Pretends to fly.

His flight has piqued, his glitter caught her ;
And soon her mammy's darling daughter,
Whose eyes have made such mighty slaughter,
    Charm'd by a fop,
Is fairly hit 'twixt wind and water,
    And, miss ! you drop !

Then certain fate of fallen lasses,
When short-lived bliss more frail than glass is,
To eyes of all degrees and classes
    Exposed you stand,
And soon your beauty circling passes
    From hand to hand.

In vain your flattering charms display you ;
From home and parents far away, you
See former friends with scorn survey you ;
    While fools and brutes
May take you up, or down may lay you,
    As humour suits.

Oh! mark, dear girls, the moral story
Of one, who breathes but to adore ye!
Let no rash action mar your glory;
    But when you wish
To catch some coxcomb, place before ye
    The flying fish.

## APRIL 20.

Two or three years ago, our captain, while his vessel was lying in Black River Bay, for the purpose of loading, was informed by his sailors, that their beef and other provisions frequently disappeared in a very unaccountable manner. However, by setting a strict watch during the night, he soon managed to clear up the mystery : and a negro, who had made his escape from the workhouse, and concealed himself on board among the bags of cotton, was found to be the thief. He was sent back to the workhouse, of which the chain was still about his neck. But another negro had better luck in a similar attempt on board of a different vessel. He contrived to secrete himself in the lower part of it, where the sugar hogsheads are stored, unknown to any one. As soon as the cargo was completed, the planks above it were caulked down, and raised no more till their ship reached Liverpool; when, to the universal astonishment, upon opening the hold, out walked Mungo, in a wretched condition to be sure, but still at least alive, and a freeman in Great Britain. During his painful voyage, he had subsisted entirely upon sugar, of which he had consumed nearly an hogs-head; how he managed for water I could not learn, nor can imagine.

## APRIL 23.

The old steward, this morning, told one of the sailors, who complained of being ill, that he would get well as soon as he should reach England, and could have plenty of vegetables; "for," he said, "the man had only got a *stomachick* complaint; nothing but just scurvy!"

## APRIL 24.

Sea Terms.—The *sheets,* a term for various ropes; the *halyards,* ropes which extend the top-sails; the *painter,* the rope which fastens the boat to the vessel; the *eight points of the compass,* south, south and by east, south-south east, south east and by east, south-east, east south and by east, east south east, east and by south east. The knowledge of these points is termed "knowing how to box the compass."

## APRIL 27.

Many years ago, a new species of grass was im-ported into Jamaica, by Mr. Vassal, (to whom an estate near my own then belonged), as he said "for the purpose of feeding his pigs and his book-keepers." Its seeds being soon scattered about by the birds, it has taken possession of the cane-pieces, whence to eradicate it is an utter impossibility, the roots being as strong as those of ginger, and insinuating themselves under ground to a great extent; so that the only means of preventing it from entirely choking up the canes, is plucking it out with the hand, which is obliged to be done frequently, and has increased the labour of the plantation at least one third. This nuisance, which is called " Vassal's grass," from its original introducer, has now completely over-run the parish of Westmoreland, has begun to show itself in the neighbouring parishes, and probably in time will get a footing throughout the island. St. Thomas's in the East has been inoculated with another self-inflicted plague, under the name of " the rifle-ant," which was imported for the purpose of eating up the ants of the country; and so to be sure they did, but into the bargain they eat up every thing else which came in their way, a practice in which they persist to this hour; so that it may be doubted whether in Jamaica most execrations are bestowed in the course of the day upon Vassal's grass, the rifle-ants, Sir Charles Price's rats, or the Reporter of the African Society; only that the maledictions uttered against the three first are necessarily local, while the Reporter of the African Society comes in for curses from all quarters.

### April 30. (Tuesday.)

A whole calendar month has elapsed since our quitting Jamaica, during which the wind has been favourable for something less than four-and-twenty hours; either it has blown precisely from the point on which we wanted to sail, or has been so faint, that we scarcely made one knot an hour. However, on Tuesday last, finding ourselves in the latitude of the "still-vexed Bermoothes," by way of variety, a sudden squall carried away both our lower stunsails in the morning; and at nine in the evening there came on a gale of wind truly tremendous. The ship pitched and rolled every minute, as if she had been on the point of overturning; the hen-coops floated about the deck, and many of the poultry were found drowned in them the next morning. Just as the last dead-light was putting up, the sea embraced the opportunity of the window being open, to whip itself through, and half filled the after-cabin with water; and in half an hour more a mountain of waves broke over the vessel, and pouring itself through the sky-light, paid the same compliment to the fore-cabin, with which it had already honoured the after one. About four in the morning the storm abated, and then we relapsed into our good old jog-trot pace of a knot an hour. Our passengers consist of a Mrs. Walker with her two children, and a sick surgeon of the name of Ashman.

## May 5. (Sunday.)

We continue to proceed at such a tortoise-pace, that it has been thought advisable to put the crew upon an allowance of water.

## May 7.

A negro song.—" Me take my cutacoo, (i. e. a basket made of matting,) and follow him to Lucea, and all for love of my bonny man-O — My bonny man come home, come home! Doctor no do you good. When neger fall into neger hands, buckra doctor no do him good more. Come home, my gold ring, come home!" This is the song of a wife, whose husband had been Obeahed by another woman, in consequence of his rejecting her advances. A negro riddle: " Pretty Miss Nancy was going to market, and she tore her fine yellow gown, and there was not a taylor in all the town who could mend it again." This is a ripe plantain with a broken skin. The negroes are also very fond of what they call Nancy stories, part of which is related, and part sung. The heroine of one of them is an old woman named Mamma Luna, who having left a pot boiling in her hut, found it robbed on her return. Her suspicions were divided between two children whom she found at play near her door, and some negroes who had passed that way to market. The children denied the theft positively. It was necessary for the negroes, in order to reach their own estate, to wade through a river at that time almost dry; and on their return, Mammy Luna (who it should seem, was not without some skill in witchcraft,) warned them to take care in venturing across the stream, for that the water would infallibly rise and carry away the person who had stolen the contents of her pot; but if the thief would but confess the offence, she engaged that no harm should happen, as she only wanted to exculpate the innocent, and not to punish the guilty. One and all denied the charge, and several crossed the river without fear or danger; but upon the approach of a *belly-woman* to the bank, she was observed to hesitate. "My neger, my neger," said Mammy Luna, "why you stop? me tink, you savee well, who thief me?" This accusation spirited up the woman, who instantly marched into the river, singing as she went (and the woman's part is always chanted frequently in chorus, which the negroes call, "taking up the sing").

> "If da me eat Mammy Luna's pease-O,
> Drowny me water, drowny, drowny!"

"My neger, my neger," cried the old woman, "me sure now you the thief! me see the water wet you feet. Come back, my neger, come back." Still on went the woman, and still continued her song of

> "If da me eat Mammy Luna's pease, &c."

"My neger, my neger," repeated Mammy Luna, "me no want punish you; my pot smell good, and you belly-woman. Come back, my neger, come back; me see now water above your knee!" But the woman was obstinate; she continued to sing and to advance, till she reached the middle of the river's bed, when down came a tremendous flood, swept her away, and she never was heard of more; while Mammy Luna warned the other negroes never to take the property of another; always to tell the truth; and, at least, if they should be betrayed into telling a lie, not to persist in it, otherwise they must expect to perish like their companion. Observe, that a moral is always an indispensable part of a Nancy story. Another is as follows: — "Two sisters had always lived together on the best terms; but, on the death of one of them, the other treated very harshly a little niece, who had been left to her care, and made her a common drudge to herself and her daughter. One day the child having broken a water-jug, was turned out of the house, and ordered not to return till she could bring back as good a one. As she was going along, weeping, she came to a large cotton-tree, under which was sitting an old woman without a head. I suppose this unexpected sight made her gaze rather too earnestly, for the old woman immediately enquired—'Well, my piccaniny, what you see?' 'Oh, mammy,' answered the girl, 'me no see nothing.' 'Good child!' said

again the old woman; 'and good will come to
you.' Not far distant was a cocoa-tree; and here
was another old woman, without any more head
than the former one. The same question was
asked her, and she failed not to give the same
answer which had already met with so good a reception. Still she travelled forwards, and began
to feel faint through want of food, when, under a
mahogany tree, she not only saw a third old woman,
but one who, to her great satisfaction, had got a
head between her shoulders. She stopped, and
made her best courtesy — 'How day, grannie!'
'How day, my piccaniny; what matter, you no
look well?' 'Grannie, me lilly hungry.' 'My
piccaniny, you see that hut, there's rice in the pot,
take it, and yam-yamme; but if you see one black
puss, mind you give him him share.' The child
hastened to profit by the permission; the 'one
black puss' failed not to make its appearance, and
was served first to its portion of rice, after which
it departed; and the child had but just finished her
meal, when the mistress of the hut entered, and
told her that she might help herself to three eggs out
of the fowl-house, but that she must not take any of
the *talking* ones: perhaps, too, she might find the
black puss there, also; but if she did, she was to
take no notice of her. Unluckily all the eggs
seemed to be as fond of talking as if they had been
so many old maids; and the moment that the child
entered the fowl-house, there was a cry of 'Take

*me!* Take *me!*' from all quarters. However she was punctual in her obedience; and although the conversable eggs were remarkably fine and large, she searched about till at length she had collected three little dirty-looking eggs, that had not a word to say for themselves. The old woman now dismissed her guest, bidding her to return home without fear; but not to forget to break one of the eggs under each of the three trees near which she had seen an old woman that morning. The first egg produced a water-jug exactly similar to that which she had broken; out of the second came a whole large sugar estate; and out of the third a splendid equipage, in which she returned to her aunt, delivered up the jug, related that an old woman in a red docker (i. e. petticoat) had made her a great lady, and then departed in triumph to her sugar estate. Stung by envy, the aunt lost no time in sending her own daughter to search for the same good fortune which had befallen her cousin. She found the cotton-tree and the headless old woman, and had the same question addressed to her; but instead of returning the same answer — ' What me see ?' said she; ' me see one old woman without him head!' Now this reply was doubly offensive; it was rude, because it reminded the old lady of what might certainly be considered as a personal defect; and it was dangerous, as, if such a circumstance were to come to the ears of the buckras, it might bring her into trouble, women being seldom known to walk and talk without their heads, indeed, if ever, except by the assistance of Obeah. 'Bad child!' cried the old woman; 'bad child! and bad will come to you!' Matters were no better managed near the cocoa-tree; and even when she reached the mahogany, although she saw that the old woman had not only got her head on, but had a red docker besides, she could not prevail on herself to say more than a short 'How day?' without calling her 'grannie.' [Among negroes it is almost tantamount to an affront to address by the name, without affixing some term of relationship, such as 'grannie,' or 'uncle,' or 'cousin.' My Cornwall boy, George, told me one day, that 'Uncle Sully wanted to speak to massa.' 'Why, is Sully your uncle, George?' 'No, massa; me only call him so for honour.'] However, she received the permission to eat rice at the cottage, coupled with the injunction of giving a share to the black puss; an injunction, however, which she totally disregarded, although she scrupled not to assure her hostess that she had suffered puss to eat till she could eat no more. The old lady in the red petticoat seemed to swallow the lie very glibly, and despatched the girl to the fowl-house for three eggs, as she had before done her cousin; but having been cautioned against taking the talking eggs, she conceived that these must needs be the most valuable; and, therefore, made a point of selecting those three which seemed to be the greatest gossips of the whole poultry yard. Then, lest their chattering should betray her disobedience, she thought it best not to return into the hut, and, accordingly, set forward on her return home; but she had not yet reached the mahogany tree, when curiosity induced her to break one of the eggs. To her infinite disappointment it proved to be empty; and she soon found cause to wish that the second had been empty too; for, on her dashing it against the ground, out came an enormous yellow snake, which flew at her with dreadful hissings. Away ran the girl; a fallen bamboo lay in her path; she stumbled over it, and fell. In her fall the third egg was broken; and the old woman without the head immediately popping out of it, told her, that if she had treated her as civilly, and had adhered as closely to the truth as her cousin had done, she would have obtained the same good fortune; but that as she had shown her nothing but rudeness, and told her nothing but lies, she must be contented to carry nothing home but the empty egg-shells. The old woman then jumped upon the yellow snake, galloped away with incredible speed, and never showed her red docker in that part of the island any more."

### APRIL 8.

At breakfast the captain was explaining to me the dangerous consequences of breaking the wheelrope: two hours afterwards the wheel-rope broke, and round swung the vessel. However, as the accident fortunately took place in the day time, and when the sea was perfectly calm, it was speedily remedied : but this was " talking of the devil and his imps" with a vengeance.

### APRIL 10.

During the early part of my outward-bound voyage I was extremely afflicted with sea-sickness; and between eight o'clock on a Monday morning, and twelve on the following Thursday, I actually brought up almost a thousand lines, with rhymes at the end of them. Having nothing better to do at present, I may as well copy them into this book. Composed with such speed, and under such circumstances, I take it for granted that the verses cannot be very good; but let them be ever so bad, I defy any one to be more sick while reading them than the author himself was while writing them. This strange story was found by me in an old Italian book, called " Il Palagio degli Incanti," in which it was related as a fact, and stated to be taken from the " Annals of Portugal," an historical work. I will not vouch for the truth of it myself; and, at all events, I earnestly request that no person who may read these verses will ask me " who the hero really was?" If he does, I shall only return the same answer which the lady gave her husband when, being on the point of shipwreck, he requested her to tell him whether she had really ever wronged his bed ? " My dear," said she, " sink or swim, that secret shall go to the grave with me."

# THE ISLE OF DEVILS.

## A METRICAL TALE.

---

" Should I report this now, would they believe me?
If I should say, I saw such islanders,
Who, though they were of monstrous shape, yet, note,
Their manners were more gentle-kind, than of
Our human generation you shall find
Many; nay, almost any!" —

*Tempest,* Act 3.

---

## I.

SPEED, Halcyon, speed, and here construct thy nest:
Brood on these waves, and charm the winds to rest!
No wave should dare to rage, no wind to roar,
Till lands yon blooming maid on Lisbon's shore.
That maid, as Venus fair and chaste is she,
When first to dazzled sky and glorying sea
The bursting conch Love's new-born queen exposed,
The fairest pearl that ever shell inclosed.
    While love's fantastic hand had joyed to braid
Her locks with weeds and shells like some sea-maid,
High seated at the stern was Irza seen,
And seemed to rule the tide, as ocean's queen.
Smooth sailed the bark; the sun shone clear and bright;
The glittering billows danced along in light;
While Irza, free from fear, from sorrow free,
Bright as the sun, and buoyant as the sea,
Bade o'er the lute her flying fingers move,
And sang a Spanish lay of Moorish love.

s 3

## ZAYDE AND ZAYDA.

(*From Las Guerras Civiles de Granada.*)

Lo! beneath yon haughty towers,
   Where the young and gallant Zayde
Fondly chides the lingering hours,
   Till they bring his lovely maid.

Evening shades are gathering round him;
   Doubting fear his heart alarms;
But nor doubt nor fear can wound him,
   If he views his lady's charms.

Hark! the window softly telling,
   Zayda comes to bless his sight;
Bright as sun-beams clouds dispelling,
   Mild as Cynthia's trembling light.

" Dearest, say, to what I'm fated!"
   Cried the Moor, as near he drew:
" Is the tale my page related,
   Loveliest lady, is it true?

" To an ancient lord thy beauty
   Does thy tyrant father doom?
Must my love, the slave of duty,
   Waste in age's arms her bloom?

" If my lot be still to languish,
   Thine, another's bride to be,
Let thy lips pronounce my anguish;
   'Twill be bliss to die by thee!"

Rising sighs her grief discover;
   Fast her tears, while speaking, pour —
" Zayde, my Zayde, our loves are over!
   Zayde, my Zayde, we meet no more!

" Allah knows, I cherished dearly,
 Fondest hopes of being thine !
Allah knows, I grieve sincerely,
 When I those fond hopes resign !

" May some lady, happier, fairer,
 Blest with every charm and grace,
Whose kind friends would grieve to tear her
 From all comfort, fill my place:

" May all pleasures greet your bridal;
 May she give you heart for heart !
Never be she from her idol
 Forced, as I am now, to part ! "

" Rumour did not then deceive me ! "
 Wild the Moor in anguish cries :
" Then 'tis true ! for wealth you leave me !
 Wealth has charms for Zayda's eyes !

" Blind to beauty, cold to pleasure,
 Ozmyn shall my hopes destroy !
Yes; though worthless such a treasure,
 *He* shall Zayda's charms enjoy !

" Fare thee well ! so soon to sever
 Little thought I, when you said,
' Thine it is, and thine for ever
 ' Shall be Zayda's heart, my Zayde ! ' "

## II.

Scarce moved the zephyr's wings, while breathed the song,
And waves in silence bore the bark along.
'Twas Irza sang ! Rosalvo at her side
Gazed on his cherub-love, his destined bride,
Felt at each look his soul in softness melt,
Nor wished to feel more bliss than then he felt.

'Gainst the high mast, intent on book and beads,
A reverend abbot leans, and prays, and reads :
Yet oft with secret glance the pair surveys,
Marks how *she* looks, and listens what *he* says.
An idle task !   The terms which speak their love
Had served for prayer, and passed unblamed above.
He finds each tender phrase so free from harm,
So pure each thought, each look so chaste though warm,
Still to his book and beads he turns again,
Pleased to have found his guardian care so vain;
While oft a blush of shame his pale cheek wears,
To find his thoughts so much less pure than theirs.
    Oh ! they *were* pure ! pure as the moon, whose ray
Loves on the shrines of virgin-saints to play;
Pure as the falling snow, ere yet its shower
Bends with its weight its own pale fragile flower.
Not fourteen years were Irza's ; nay, 'tis true,
Most maids at twelve know more than Irza knew :
And scarce two more had spread with silken down
Her youthful cousin's cheek of glowing brown.
His tutor sage (in fact, not show, a saint)
Had kept his heart and mind secure from taint.
In liberal arts, in healthful manly sports,
In studies fit for councils, camps, and courts,
His moments found their full and best employ,
Nor left one leisure hour for guilty joy.
Since her blue dove-like eyes six springs had seen,
Immured in cloistered shades had Irza been,
From duties done her sole delight deriven,
And her sole care to please the queen of heaven.
None e'er approached her, save the pure and good :
Her promised spouse ; that monk who near them stood;
Her viceroy uncle, and some guardian nun
Were all she e'er had seen by moon or sun.
No amorous forms, by wanton art designed,
Had e'er inflamed her blood, or stained her mind :

No hint in books, no coarse or doubtful phrase
E'er bade her curious thought explore the maze
No glowing dream by memory's pencil drawn
Had e'er profaned her sleep, and made her blush at dawn.
With flowers she decked the virgin mother's shrine,
Nor guessed a wonder made that name divine.
The very love, which lent her looks such fire,
Ne'er raised one blameful thought, nor loose desire;
Like streams of gold, which in alembic roll,
The flames she suffered but refined her soul;
Made it more free from stain, more light from dross,
With brighter lustre, and with softer gloss.
That, which she bore her bridegroom, well might claim
A brother's love, and bear a sister's name:
And e'en where now her lips in playful bliss
Sealed on Rosalvo's eyes a balmy kiss,
Love's highest, dearest grace she meant to show,
Nor thought he more could ask, nor she bestow.

### III.

From Goa's precious sands to Lisbon's shore,
The viceroy's countless wealth that vessel bore:
In heaps there jewels lay of various dyes,
Ingots of gold, and pearls of wondrous size;
And there (two gems worth all that Cortez won)
He placed his angel niece and only son.
Sebastian sought the Moors! With loyal zeal
Rosalvo cased his youthful limbs in steel;
To die or conquer by his sovereign's side
He came; and with him came his destined bride.
E'en now in Lisbon's court for Irza's hair
Virgins the myrtle's nuptial crown prepare,
And Hymen waves his torch from Cintra's towers,
Hails the dull bark, and chides the slow-winged hours.
Seldom in this bad world two hearts we see
So blest, and meriting so blest to be;

Then oh! ye winds, gently your pinions move,
And speed in safety home the bark of love.
Brood, Halcyon, brood: thy sea-spell chaunt again,
And keep the mirror of the enchanted main,
Where his white wing the exulting tropic dips,
Calm as their hearts, and smiling as their lips.
   The charm prevails! Hushed are the waves and still;
The expanded sails light favouring zephyrs fill,
Wafting with motion scarce perceived; and now
In rapture Irza from the vessel's prow
Gazed on an isle with verdure gay and bright,
Which seemed (so green it shone in solar light)
An emerald set in silver. Long her eyes
Dwelt on its rocks; and "Oh! dear friend," she cries,
And clasps Rosalvo's hand, — "admire with me
Yon isle, which rising crowns the silent sea!
How bold those mossy cliffs, which guard the strand,
Like spires, and domes, and towers in fairy-land!
How green the plains! how balsam-fraught the breeze!
How bend with golden fruit the loaded trees;
While, fluttering midst their boughs in joyful notes,
Myriads of birds attune their warbling throats!
Blooms all the ground with flowers! and mark, oh! mark
That giant palm, whose foliage broad and dark
Plays on the sun-clad rock! — Beneath, a cave
Spreads wide its sparry mouth: while loosely wave
A thousand creepers, dyed with thousand stains,
Whose wreaths enrich the trees, and cloathe the plains.
Dear friend, how blest, if passed my life could be
In that fair isle, with God alone and thee,
Far from the world, from man and fiend secure,
No guilt to harm us, and no vice to lure!
Bright round the virgin's shrine would blush and bloom
That world of flowers, which pour such rich perfume;
And sweet yon caves repeat with mellowing swell
Eve's closing hymn, when chimed the vesper-bell."

The pilot heard — " Oh ! spring of life," he cried,
" How bright and beauteous seems the world untried !
I too, like you, in youth's romantic bowers
Dreamt not of wasps in fruit, nor thorns in flowers ;
And when on banks of sand the sunbeams shone,
I deemed each sparkling flint a precious stone.
Ah ! noble lady, learn, that isle so fair,
The fields all roses, and all balm the air,
That isle is one, where every leaf's a spell,
Where no good thing e'er dwelt, nor e'er shall dwell.
No fisher, forced from home by adverse breeze,
Would slake his thirst from yon infernal trees :
No shipwrecked sailor from the following waves
Would seek a shelter in those haunted caves.
There flock the damned ! there Satan reigns, and revels !
And thence yon isle is called " The Isle of Devils ! "
Nor think, on rumour's faith this tale is given :
Once, hot in youthful blood, when hell nor heaven
Much claimed my thoughts, (the truth with shame I tell ;
Holy St. Francis, guard thy votary well ! )
In quest of water near that isle I drew :
When lo ! such monstrous forms appalled my view,
Such shrieks I heard, sounds all so strange and dread,
That from the strand with shuddering haste I fled,
Plyed as for life my oars, nor backward bent my head.
And though since then hath flown full many a year,
Still sinks my heart, still shake my limbs with fear,
Soon as yon awful island meets mine eye !
Cross we our breasts ! say, ' Ave ! ' and pass by ! "

## IV.

The isle is past.    And still in tranquil pride
Bears the rich bark its treasures o'er the tide.
And now the sun, ere yet his lamp he shrouds,
Stains the pure western sky with crimson clouds :
Now from the sea's last verge he sheds his rays,
And sinks triumphant in a golden blaze.

Still o'er the heavens reflected splendours flow,
Which make the world of waters gleam and glow:
Wide and more wide each billow shines more bright,
Till all the empurpled ocean floats in light.
Soon as fair Irza marked the evening's close,
Grave from her seat the young enthusiast rose,
Told o'er her beads, and when the string was said,
"Ave Maria!" sang the enraptured maid;
Her look so humble, so devout her air,
Each worldly wish appeared so lost in prayer,
All felt, no thought could to her mind be near,
That man her form could see, her voice could hear:
Hushed all the ship!—Each sailor checked his glee,
Clasped his hard hands, and bent his trembling knee;
And each (as rose that soft mysterious strain,
Best help in trouble, and sweet balm in pain)
Gazed on the maid with mingled awe and fear,
Damp on his cheek perceived the unwonted tear,
Then raised to Heaven his eyes in earnest prayer,
And half believed himself already there.
Low too Rosalvo knelt, nor knew, if now
For Mary's grace, or Irza's, rose his vow.
Scarce e'en the monk forbore to kneel; his child
Fondly he viewed, and sweetly, gravely smiled,
And blessed that God, as swelled each melting note,
Who gave such heavenly powers to human throat!
  Melodious strains, oh! speed your flight above
On Neptune's wings, and reach the ear of Love!
Oh! spread thy starry robe, celestial queen,
(For much thine aid she needs!) from ills to screen
Thy virgin-votaress!—Silence holds the deep,
And e'en the helmsman's eyes are sealed by sleep:
Yet mark yon gathering clouds!—the moon is fled!—
Mark too that deathlike stillness, deep and dread!
And hark!—from yon black cloud an awful voice
Pours the wild chaunt, and bids the winds rejoice!

## SONG OF THE TEMPEST-FIEND.

I marked her!—the pennants, how gaily they streamed!—
　How well was she armed for resistance!
The waves that sustained her, how brightly they beamed
In the sun's setting rays, and the sailors all seemed
　To forget the storm-spirit's existence.

But I marked her!—and now from the clouds I descend!
　My spells to the billows I mutter!
I clap my black pinions! my wand I extend,
In darkness the sky and the ocean to blend,
　And the winds mark the charms which I utter.

Now more and more rapid in eddies I whirl,
　In my voice while the thunder-clap rumbles:
And now the white mountainous waves, as they curl,
I joy o'er the deck of the vessel to hurl,
　And laugh, as she tosses and tumbles.

The crew is alarmed; but the tempest prevails,
　No care from my fury delivers!
Ere there's time for their furling the canvass, the sails
From the top to the bottom I split with my nails,
　And they stream in the blast, rent in shivers!

The sky and the ocean, fierce battle they wage;
　The elements all are in action!
No sailor the storm longer hopes to assuage:
What clamours, what hurry, what oaths, and what rage!
　Oh, brave! what despair, what distraction!

Their heart-strings, they ache, while my ravage they view;
　Each knee 'gainst its fellow is knocking!
My eyes, darting lightnings to dazzle the crew,
Burn and blaze; and those lightnings so forked and so blue
　Make the darkness of midnight more shocking.

The morn to that vessel no succour shall bring!
   Now high o'er the main-mast I hover;
Now I plunge from the sky to the deck with a spring,
And I shatter the mast with one flap of my wing;
   It cracks! and it breaks! and goes over!

Hew away, gallant seamen! fatigue never dread;
   You shall all rest to-night from your labours!
The ocean's wide mantle shall o'er you be spread,
The white bones of mariners pillow your head,
   And the whale and the shark be your neighbours.

For I swoop from aloft, and I blaze, and I burn,
   While my spouts the salt billows are drinking:
And I drive 'gainst the vessel, and beat down the stern,
And pour in a flood, which shall never return,
   And all cry — " She's sinking! she's sinking!"—

The barge?—well remembered!—'tis strong, and 'tis large,
   And will live in the billows' commotion;
But now all my spouts from the clouds I discharge,
And down goes the vessel, and down goes the barge!
   Hurrah! I reign lord of the ocean!

How their shrieks rose in chorus! Now all is at rest;
   The tempest no longer is brewing!
My dreams by the harm newly done will be blest,
So I'll sleep for a while on a thunder-cloud's breast,
   Then rouze to hurl round me fresh ruin.

### V.

   Hushed is the storm: the heavens no longer frown;
And o'er that spot, where late the bark went down,
All bright and smiling flows the treacherous wave,
Like sunshine playing on a new-made grave.
Full rose the watery moon: it showed a plank,
To which, all deadly pale, with tresses dank,
And robes of white, on which the sea had flung
Loose wreaths of ocean-flowers, unconscious clung

A fair frail form:—'twas Irza!—to the shore
Each following wave the virgin nearer bore;
And now the mountain surge o'erwhelmed the land,
Then flying left her on the wished-for strand.
  Soon hope and love of life her powers renew;
Swift tow'rds a cliff she speeds, which towers in view,
Nor waits the wave's return; and now again
Safe on the shore, and rescued from the main,
Prostrate she falls, and thanks the Sire of life,
Whose arm hath snatched her from the billowy strife.
That duty done, she rose, and gazed around:
Mossed are the rocks, and flowers bestrew the ground.
Not distant far, a group of fragrant trees
Bend with their golden fruit. The ocean-breeze
Shakes a gigantic palm, which o'er a cave
Its dark green foliage spreads, and wildly wave
Their blooming wreaths, all starred with midnight dews,
A thousand creeping plants of thousand hues.
Then flashed the dreadful truth on Irza's view!
That cave — those trees — that giant palm she knew!
Then from her lips for ever fled the smile:
—" Mother of God!" she shrieked, " the Demon-Isle!"—
  Long on a broken crag she knelt, and prayed,
And wearied every saint for strength and aid;
Then speechless, heedless, senseless lay; when, lo!
Strange mutterings near her roused from torpid woe
Her soul to fresh alarms. Her head she reared,
And near her face an hideous face appeared;
But straight 'twas gone!—In trembling haste she rose,
And saw a ring of monstrous dwarfs inclose
Her rugged couch. Not Teniers' hand could paint
Forms more grotesque to scare the tempted saint,
Than here, as on they pressed in circling throng,
With gnashing teeth seemed for her blood to long,
And grinned, and glared, and gloated! Quicker grew
Her breath! Death hemmed her round! As yet, 'tis true,

Far off they kept; but soon, more daring grown,
More near they crept, oft sharpening on some stone
Their long crookt claws; and still, as on they came,
They screeched and chattered; and their eyes of flame,
Twinkling and goggling, told, what pleasure grim
'Twould give to rack and rend her limb from limb:
—"Heaven take my soul!" she cried,—when, hark! a
     moan,
So full, so sad, so strange — not shriek — not groan —
Something scarce earthly — breathed above her head —
'Twas heard, and instant every imp was fled.
    What was that sound?　What pitying saint from high
Had stooped to save her?　Now to heaven her eye
Grateful she raised.　Almighty powers ! — a form,
Gigantic as the palm, black as the storm,
All shagged with hair, wild, strange in shape and show,
Towered on the loftiest cliff, and gazed below.
On *her* he gazed, and gazed so fixed, so hard,
Like knights of bronze some hero's tomb who guard.
Bright wreaths of scarlet plumes his ᵖmples crowned,
And round his ankles, arms, and wrists were wound
Unnumbered glassy strings of crystals bright,
Corals, and shells, and berries red and white.
On *her* he gazed, and floods of sable fires
Rolled his huge eyes, and spoke his fierce desires,
As on his club, a torn-up lime, he leaned.—
" Help, Heaven !" thought Irza, " 'tis the master-fiend !"
    Not long he paused: he now with one quick bound
Sprang from the cliff, and lighted on the ground.
Back fled the maid in terror; but her fear
Was needless.　Humbly, slowly crept he near,
Then kissed the earth, his club before her laid,
And of his neck her footstool would have made:
But from his touch she shrank.　He raised his head,
And saw her limbs convulsed, her face all dread,

And felt the cause his presence! Sad and slow
He rose, resumed his club, and turn'd to go.
Reproachful was his look, but still 'twas kind;
He climb'd the rock, but oft he gazed behind;
He reach'd the cave; one look below he threw;
Plaintive again he moan'd, and with slow steps withdrew.
   She is alone; she breathes again! — Fly, fly! —
Ah! wretched girl, too late! with frenzied eye,
(Scarce gone the master-fiend) his imps she sees,
Pour from the rocks, and drop from all the trees
With yell, and squeak, and many a horrid sound,
And form a living fence to hedge her round:
—" Now then," she cried, " all's over! — oh! farewell,
Farewell, Rosalvo!" On her knee she fell,
And told her beads with trembling hands. Yet still
On came the throng; and soon, with wanton skill
(Lured by its coral glow and cross of gold),
One snatch'd her chaplet, nor forsook his hold,
Though hard she struggled: while more bold, more fierce
Another seized her arm, and dared to pierce
With his sharp teeth its snow. The pure blood stream'd
Fast from the wound, and loud the virgin scream'd;
And strait again was heard that sad strange moan,
And instant all the dwarfs again were flown.
   Scarce conscious that she lived, scarce knowing why,
Half grieved, half grateful, Irza raised her eye:
Still on the rock (not dared he down to spring)
Dark and majestic stood the demon-king;
Then lowly knelt, and raised his arm to wave
An orange bough, and court her to his cave.
Lost are her friends; no help, no hope is nigh;
What can she do, and whither can she fly?
To *him* already twice her life she owes,
And but his presence now restrains her foes.
On wings of flame the sun had left the main;
And peeping from the trees, the imps too plain

T

Shot darts of rage from their green orbs of sight:
She heard their gibberings, and she mark'd their spite;
And, while they eyed her form, their care she saw
To grind their teeth, and whet each cruel claw.
Demons alike, the monarch-demon's breast
Appear'd least fierce; of ills she chose the best,
Sought, where profaned her coral rosary lay,
Then slowly mounted where he show'd the way.
 Cautious he led her tow'rds his lone abode,
And clear'd each stone that might impede her road.
With pain she trod: she reach'd the cave; but there
No more their weight her wearied limbs could bear.
Exhausted, fainting, anguish, terror, thirst,
Fatigue o'erpower'd her frame: her heart must burst,
Her eyes grow dim! Sunk on the rock she lies,
And sinking, prays she never more may rise.

## VI.

 Long in this deathlike swoon she lay: at length
Exhausted nature show'd forth all its strength,
And call'd her back to life. Her opening eyes
Beheld a grotto vast in depth and size,
Whose high straight sides forbade all hopes of flight:
The fractured roof gave ample space for light,
Through which in gorgeous guise the day-star shone
On many a lucid shell and brilliant stone.
Through pendent spars and crystals as it falls,
Each beam with rainbow hues adorns the walls,
Gilds all the roof, emblazes all the ground,
And scatters light, and warmth, and splendour round.
Gently on pillowing furs reposed her head;
With many a verdant rush her couch was spread;
A gourd with blushing fruits was near her placed,
Whose scent and colour woo'd alike her taste;
And round her strewn there bloom'd unnumber'd flowers;
Charming her sense with aromatic powers.

One only object chill'd her blood with ear:
Far off removed (but still, alas! too near),
Scarce breathing, lest a breath her sleep might break,
There stood the fiend, and watch'd to see her wake.
  In sooth, if credit outward show might crave,
Than Irza, ne'er had nymph an humbler slave.
He watched her every glance; her frown he fear'd;
And if his pains to meet her wish appear'd,
All pains seem'd far o'er-paid, all cares appeased,
And so *she* found but pleasure, *he* was pleased.
One power he claim'd, but claim'd that power alone:
Still, when he left her side, a mass of stone
Barr'd up the grotto, nor allow'd her feet
To pass the limits of her bright retreat.
But when in quest of food not forced to stray,
In Irza's sight he wore the livelong day,
And show'd her living springs and noontide shades,
Spice-breathing groves, and flower-enamell'd glades.
For her he still selects the sweetest roots,
The coolest waters, and the loveliest fruits;
To deck her charms the softest furs he brings,
And plucks their plumage from flamingo wings;
Bids blooming shrubs, to shade her, bend in bowers,
And strews her couch with fragrant herbs and flowers;
While many an ivy-twisted grate restrains
The splendid tenants of the etherial plains.
Then, when she sought her lonesome grot at eve,
And waved her hand, and warn'd him take his leave,
Her will was his: he breathed his plaintive moan,
Gazed one last look, then gently roll'd the stone.
  Perhaps, such constant care and worship paid,
More fit for angel than for mortal maid,
At length had won her, with more grateful mind
To view his gifts, and pay respect so kind;
But, as her giant-gaoler she esteem'd
Some prince of subterraneous fire, she deem'd

His favours snares, his presents only given
To shake her faith, and steal her soul from heaven.
Still then her loathing heart remain'd the same,
Joy'd when he went, and shudder'd when he came;
And when to share his fruits by hunger press'd,
Ever she bless'd them first, and cross'd her breast.

## VII.

Days creep — months roll — no change! no hope! and oh!
Rosalvo lost, what hope can life bestow?
Death, only death, she feels, can end her woes;
Nor doubts death soon will bring that wish'd-for close;
For now her frame, her mind, confess disease;
Painful and faint she moves; her tottering knees
Scarce bear her weight; and oft, by humour moved,
Her sickening soul now loathes what late it loved.
It comes! the moment comes!    Her frame is rent
By sharper pangs; her nerves, too strongly bent,
Seem on the point to break; her forehead burns;
Her curdling blood is fire, is ice by turns;
Her heart-strings crack! — " This hour is sure her last!'
Fainting she sinks, and hopes " that hour is pass'd!"
    Wake, Irza, wake to grief most strange and deep!
Still must thou live, and only live to weep!
Oh, lift thine aching head, thy languid eyes,
And mark what hideous stranger near thee lies.
" Guard me, all blessed saints!" — A monster child
Press'd her green couch; and, as it grimly smiled,
Its shaggy limbs, and eyes of sable fire,
Betray'd the crime, and claim'd its hellish sire!
    " Lost! lost!  My soul is lost!" the affrighted maid,
(Ah, now a maid no more!) distracted, said,
And wrung her hands. Those words she scarce could say;
Yet *would* have pray'd, but fear'd 't was sin to pray!
That only veil which ne'er admits a stain,
The veil of ignorance, was rent in twain:

In spite of virtue, cloisters, horror, youth,
She knows, and feels, and shudders at the truth.
That night accursed! — In death-like swoon she slept —
Then near her couch if that dark demon crept —
Oh! where was then her guardian angel's aid?
And would not heavenly Mary save her maid?
Deprived of sense — betray'd by place and time —
Then was she doom'd to share the unconscious crime?
Debased, deflower'd, and stamp'd a wretch for life,
A monster's mother, and a demon's wife?
   Oh! at that thought her soul what passions tear!
How then she beats her breast, how rends her hair,
And bids, with golden ringlets scatter'd round,
Stream all the air, and glitter all the ground!
Sighs, sobs, and shrieks the place of words supply;
And still she mourns to live, and prays to die,
Till heart denies to groan, and eyes to flow;
Then, on her couch of rushes sinking low,
Languid and lost she lies, in silent, senseless woe.
   What lifts her burning head? why opes her eye?
What makes her blood run back? A faint shrill cry!
Too well, alas! that cry was understood:
The monster pined for want, and claim'd its food.
Then in her heart what rival passions strove!
How shrinks disgust, how yearns maternal love!
Now to its life her feelings she prefers;
Now Nature wakes, and makes her own — "'T is hers!"
Loathing its sight, she melts to hear its cries,
And, while she yields the breast, averts her eyes.
   Not so the demon-sire: the child he raised,
He kiss'd it — danced it — nursed it — knelt, and gazed,
Till joyful tears gush'd forth, and dimm'd his sight:
Scarce Irza's self was view'd with more delight.
He held it tow'rds her — horror seem'd to thrill
Her frame. He sigh'd, and clasp'd it closer still.
Once, and but once, his features wrath express'd:
He saw her shudder, as it drain'd her breast;

And, while reproach half mingled with his moan,
Snatch'd it from her's, and press'd it to his own.

### VIII.

Three months had pass'd; still lived the monster-brat:
Its sire had sought the wood; alone she sat:
She sheds no tears — no tears are left to shed;
Unmoisten'd burn her eyes — her heart seems dead —
Her form seems marble.   Lo ! from far the sound
Of music steals, and fills the caves around.
She starts ! — scarce breathing — trembling; — "Oh ! for
    wings !" —
But hark ! for nearer now the minstrel sings.

### SONG.

#### 1.

When summer smiled on Goa's bowers
    They seem'd so fair;
All light the skies, all bloom the flowers,
    All balm the air !
The mock-bird swell'd his amorous lay,
    Soft, sweet, and clear;
And all was beauteous, all was gay,
    For *she* was near.

#### 2.

But now the skies in vain are bright
    With Summer's glow;
The pea-dove's call to Love's delight
    Augments my woe;
And blushing roses vainly bloom;
    Their charms are fled,
And all is sadness, all is gloom,
    For *she* is dead !

3.

Now o'er thy head, my virgin love,
    Rolls Ocean's wave;
But fond regret, in myrtle grove,
    Hath dug thy grave.
Sweet flowers, around her vacant urn
    Your wreaths I 'll twine,
And pray such flowers, ere Spring's return,
    May garland mine!


" He! he!" — That love-lorn dirge — that heavenly
    tongue —
That air, *she* taught him; 't was Rosalvo sung!
Rosalvo, whom the waves, which wreck'd their bark,
Had borne, like her, for purpose sad and dark,
To that strange isle; though far remote the beach
From Irza's grot, which Fate ordain'd him reach;
But now at length his curious search explores
These rude and slippery crags and distant shores;
And while he treads his dangerous path, the strains
Which Irza taught him soothe her lover's pains.
    She hears his steps, and hears them soon more near;
And loud she cries — " Rosalvo! Hear! oh, hear!
'T is Irza calls!" and now more quick, more nigh,
Down the steep rock she hears those footsteps fly.
Again she calls. He comes! He searches round;
He seeks the gate, and soon the gate is found.
Alas! 't is found in vain! the marble guard
Seem'd rooted as the rock, whose mouth it barr'd.
Yet still, with labouring nerves, to move the stone
He struggles. Now he stops; and, hark! A groan!
But one; then all was hush'd! A sickening chill
Seized Irza's heart, and seem'd her veins to thrill.
Fain had she call'd her youthful bridegroom's name;
Her tongue Fear's numbing fingers seem'd to lame.

Footsteps! — more near they drew: — slow rolled the
     stone —
The infernal gaoler came, but came alone.
With anxious glance his eye explored the cell;
But when it fix'd on her's, abash'd it fell.
He knelt, and seem'd to fear her frown.  He bore
His club.  'T was splash'd with brains! 't was wet with
     gore!
She fear'd — she guess'd — she rush'd — she ran — she
     flew, —
Nor dared the fiend her frantic course pursue.
" Rosalvo! speak! Rosalvo!"  Shrill, yet sweet,
She wakes the echoes.  What obstructs her feet?
'T is he, the young, the good, the kind, the fair!
As some frail lily, which the passing share*
Or wanton boy hath wounded, droops its head,
Its whiteness wither'd, and its fragrance fled,
Low lay the youth, and from his temple's wound
With precious streams bedew'd the ensanguin'd ground.
   Then reason fled its seat!  She shrieks! she raves!
And fills with hideous yells the ocean caves;
Rends her bright locks, and laughs to see them fly,
And bids them seek Rosalvo in the sky.
To dig his grave she fiercely ploughs the ground,
Loud shrieks his name, nor feels the flints that wound
Her bosom's globes, and stain their snow with gore,
As wild she dashes down, and beats in rage the floor.
   Now fail her strength, her spirits; mute she sits,
Silent and sad; then laughs and sings by fits.
A statue now she seems, or one just dead,
Her looks all gloom, her eyes two balls of lead:
Then simply smiles, and chaunts, with idiot glee,
" Ave Maria!  Benedicite!"
Till, Nature's powers revived by rest, again
The fury passions riot in her brain,
And all is rage, revenge, and helpless, hopeless pain.

     " Purpureus veluti flos," &c. — VIRGIL.

### IX.

Days, weeks, months pass.  Time came with slow relief;
But still at length it came.   No more her grief
Disturbs her brain: she knows " that groan was his ! "
And fully feels herself the wretch she is.
She rises: towards the grotto's mouth she goes,
Nor dares the fiend her wandering steps oppose.
She seeks the spot on which Rosalvo fell,
On which he died !   She knows that spot too well !
But, lo ! no corse was there !   All smooth and green
A velvet turf o'erstrewn with flowers was seen,
And fenced with roses.   " Oh ! whose pious care
Hath deck'd this grave?   Hear, gracious Heaven, his
   prayer,
When most he needs ! "   While thus in doubt she stands,
She marks the fiend's approach.   His ebon hands
Sustain'd a gourd of flowers of various hue;
He pour'd them, kiss'd the turf, and straight withdrew·
 Hither each morn his blooming gifts he bore,
Smooth'd the green sod, and strew'd it o'er and o'er.
Hither, each morn, came Irza; on those flowers
She wept, she pray'd, she sang away her hours.
So mourns the nightingale on poplar spray *,
Her callow brood by shepherds borne away,
Weeps all the night, and from her green retreat
Fills the wide groves with warblings sad as sweet.

### X.

And still fresh woes succeed.   She feels again
Mysterious pangs, nor doubts her cause of pain.
Too sure, while lost in maniac state she lay,
Her sense, her wits, her feeling all away,
The fiend once more had seized the unguarded hour
To force her weakness, and abuse his ower.

---

 * " Qualis populeâ," &c. — VIRGIL.

Again Lucina came.   That new-born cry,
Shuddering, again she heard ; her fearful eye
Wander'd around awhile, nor dared to stay.
" There, there he lies ! my child !"   With fresh essay
Once more she turn'd.   But when at length her sight
Dwelt on its face, her wonder — her delight —
Can ne'er by tongue be told, by fancy guess'd !
Frantic she caught, she kiss'd, and lull'd him on her breast.
    Oh ! who can paint how Irza loved that child !
Grieved when he moan'd, and smiled whene'er he smiled !
His dimpled arm soft on the rushes lay ;
Through his fine skin the blood was seen to play ;
That skin than down of swans more smooth and white ;
Nor e'er shone summer sky so blue and bright,
As shone the eyes of that same cherub elf ;
In small the model of her beauteous self.
The scant gold locks which gilt his ivory brow,
Were sun-beams gleaming on a globe of snow ;
And on his coral lips the red which stood,
Shamed the first rose, whose milk was Paphia's blood.
By fairy-thefts since nurses were beguiled,
Never stole fairy yet a lovelier child !
In Nature's costlier charms no babe array'd,
At length a mother's fears and throes repaid :
Not when Lucina first in myrtle grove,
To Beauty's kiss presented new-born Love ;
And while, with wond'ring eyes, the immortal boy
Imbibed new light, and pour'd ecstatic joy :
He kiss'd and drain'd by turns her fragrant breast,
Till amorous ring-doves coo'd the god to rest.
    Mothers may love as much, but never more,
Nor e'er did mother love so well before,
As Irza loved that child !   Her sable lord
Mark'd well that love ; and now, to health restored,
He felt her child to home would chain her feet,
Nor roll'd the stone to close her lone retreat.

Still, when he went, he with him bore away
That fav'rite babe, nor fear'd she far would stray.
Arm'd with his club, she now might safely rove
Through verdant vale, or weep in shadowy grove;
For soon the dwarfs were used to bear her sight,
Knew that dread club, nor dared indulge their spite.
Still from afar off looks of rage they cast,
And shrilly squeal'd and clamour'd as she pass'd;
But by their flight when near she came, 't was seen,
They own'd allegiance, and confess'd their queen.

### XI.

One morn her savage lord, in quest of food,
Forsook the cave, and sought th' adjacent wood;
And as her darling boy he with him bore,
Irza, unwatch'd, might pace the sounding shore.
Listless and slow she moved, and climb'd with pain
A tow'ring cliff, which beetled o'er the main.
Now three full years had flown, since Irza's eye
Had dwelt on human form, and since reply
From human tongue had blest her ear.   'Tis true,
Throned on a rock, which spread before her view
The sea's wide-stretching plains, she once descried
A gallant vessel plough the neighbouring tide.
By cries to draw it near she long essay'd,
And oft a palm-bough waved in sign for aid:
But all her cries and all her signs were vain;
On sail'd the bark, nor e'er return'd again!
On that same rock she sat, and eyed the wave,
And wish'd she there had found her wat'ry grave!
Fain had she sought one then, plunged from the steep,
And buried all her suff'rings in the deep;
But faith alike and reason bade her shun
That wish, nor break a thread which God had spun.
Hark! — was it fancy? — hark again! — the shores
Echo the sound of fast approaching oars.

Oh! how she gazed! —a barge (by friars 't was mann'd)
Cut the smooth waves, and sought the rocky strand.
Soon (while his wither'd hands a crosier hold,
All rich with gems, and rough with sculptured gold),
Landing alone, a reverend monk appear'd: —
His jewell'd cross — his flowing silver beard —
" 'Tis he! — 'tis he!" — swift down the steep she flies,
Falls at the stranger's feet, and frantic cries,
Down her pale cheek while tears imploring roll,
" Help, father abbot! save me! save my soul!"
'Twas he indeed! that bark which ne'er return'd,
Well on the cliff her fair wild form discern'd,
But deem'd some island-fiend had spread a snare
To lure them with a form so wild and fair.
Yet oft in Lisbon would those seamen tell,
How angled for their souls the prince of hell;
And warmly paint, their leisure to beguile,
The fallen angel of th' enchanted isle.
At length this wonder reach'd the abbot's ear,
And prompt affection made the wonder clear: —
" 'Twas Irza! shipwreck'd Irza! none but she
So heav'nly fair, so lonely lost could be!"
Straight he prepares anew that sea to brave,
Which once already seem'd to yawn his grave;
Nor ask, how chanced it that he reach'd the shore:
'Twas through a miracle and nothing more.
Whether on monkish frock as safe rode he,
As night-hags skim in sieves o'er Norway's sea;
Or like Arion plough'd the wat'ry plain,
Horsed on some monster of the astonish'd main,
Some shark, some whale, some kraken, some sea-cow —
St. Francis saved him, and it boots not how.
And now again the saint his priest survey'd,
From waves and winds imploring heavenly aid;
Resolved for Irza's sake to brave the worst
Which fate could offer on that isle accurst.

Far off his ship was anchor'd; on that strand
Not India's wealth could make a layman land!
Therefore with none but monks he mann'd his barge,
Which bore of beads and bells a sacred charge;
Whole heaps of relics lent by Cintra's nuns,
And holy water (blest at Rome) by tons!
His toils were all o'erpaid! he saw again
His fav'rite child, and kindly soothed her pain;
And while her tale he heard, oft dropp'd a tear,
And sign'd his beard-swept breast in awe and fear:
Then bade her speed the friendly bark to gain,
And fly the infernal monarch's green domain;
Nor yield her tyrant time to cast a spell,
And rouse to cross her flight the powers of hell.
Then first from Irza's cheek the glow of red,
By hope of rescue raised, grew faint, and fled;
Trembling she nam'd her cherub-boy, confess'd
A mother's fondness fill'd his mother's breast;
Described how fair he look'd, how sweet he smiled,
And fear'd her flight might quite destroy her child.
Then rose the abbot's ire — " Oh, guilty care ! "
Frowning, he cried, and shook his hoary hair:
" Fair is the imp? and shall he therefore breathe
To win new subjects for the realms beneath?
The fiends most dangerous are those spirits bright,
Who toil for hell, and show like sons of light;
And still when Satan spreads his subtlest snares,
The baits are azure eyes, the lines are golden hairs.
Name thou the brat no more!   To Cintra's walls
Fly, where thy footsteps mild repentance calls.
I'll hear no plaint! kneel not! I'm deaf to prayer!
Swift, brethren, to the barge this maniac bear;
Speed ! speed ! — no tears ! — no struggling ! — no delay!
Row, brethren, row, and waft us swift away ! "

## XII.

The monks obeyed. Then, ᶜ ⸳ ᵢᵤ Irza's soul
What various passions raged, aɪ    :k'd control!
Now how she mourn'd, now how    vept for joy,
How loathed the sire, and how adoɪ⸗ the boy!
The barge is gain'd; they row. When, lo! from high
Her ear again receives that well-known cry,
That sad, strange moan! she starts, and lifts her eye.
There, on a rock which fenced the strand, once more
She saw her demon-husband stand: he bore
Her beauteous babe; and, while he view'd the barge,
Keen anguish seem'd each feature to enlarge,
And shake each giant limb. With piteous air
His arms he spread, his hands he clasp'd in prayer;
Knelt, wept, and while his eye-balls seem'd to burn,
Oft show'd the child, and woo'd her to return.
His suit the monks disdain; the barge recedes;
More humbly now he kneels, more earnest pleads.
But when he found no tears their course delay,
And still the boat pursued its watery way;
Then, 'gainst his grief and rage no longer proof,
He gnash'd his teeth, he stamp'd his iron hoof,
Whirl'd the boy wildly round and round his head,
Dash'd it against the rocks, and howling fled.
    Loud shrieks the mother! changed to stone she stands,
And silent lifts to heav'n her clay-cold hands:
Then, sinking down, stretch'd on the deck she lies,
Hid her pale face, and closed her aching eyes.
But hark! why shout the monks?—"Again," they said,
"Again the demon comes!" with desperate dread
Starts the poor wretch, and lifts her anguish'd head.
Yes! there the infant-murderer stood once more,
But now far different were the looks he wore.
No bending knee, no suppliant glance was seen,
Proud was his port, and stern and fierce his mien.
His blood-stain'd eye-balls glared with vengeful ire;
His spreading nostrils seem'd to snort out fire.

Swiftly from crag to crag he following sprung,
While round his neck his shaggy offspring clung;
And now, like some dark tow'r, erect he stood,
Where the last rock hung frowning o'er the flood : —
 " Look ! look !" he seem'd to say, with action wild,
" Look, mother, look ! this babe is still your child !
With him as me all social bonds you break,
Scorn'd and detested for his father's sake :
My love, my service only wrought disdain,
And nature fed his heart from yours in vain !
Then go, Ingrate, far o'er the ocean go,
Consign your friend, your child to endless woe !
Renounce us ! hate us ! pleased, your course pursue,
And break their hearts who lived alone for you ! "
His eyes, which flash'd red fire — his arms spread wide,
Her child raised high to heaven — too plain implied,
Such were his thoughts, though nature speech denied.
And now with eager glance the deep he view'd,
And now the barge with savage howl pursued;
Then to his lips his infant wildly press'd,
And fondly, fiercely, clasp'd it to his breast :
Three piteous moans, three hideous yells he gave,
Plunged headlong from the rock, and made the sea his
　　　grave.

### XIII.

Where, screen'd by orange groves and myrtle bowers,
Saint-favour'd Cintra rears her gothic towers;
A nun there dwells, most holy, sad, and fair,
Her only business penance, fasts, and prayer;
Her only joy with flowers the shrines to dress,
Weep with the suff'ring, and relieve distress.
A poor lay-sister she; yet golden rain
Showers from her hand to glad each barren plain :
In other eyes she lights up joy, but ne'er
Those eyes of hers were seen a smile to wear :
From other breasts she plucks the thorn of grief,
But feels, her own admits of no relief.

Where age and sickness count the hours by groans,
Uncall'd, she comes to hear and hush their moans.
There, ever humble, watchful, patient, kind,
No nauseous task, no servile care declined,
O'er the sick couch, all day, all night she hangs,
Till health or death relieves the sufferer's pangs.
No thanks she takes, no praise from man receives,
Her duty done, the rest to God she leaves;
But only when her care redeems a life,
Parting she says — " Pray for a demon's wife ! "
With blessings still, whene'er that nun they view,
The young, the aged her sainted steps pursue,
And cry, with bended knee and suppliant air,
" Sister of mercy, name us in thy prayer! "
With beads the night, in gracious acts the day,
So wore her youth, so wears her age away.
Now cease, my lay ! thy mournful task is o'er;
Irza, farewell ! I wake thy lute no more.

## XIV.

" Was such her fate? and did her days thus creep
So sad, so slow, till came the long last sleep?
And did for this her hands with roses twine
The Saviour's altars and the Virgin's shrine?
Pure, beauteous, rich, did all these blessings tend,
But from the world in prime of life to send
This gifted maid, in prayer to waste her hours,
And weep a fancied crime in cloister'd bowers?"
  Oh, blind to fate ! perhaps that fancied crime
Which bade her quit the world in youthful prime,
Snatch'd her from paths, where beauty, wealth, and fame
Had proved but snares to load her soul with shame,
And spared her pangs from wilful guilt which flow,
The only serious ills that man can know !
Ah ! what avails it, since they ne'er can last,
If gay or sad our span of days be past?

Pray, mortals, pray, in sickness or in pain,
Not long nor blest to live, but pure from stain.
A life of pleasure, and a life of woe,
When both are past, the difference who can show?
But all can tell, how wide apart in price
A life of virtue, and a life of vice.
   Then still, sad Irza, tread your thorny way,
Since life must end, and merits ne'er decay.
Wounded past hope, still prize the pleasure pure,
To heal those hearts which yet can hope a cure;
Nor doubt, the soul which joys in noble deeds
Shall reap a rich reward when most it needs.
When comes that day to conscious guilt so dread,
Angels unseen shall bathe your burning head:
The prayers of orphans fan with balmy breath,
And widow's blessings drown the threats of death;
Each sigh your pity hush'd shall swelling rise
In loud hosannas when you mount the skies;
And every tear on earth to sorrow given,
Be precious pearls to wreathe your brows in heaven!

## APRIL 17.

" Piansi i riposi di quest' umil vita,
   E sospirai la mia perduta pace ! "

I regret the loss of our dead calm and our crawling pace of a knot and a half an hour; for during
the last four days we have had nothing but gales
and squalls, mountainous waves, the vessel rolling
and pitching incessantly, and the sea perpetually
pouring in at the windows and down through the
hatchway. Into the bargain, we are now sufficiently towards the north to find the weather perish-
ingly.cold, and we have neither wood nor coals
enough on board to allow a fire for the cabin.

But, among all our inconveniences, that which is the most intolerable undoubtedly arises from the sick apothecary. It seems that his complaint is the consequence of dram-drinking, which has affected his liver. Since his coming on board, he has continued to indulge his taste; and growing worse (as might be expected), he has now thought proper to put himself in a state of salivation: the consequence is, that what with the mercury and what with the man, aided by the concomitant effluvia of our cargo of sugar, rum, and coffee, for a combination of villanous smells, Falstaff's buck-basket was nothing to the cabin of the Sir Godfrey Webster. I could almost fancy myself Slawken-bergius's Don Diego just returned from the Promontory of Noses, and that I had exchanged my snub for a proboscis; so much do all my other senses appear to be absorbed in that of smelling, and so completely do I seem to myself to be nose all over. As to the poor apothecary, his mercury annoys us without any signs as yet of its benefiting himself. He grows worse daily, and I greatly doubt his ever reaching England.

### April 19. (Sunday.)

I have not been able to ascertain exactly the negro notions concerning the *Duppy;* indeed, I believe that his character and qualities vary in different parts of the country. At first, I thought that the term Duppy meant neither more nor less than a ghost; but sometimes he is spoken of as "the Duppy," as if there were but one, and then he seems to answer to the devil. Sometimes he is a kind of malicious spirit, who haunts burying-grounds (like the Arabian gouls), and delights in playing tricks to those who may pass that way. On other occasions, he seems to be a supernatural attendant on the practitioners of Obeah, in the shape of some animal, as familiar imps are supposed to belong to our English witches; and this latter is the part assigned to him in the following "Nancy-story:"—

"Sarah Winyan was scarcely ten years old, when her mother died, and bequeathed to her considerable property. Her father was already dead; and the guardianship of the child devolved upon his sister, who had always resided in the same house, and who was her only surviving relation. Her mother, indeed, had left two sons by a former husband, but they lived at some distance in the wood, and seldom came to see their mother; chiefly from a rooted aversion to this aunt; who, although from interested motives she stooped to flatter her sister-in-law, was haughty, ill-natured, and even suspected of Obeahism, from the occasional visits of an enormous black dog, whom she called Tiger, and whom she never failed to feed and caress with marked distinction. In case of Sarah's death, the aunt, in right of her brother, was the heiress of his property. She was determined to remove this obstacle to her wishes; and after treating her for some time with harshness and even cruelty, she one night took occasion to quarrel with her for some trifling fault, and fairly turned her out of doors. The poor girl seated herself on a stone near the house, and endeavoured to beguile the time by singing —

  ' Ho-day, poor me, O !
    Poor me, Sarah Winyan, O !
    They call me neger, neger !
    They call me Sarah Winyan, O !'

But her song was soon interrupted by a loud rusk-ing among the bushes; and the growling which accompanied it announced the approach of the dreaded Tiger. She endeavoured to secure herself against his attacks by climbing a tree: but it seems that Tiger had not been suspected of Obeahism without reason; for he immediately growled out an assurance to the girl, that come down she must and should! Her aunt, he said, had made her over to him by contract, and had turned her out of doors that night for the express purpose of giving him an opportunity of carrying her away. If she would descend from the tree, and follow him willingly to his own den to wait upon him, he engaged to do her no harm; but if she refused to do this, he threatened to gnaw down the tree with-out loss of time, and tear her into a thousand pieces. His long sharp teeth, which he gnashed occasionally during the above speech, appeared

perfectly adequate to the execution of his menaces,
and Sarah judged it most prudent to obey his com-
mands.   But as she followed Tiger into the wood,
she took care to resume her song of

'Ho-day, poor me, O!'

in hopes that some one passing near them  might
hear her name, and come to her rescue.   Tiger,
however, was aware of this, and positively forbad
her singing.   However, she contrived every now
and then to loiter behind;  and when she thought
him out of hearing, her

'Ho-day! poor me, O!'

began again; although she was compelled to sing
in so low a voice, through fear of her four-footed
master, that she had but faint hopes of its reaching
any ear but her own. Such was, indeed, the event,
and Tiger conveyed her to his den without molest-
ation.   In the meanwhile, her two half-brothers
had heard of their mother's death, and soon arrived at the house to enquire what was become of
Sarah.  The aunt received them with every appearance of welcome; told them that grief for the loss
of her only surviving parent had already carried
her niece to the grave, which she showed them in
her garden; and acted her part so well, that the
youths departed perfectly satisfied of the decease
of their sister.   But while passing through the
wood on their return, they heard some one singing, but in so low a tone that it was impossible to

distinguish the words. As this part of the wood was the most unfrequented, they were surprised to find any one concealed there. Curiosity induced them to draw nearer, and they soon could make out the

> ' Ho-day ! poor me, O !
> Poor me, Sarah Winyan, O !'

There needed no more to induce them to hasten onwards; and upon advancing deeper into the thicket, they found themselves at the mouth of a large cavern in a rock. A fire was burning within it; and by its light they perceived their sister seated on a heap of stones, and weeping, while she chanted her melancholy ditty in a low voice, and supported on her lap the head of the formidable Tiger. This was a precaution which he always took when inclined to sleep, lest she should escape; and she had taken advantage of his slumbers to resume her song in as low a tone as her fears of waking him would allow. She saw her brothers at the mouth of the cave: the youngest fortunately had a gun with him, and he made signs that Sarah should disengage herself from Tiger if possible. It was long before she could summon up courage enough to make the attempt; but at length, with fear and trembling, and moving with the utmost caution, she managed to slip a log of wood between her knees and the frightful head, and at length drew herself away without waking him. She then crept softly out of the cavern, while the youngest brother crept as softly into it: the monster's head still reposed upon the block of wood; in a moment it was blown into a thousand pieces; and the brothers, afterwards cutting the body into four parts, laid one in each quarter of the wood."

From that time only were dogs brought into subjection to men; and the inhabitants of Jamaica would never have been able to subdue those ferocious animals, if Tiger had not been killed and quartered by Sarah Winyan's brothers. As to the aunt, she received the punishment which she merited, but I cannot remember what it was exactly. Probably, the brothers killed and quartered *her* as well as her four-footed ally: or, perhaps, she was turned into a wild beast, and supplied the vacancy left by Tiger, as was the case with the celebrated Zingha, queen of Angola; who, although she embraced Christianity on her death-bed, and died according to the most orthodox forms of the Romish religion, still had conducted herself in such a manner while alive, that shortly after her decease, the kingdom being ravaged by a hyena, her subjects could not be persuaded but that the soul of this most Christian queen had transmigrated into the body of the hyena. Yet this was surely doing the hyena great injustice; for she, at least, had never been in the habit of composing ointments by pounding little children in a mortar with her own hands; an amusement which Zingha had introduced at the court of Angola. It took surprisingly; shortly, no woman thought her toilette completed, unless she had used some of this ointment. Pounding children became all the rage; and ladies who aspired to be the leaders of fashion, pounded their own.

## APRIL 20.

### EPIGRAM. — (From the French.)

" Whose can that little monster be?
   Its parents really claim one's pity !"
" Madam, that child belongs to me." —
   " Well, I protest, she's vastly pretty !"

## APRIL 21.

The weather gets no better, the apothecary gets no worse, and both are as foul and as disagreeable as they can well be. As to the man, it is wonderful that he is still alive, for he has swallowed nothing for the last three weeks except drams and laudanum. He drinks, and he stinks, and he does nothing else earthly or celestial. The quantity of spirits which he pours down his throat incessantly should, of itself, be sufficient to finish him; but he seems to have accustomed himself to drams, as Mithridates used himself to poisons, till his stomach is completely proof against them; or like the Scythian princess, who was fed upon ratsbane pap from her infancy, for the express purpose of one day or other poisoning Alexander in her embraces; and who arrived at such perfection, that although the venom did no harm to her own constitution, she killed a condemned criminal with a single kiss. The consequence was, that hemp fell fifty per cent, and Jack Ketch's nose was put out of joint completely; for the devil a culprit of any pretensions to taste could be found in all Scythia, who could be prevailed upon to be executed except by her royal highness's own lips. I am afraid this story is not strictly historical, and that we should look for it in vain in Quintus Curtius.

### APRIL 23.

A gale of wind began to show itself on Monday night; it has continued to blow ever since with increasing violence, and is now become very serious. The captain says that he never experienced weather so severe at this season: this is only my usual luck. Certainly nothing can be more disagreeable than a ship on these occasions. The sea breaks over the vessel every minute, and it is really something awful to see the waves raised into the air by the force of the gale, hovering for a while over the ship, and then coming down upon us swop, to inundate every thing below deck as well as upon it. The wind is piercingly cold; the floors and walls are perpetually streaming. But a fire is quite out of the question; and, indeed, at one time to-day, our eating appeared to be out of the question too; for at four o'clock the cook sent us word, that the sea put the kitchen-fire out as fast as he could light it; that he was almost frozen, having been for the last eight hours up to his waist in water; and that we must make up our minds to get no dinner to-day. However, the steward coaxed him, and encouraged him, and poured spirits down his throat, and at last a dinner of some kind was put upon the table; but it had not been there ten minutes, before a tremendous sea poured itself down the companion stairs and through the hatchway, set every thing on the table afloat, deluged the cabin, ducked most of the company, and drove us all into the other room. I was lucky enough to escape with only a sprinkling; but Mrs. Walker was soaked through from head to foot. We can only cross the cabin by creeping along by the sides as if we were so many cats. Walking the deck, even for the sailors, is absolutely out of the question; and the little cabin-boy has so fairly given up the attempt, that he goes crawling about upon all fours. Even our Spanish mastiff, Flora, finds it impossible to keep her four legs upon deck. Every five minutes up they all go, away rolls the dog over and over; and when she gets up again, shakes her ears, and howls in a tone of the most piteous astonishment.

APRIL 24.

Though the gale was itself sufficiently serious, its effects at first were ludicrous enough; but yesterday it produced a consequence truly shocking and alarming. Edward Sadler, the second mate, was at breakfast in the steerage : the boatswain had been cutting some beef with a large case-knife, which he had afterwards put down upon the chest on which they were sitting: a sudden heel o.' the ship threw them all to the other side of the cabin : the knife fell with its haft against the ladder; and poor Edward falling against it, at least three inches of the blade were forced into his right side. The wound was dressed without the loss of a moment; but, from its depth, the jaggedness of the weapon with which it was made, and from a pain which immediately afterwards seized the poor fellow in his chest, the apothecary thinks that his recovery is very improbable : he says that the liver is certainly perforated, and so probably are the lungs. If the latter have escaped, it must have been only by the breadth of a hair. Every one in the ship is distressed beyond measure at this accident, for the young man is a universal favourite. He is but just one and twenty, good-looking, with manners much superior to his station; and so unusually steady, as well as active, that if Providence grants him life, he cannot fail to raise himself in his profession.

## APRIL 25.

Edward complains no longer of the pain in his chest; he sleeps well, eats enough, has no fever, and every symptom is so favourable, that Dr. Ashman encourages us to hope that he has re-

ceived no material injury. Our ship-carpenter has
always appeared to be the sulkiest and surliest of
sea-bears: yet, on the day of Edward's accident,
he passed every minute that he could command
by the side of his sofa, kneeling, and praying, and
watching him as if he had been his son; and every
now and then wiping away his "own tears" with the
dirtiest of all possible pocket-handkerchiefs. So
that what Goldsmith said of Dr. Johnson may be
applied to this old man: " He has nothing of a
bear but his skin." After tearing every sail in the
ship into shivers, and being as disagreeable as ever
it could be, the gale has at length abated. Yesterday it was a storm, and we were going to Ireland,
Lisbon, Brest — in short, every where except to
England; to-day, it is a dead calm, and we are
going nowhere at all.

### April 26. (Sunday.)

The gale has returned with increased violence,
and we are once more at our old trade of dead
lights; however, for this time, the wind, at least,
is in our favour.

### April 28.

The wounded mate is so much recovered as to
come upon deck for a few hours to-day, and may
now be considered as completely out of danger;
although Dr. Ashman is positive (from his difficulty of breathing at first, and the subsequent

pain in his chest) that his lungs must actually have been wounded, however slightly. We are now nearly abreast of Scilly; we fell in with several Scilly boats to-day, from whom we obtained a very acceptable supply of fish, vegetables, and news-papers.

APRIL 29.

*An African Nancy-story.*—" The headman (*i. e.* the king) of a large district in Africa, in one of his tours, visited a young nobleman, to whom he lost a considerable sum at play. On his departure he load-ed his host with caresses, and insisted on his coming in person to receive payment at court; but his pretended kindness had not deceived the nurse of the young man. She told him, that the headman was certainly incensed against him for having conquered him at play, and meant to do him some injury; that having been so positively ordered to come to court, he could not avoid obeying; but she advised him to take the river-road, where, at a particular hour, he would find the king's youngest and favourite daughter bathing; and she instructed him how to behave. The youth reached the river, and concealed himself, till he saw the princess enter the stream alone; but when she thought fit to regain the bank, she found herself extremely embarrassed. —' Ho-day! what is become of my clothes? ho-day! who has stolen my clothes? ho-day! if any one will bring me back my clothes, I promise that no harm shall happen to him this day—O!'—This was the cue for which the youth had been instructed to wait. ‘Here are your clothes, missy!’ said he, stepping from his concealment: ‘a rogue had stolen them, while you were bathing; but I took them from him, and have brought them back.’—‘Well, young man, I will keep my promise to you. You are going to court, I know; and I know also, that the headman will chop off your head, unless at first sight you can tell him which of his three daughters is the youngest. Now I am she; and in order that you may not mistake, I will take care to make a sign; and then do not you fail to pitch upon me.’ The young man assured her, that, having once seen her, he never could possibly mistake her for any other, and then set forwards with a lightened heart. The headman received him very graciously, feasted him with magnificence, and told him that he would present him to his three daughters, only that there was a slight rule respecting them to which he must conform. Whoever could not point out which was the youngest, must immediately lose his head. The young man kissed the ground in obedience, the door opened, and in walked three little black dogs. Now, then, the necessity of the precaution taken by the princess was evident; the youth looked at the dogs earnestly; something induced the headman to turn away his eyes for a moment, and in that moment one of the dogs lifted up its fore paw.

' This,' cried the youth —' this is your youngest
daughter;'—and instantly the dogs vanished, and
three young women appeared in their stead.
The headman was equally surprised and incensed;
but concealing his rage, he professed the more
pleasure at that discovery; because, in consequence, the law of that country obliged him to
give his youngest daughter in marriage to the
person who should recognise her; and he charged
his future son-in-law to return in a week, when he
should receive his bride. But his feigned caresses
could no longer deceive the young man: as it was
evident that the headman practised Obeah, he did
not dare to disobey him; and knew that to escape
by flight would be unavailing. It was, therefore,
with melancholy forebodings that he set out for
court on the appointed day; and (according to
the advice of his old nurse) he failed not to take
the road which led by the river. The princess
came again to bathe; her clothes again vanished; she had again recourse to her ' Ho-day!
what is become of my clothes?' and on hearing
the same promise of protection, the youth again
made his appearance. ' Here are your clothes,
missy,' said he; ' the wind had blown them away
to a great distance; I found them hanging upon
the bushes, and have brought them back to you.'
Probably the princess thought it rather singular,
that whenever her petticoats were missing, the
same person should always happen to be in the

way to find them : however, as she was remarkably
handsome, she kept her thoughts to herself, swallowed the story like so much butter, and assured
him of her protection. ' My father,' said she,
' will again ask you which is the youngest daughter;
and as he suspects me of having assisted you
before, he threatens to chop off *my* head instead
of yours, should I disobey him a second time.
He will, therefore, watch me too closely to allow
of my making any sign to you ; but still I will contrive something to distinguish me from my sisters;
and do you examine us narrowly till you find it.'
As she had foretold, the headman no sooner saw
his destined son-in-law enter, than he told him
that he should immediately receive his bride; but
that if he did not immediately point her out, the
laws of the kingdom sentenced him to lose his
head. Upon which the door opened, and in walked
three large black cats, so exactly similar in every
respect, that it was utterly impossible to distinguish
one from the other. The youth was at length on
the point of giving up the attempt in despair,
when it struck him, that each of the cats had a
slight thread passed round its neck ; and that while
the threads of two were scarlet, that of the third
was blue. ' *This* is your youngest daughter;'
cried he, snatching up the cat with the blue thread.
The headman was utterly at a loss to conceive by
what means he had made the discovery; but could
not deny the fact, for there stood the princesses in

their own shape. He therefore affected to be greatly pleased, gave him his bride, and made a great feast, which was followed by a ball; but in the midst of it the princess whispered her lover to follow her silently into the garden. Here she told him, that an old Obeah woman, who had been her father's nurse, had warned him, that if his youngest daughter should live to see the day after her wedding, he would lose his power and his life together; that she, therefore, was sure of his intending to destroy both herself and her bridegroom that night in their sleep; but that, being aware of all these circumstances, she had watched him so narrowly as to get possession of some of his magical secrets, which might possibly enable her to counteract his cruel designs. She then gathered a rose, picked up a pebble, filled a small phial with water from a rivulet; and thus provided, she and her lover betook themselves to flight upon a couple of the swiftest steeds in her father's stables. It was midnight before the headman missed them: his rage was excessive; and immediately mounting his great horse, Dandy, he set forwards in pursuit of the lovers. Now Dandy galloped at the rate of ten miles a minute. The princess was soon aware of her pursuer: without loss of time she pulled the rose to pieces, scattered the leaves behind her, and had the satisfaction of seeing them instantly grow up into a wood of briars, so strong and so thickly planted, that Dandy vainly attempted to force his way through them. But, alas! this fence was but of a very perishable nature. In the time that it would have taken to wither its parent rose-leaves, the briars withered away; and Dandy was soon able to trample them down, while he continued his pursuit. Now, then, the pebble was thrown in his passage; it burst into forty pieces, and every piece in a minute became a rock as lofty as the Andes. But the Andes themselves would have offered no insurmountable obstacles to Dandy, who bounded from precipice to precipice; and the lovers and the headman could once more clearly distinguish each other by the first beams of the rising sun. The headman roared, and threatened, and brandished a monstrous sabre; Dandy tore up the ground as he ran, neighed louder than thunder, and gained upon the fugitives every moment. Despair left the princess no choice, and she violently dashed her phial upon the ground. Instantly the water which it contained swelled itself into a tremendous torrent, which carried away every thing before it, — rocks, trees, and houses; and ‘the horse and his rider’ were carried away among the rest.—‘ *Hic finis Priami fatorum!*’ There was an end of the headman and Dandy! The princess then returned to court, where she raised a strong party for herself; seized her two sisters, who were no better than their father, and had assisted him in his witchcraft; and having put them and all their partisans to death by a summary mode of proceeding, she established herself and her husband on the throne as headman and headwoman. It was from this time that *all* the kings of Africa have been uniformly mild and benevolent sovereigns. Till then they were all tyrants, and tyrants they would all still have continued, if this virtuous princess had not changed the face of things by drowning her father, strangling her two sisters, and chopping off the heads of two or three dozen of her nearest and dearest relations."

It seems to be an indispensable requisite for a Nancy-story, that it should contain a witch, or a duppy, or, in short, some marvellous personage or other. It is a kind of "*pièce à machines.*" But the creole slaves are very fond of another species of tale, which they call " Neger-tricks," and which bear the same relation to a Nancy-story which a farce does to a tragedy. The following is a specimen:—

*A Neger-trick.*—" A man who had two wives divided his provision-grounds into two parts, and proposed that each of the women should cultivate one half. They were ready to do their proper share, but insisted that the husband should at least take his third of the work. However, when they were to set out, the man was taken so ill, that he found it impossible to move; he quite roared with pain, and complained bitterly of a large lump which had formed itself on his cheek during the night. The wives did what they could to relieve him, but in vain ; they boiled a negro-pot for him, but he was too ill to swallow a morsel: and at length they were obliged to leave him, and go to take care of the provision-grounds. As soon as they were gone, the husband became perfectly well, emptied the contents of the pot with great appetite, and enjoyed himself in ease and indolence till evening, when he saw his wives returning; and immediately he became worse than ever. One of the women was quite shocked to see the size to which the lump had increased during her absence: she begged to examine it; but although she barely touched it with the tip of her finger as gingerly as possible, it was so tender that the fellow screamed with agony. Unluckily, the other woman's manners were by no means so delicate; and seizing him forcibly by the head to examine it, she undesignedly happened to hit him a great knock on the jaw, and, lo and behold! out flew a large lime, which he had crammed into it. Upon which both his wives fell upon him like two furies; beat him out of the house; and whenever afterwards he begged them to go to the provision-grounds, they told him that he had got no lime in his mouth *then*, and obliged him from that time forwards to do the whole work himself."

A negro was brought to England; and the first point shown him being the chalky cliffs of Dover, "O ki!" he said; "me know now what makes the buckras all so white!"

## May 29.

We once more saw the "Lizard," the first point of England; and, indeed, it was full time that we should. Besides that our provisions were nearly exhausted by the length of the voyage, our crew was in a great measure composed of fellows of the most worthless description; and the captain lately discovered that some of them had contrived to break a secret passage into the hold, where they had broached the rum-casks, and had already passed several nights in drinking, with lighted candles: a single spark would have been sufficient to blow us all up to the moon!

## June 1. (Saturday.)

We took our river pilot on board; and on Wednesday, the 5th, we reached Gravesend. I went on shore at nine in the morning; and here I conclude my JAMAICA JOURNAL.

## 1817.

### NOVEMBER 5. (Wednesday.)

I LEFT London, and embarked for Jamaica on board the same vessel, commanded by the same captain, which conveyed me thither in 1815. We did not reach the Downs till Sunday, the 9th, after experiencing in our passage a severe gale of wind, which broke the bowsprit of a vessel in our sight, but did no mischief to ourselves. On arriving in the Downs, we found all the flags lowered half way down the masts, which is a signal of mourning; and we now learnt, that, in a few hours after giving birth to a still-born son, the Princess Charlotte of Wales had expired at half-past two on Thursday morning.

### NOVEMBER 16. (Sunday.)

" Peaceful slumbering on the ocean." Here we are still in the Downs, and no symptoms of a probable removal. Indeed, when we weighed our anchor at Gravesend, it gave us a broad hint that there was no occasion as yet for giving ourselves the trouble; for, before it could be got on board, the cable was suffered to slip, and down again went the anchor, carrying along with it one of the men who happened to be standing upon it at the moment, and who in consequence went plump to the bottom. Luckily, the fellow could swim; so in a few minutes he was on board again, and no harm done.

## NOVEMBER 19.

We resumed our voyage with fine weather, but wind so perverse, that we did not arrive in sight of Portsmouth till the evening of the 21st. A pilot came on board, and conveyed us into Spithead.

## NOVEMBER 22.

This morning we quitted Portsmouth, and this evening we returned to it. The Needle rocks were already in sight, when the wind failed completely. There was no getting through the passage, and the dread of a gale would not admit of our remaining in so dangerous a roadstead. So we had nothing for it but to follow Mad Bess's example, and " return to the place whence we came." We are now anchored upon the Motherbank, about two miles from Ryde in the Isle of Wight.

## NOVEMBER 30. (Sunday.)

Edward, the young man who was so dangerously wounded on our return from my former voyage to Jamaica, is now chief mate of the vessel, and feels no other inconvenience from his accident, except a slight difficulty in raising his left arm above his head.

### December 1. (Monday.)

Here we are, still riding at anchor, with no better consolation than that of Klopstock's half-devil Abadonna; the consciousness that others are deeper damned than ourselves. Another ship belonging to the same proprietor left the West India Docks three weeks before us, and here she is still rocking cheek by jowl alongside of us,

> " One writ with us in sour misfortune's book."

### December 3.

A tolerably fair breeze at length enabled us to set sail once more.

### December 24. (Wednesday.)

I had often heard talk of " a hell upon earth," and now I have a perfect idea of " a hell upon water." It must be precisely our vessel during the last three weeks. At twelve at noon upon the 4th, we passed Plymouth, and were actually in sight of the Lizard point, when the wind suddenly became completely foul, and drove us back into the Channel. It continued to strengthen gradually but rapidly; and by the time that night arrived, we had a violent gale, which blew incessantly till the middle of Sunday, the 7th, when we were glad to find ourselves once more in sight of Plymouth, and took advantage of a temporary abatement of the wind to seek refuge in the Sound. Here, however, we soon found that we had but little reason to rejoice at the change of our situation. The Sound was already crowded with vessels of all descriptions; and as we arrived so late, the only mooring still unoccupied, placed us so near the rocks on one side, and another vessel astern, that the captain confessed that he should feel considerable anxiety if the gale should return with its former violence. So, of course, about eleven at night, the gale *did* return; not, indeed, with its former violence, but with its violence increased tenfold; and once we were in very imminent danger from our ship's swinging round by a sudden squall, and narrowly escaping coming in contact with the ship astern, which had not, it seems, allowed itself sufficient cable. Luckily, we just missed her; and our cables (for both our anchors were down) being new and good, we rode out the storm without driving, or meeting with any accident whatever. The next day was squally; and in spite of the Breakwater, the rocking of the ship from the violent agitation of the waves by the late stormy weather was almost insupportable. However, on the 9th, the wind took a more favourable turn, though in so slight a degree, that the pilot expressed great doubts whether it would last long to do us any service. But the captain felt his situation in Plymouth Sound so uneasy, that he resolved at least to make the attempt; and so we crept once more into the Channel. In a few hours the breeze strengthened; about midnight we passed the lights upon the Lizard, and the next morning England was at length out of sight. This cessation of ill luck soon proved to be only " *reculer pour mieux sauter.*" The gale, it seems, had only stopped to take breath: about four in the afternoon of Wednesday, the wind began to rise again; and from that time till the middle of the 23d it blew a complete storm day and night, with only an occasional intermission of two or three hours at a time. Every one in the ship declared that they had never before experienced so obstinate a persecution of severe weather: every rag of sail was obliged to be taken down; the sea was blown up into mountains, and poured itself over the deck repeatedly. The noise was dreadful; and as it lasted incessantly, to sleep was impossible; and I passed ten nights, one after another, without closing my eyes; so that the pain in the nerves of them at length became almost intolerable, and I began to be seriously afraid of going blind. In truth, the captain could not well have pitched upon a set of passengers worse calculated to undergo the trial of a passage so rough. As for myself, my brain is so weak, that the continuation of any violent noise makes me absolutely light-headed; and a pop-gun going off suddenly is quite sufficient at any time to set every nerve shaking, from the crown of my head to the sole of my foot. Then we had a young lady who was ready to die of sea-sickness, and an old one who was little better through fright; and I had an Italian servant into the bargain, who was as sick as the young lady, and as frightened as the old one. The poor fellow had never been on board a ship before; and with every crack which the vessel gave, he thought that to be sure, she was splitting right in half. The sailors, too, appeared to be quite knocked up from the unremitting fatigue to which they were subjected by the perseverance of this dreadful weather. Several of them were ill; and one poor fellow actually died, and was committed to the ocean. To make matters still worse, during the first week the wind was as foul as it could blow; and we passed it in running backwards and forwards, without advancing a step towards our object; till at length every drop of my very small stock of patience was exhausted, and I could no longer resist suggesting our returning to port, rather than continue buffeting about in the chops of the Channel, so much to the damage of the ship, and all contained in her. A change of wind, however, gave a complete answer to this proposal. On Thursday it became favourable as to the prosecution of our voyage, but its fury continued unabated till the evening of the 23d. It then gradually died away, and left us becalmed before the island of Madeira; where we are now rolling backwards and forwards, in sight of its capital, Funchal, on the 24th of December, being seven immortal weeks since my departure from Gravesend. The evening sun is now very brilliant, and shines full upon the island, the rocks of which are finely broken ; the height of the mountains cause their tops to be lost in the clouds; the sides are covered with plantations of vines and forests of cedars; and the white edifices of Funchal, built upon the very edge of the shore, have a truly picturesque appearance. We are now riding between the island and an isolated group of inaccessible rocks called " the Deserters;*" and the effect of the scene altogether is beautiful in the extreme.

### DECEMBER 25. (Christmas-day.)

A light breeze sprang up in the night, and this morning Madeira was no longer visible.

### DECEMBER 31. (Wednesday.)

We are now in the latitudes commonly known by the name of " the Horse Latitudes." During the union of America and Great Britain, great numbers of horses used to be exported from the latter; and the winds in these latitudes are so capricious, squally, and troublesome in every respect,— now a gale, and then a dead calm — now a fair wind, and the next moment a foul one,— that more horses used to die in this portion of the passage than during all the remainder of it. These latitudes from thence obtained their present appellation, and extend from 29° to 25° or 24½°.

* The Dezertas.

## 1818. — JANUARY 1. (Thursday.)

On this day, on my former voyage, I landed at
Black River. Now we are still at some distance
from the line, and are told that we cannot expect
to reach Jamaica in less than three weeks, even
with favourable breezes; and our breezes at present are *not* favourable. Nothing but light winds,
or else dead calms; two knots an hour, and
obliged to be thankful even for that! A-weel! this
is weary work!

## JANUARY 17. (Saturday.)

On Saturday, the 3d, we managed to crawl over
the line, and had no sooner got to the other side of
it, than we were completely becalmed; and even
when we resumed our progress, it was at such a
pace that a careless observer might have been
pardoned for mistaking our manner of moving for
a downright standing still. Day after day produced nothing better for us than baffling winds, so
light that we scarcely made two miles an hour, and
so variable that the sails could be scarcely set in
one direction before it became necessary to shift
them to another; while the monotony of our
voyage was only broken by an occasional thunder-
storm, the catching a stray dolphin now and then,
watching a shoal of flying fish, or guessing at the
complexion of the corsairs on board some vessel in
the offing: for the Caribbean Sea is now dabbed

all over like a painter's pallette with corsairs of all colours, — black from St. Domingo, brown from Carthagena, white from North America, and pea-green from the Cape de Verd Islands. On the afternoon of the 4th, one of them was at no very great distance from us; she hoisted English colours on seeing ours; but there was little doubt, from her peculiar construction and general appearance, that she was a privateer from Carthagena. She set her head towards us, and seemed to be doing her best to come to a nearer acquaintance; but the same calm which hindered us from bravely running away from her, hindered her also from reaching us, although at nightfall she seemed to have gained upon us. In the night we had a violent thunder-storm, and the next morning she was not to be seen. Still we continued to creep and to crawl, grumbling and growling, till on Sunday, the 11th, the long-looked-for wind came at last. The trade wind began to blow with all its might and main right in the vessel's poop, and sent us forward at the rate of 200 miles a day. We passed between Deseada and Antigua in the night of the 15th; and, on the 16th, the rising sun showed us the island mountain of Montserrat ; the sight of which was scarcely less agreeable to our eyes from its romantic beauty, than welcome from its giving us the assurance that our long-winded voyage is at length drawing towards its termination.

### JANUARY 19.

Yesterday morning a miniature shark chose to swallow the bait laid for dolphins, and in consequence soon made his appearance upon deck. It was a very young one, not above three feet long. I ordered a slice of him to be broiled at dinner, but he was by no means so good as a dolphin; but still there was nothing in the taste so unpalatable as to prevent the flesh from being very acceptable in the absence of more delicate food. In the evening, a bird, about the size of a large pigeon, flew on board, and was knocked down by the mate with his hat. It was sulky, and would not be persuaded to eat any thing that was offered, so he was suffered to escape this morning. It was beautifully shaped, with a swallow-tail, wings of an extraordinary spread in comparison with the smallness of the body, a long sharp bill, black and polished like a piece of jet, and eyes remarkably large and brilliant. The head, back, and outside of the wings were of a brownish slate colour, and the rest of his feathers of the most dazzling whiteness. It is called a crab-catcher.

### JANUARY 24. (Saturday.)

Our favourable breeze lasted till Tuesday, the 20th; when, having brought us half way between St. Domingo and Jamaica, it died away, and we dragged on at the rate of two or three miles an hour till Thursday afternoon, which placed us at the mouth of Black River. If we had arrived one hour earlier, we could have immediately entered the harbour; but, with our usual good fortune, we were just too late for the daylight. We therefore did not drop anchor till two o'clock on Friday, before the town of Black River; and on Saturday morning, at four o'clock, I embarked in the ship's cutter for Savannah la Mar. Every one assured us that we could not fail to have a favourable sea-breeze the whole way, and that we should be on land by eight: instead of which, what little wind there was veered round from one point of the compass to the other with the most indefatigable caprice; and we were not on shore till eleven. Here I found Mr. T. Hill, who luckily had his phaëton ready, in which he immediately conveyed me once more to my own estate. The accounts of the general behaviour of my negroes is reasonably good, and they all express themselves satisfied with their situation and their superintendents. Yet, among upwards of three hundred and thirty negroes, and with a greater number of females than men, in spite of all indulgences and inducements, not more than twelve or thirteen children have been added annually to the list of the births. On the other hand, this last season has been generally unhealthy all over the island, and more particularly so in my parish; so that I have lost several negroes, some of them young, strong, and valuable labourers in every respect; and in consequence, my sum total is rather diminished than increased since my last visit. I had been so positively assured that the custom of plunging negro infants, immediately upon their being born, into a tub of cold water, infallibly preserved them from the danger of tetanus, that, on leaving Jamaica, I had ordered this practice to be adopted uniformly. The negro mothers, however, took a prejudice against it into their heads, and have been so obstinate in their opposition, that it was thought unadvisable to attempt the enforcing this regulation. From this and other causes I have lost several infants; but I am told, that on other estates in the neighbourhood they have been still more unfortunate in regard to their children; and one was named to me, on which sixteen were carried off in the course of three days.

### January 26. (Monday.)

The joy of the negroes on my return was quite sufficiently vociferous, and they were allowed today for a holiday. They set themselves to singing and dancing yesterday, in order to lose no time; and to show their gratitude for the indulgence, not one of the five pen-keepers chose to go to their watch last night; the consequence was, that the cattle made their escape, and got into one of my very best cane-pieces. The alarm was given; my own servants and some of the head people had grace enough to run down to the scene of action; but the greatest part remained quietly in the negro-houses, beating the gumby-drum, and singing their joy for my arrival with the whole strength of their lungs, but without thinking it in the least necessary to move so much as a finger-joint in my service. The cattle were at length replaced in their pen, but not till the cane-piece had been ruined irretrievably. Such is negro gratitude, and such my reward for all that I have suffered on ship-board. To be sure, as yet there could not be a more ill-starred expedition than my present one. I only learned, yesterday, that before making the island of Madeira an Algerine corsair was actually in sight, and near enough to discern the turbans of the crew; but we lost each other through the violence of the gale.

## January 29.

There is a popular negro song, the burden of which is, —

  " Take him to the Gulley ! Take him to the Gulley !
   But bringee back the frock and board." —
  " Oh ! massa, massa ! me no deadee yet !" —
  " Take him to the Gulley ! Take him to the Gulley !"
    " Carry him along !"

This alludes to a transaction which took place some thirty years ago, on an estate in this neighbourhood, called Spring-Garden; the owner of which (I think the name was Bedward) is quoted as the cruellest proprietor that ever disgraced Jamaica. It was his constant practice, whenever a sick negro was pronounced incurable, to order the poor wretch to be carried to a solitary vale upon his estate, called the Gulley, where he was thrown down, and abandoned to his fate; which fate was generally to be half devoured by the john-crows, before death had put an end to his sufferings. By this proceeding the avaricious owner avoided the expence of maintaining the slave during his last illness; and in order that he might be as little a loser as possible, he always enjoined the negro bearers of the dying man to strip him naked before leaving the Gulley, and not to forget to bring back his frock and the board on which he had been carried down. One poor creature, while in the act of being removed, screamed out most piteously " that he was not dead yet; " and implored not to be left to perish in the Gulley in a manner so horrible. His cries had no effect upon his master, but operated so forcibly on the less marble hearts of his fellow-slaves, that in the night some of them removed him back to the negro village privately, and nursed him there with so much care, that he recovered, and left the estate unquestioned and undiscovered. Unluckily, one day the master was passing through Kingston, when, on turning the corner of a street suddenly, he found himself face to face with the negro, whom he had supposed long ago to have been picked to the bones in the Gulley of Spring-Garden. He immediately seized him, claimed him as his slave, and ordered his attendants to convey him to his house ; but the fellow's cries attracted a crowd round them, before he could be dragged away. He related his melancholy story, and the singular manner in which he had recovered his life and liberty ; and the public indignation was so forcibly excited by the shocking tale, that Mr. Bedward was glad to save himself from being torn to pieces by a precipitate retreat from Kingston, and never ventured to advance his claim to the negro a second time.

### JANUARY 30.

A man has been tried, at Kingston, for cruel treatment of a Sambo female slave, called Amey. She had no friends to support her cause, nor any other evidence to prove her assertions, than the apparent truth of her statement, and the marks of having been branded in five different places. The result was, that the master received a most severe reprimand for his inhuman conduct, and was sentenced to close confinement for six months, while the slave, in consequence of her sufferings, was restored to the full enjoyment of her freedom.

It appears to me that nothing could afford so much relief to the negroes, under the existing system of Jamaica, as the substituting the labour of animals for that of slaves in agriculture, where-

ever such a measure is practicable. On leaving
the island, I impressed this wish of mine upon the
minds of my agents with all my power; but the
only result has been the creating a very considerable additional expense in the purchase of
ploughs, oxen, and farming implements; the awk-
wardness, and still more the obstinacy, of the few
negroes, whose services were indispensable, was
not to be overcome: they broke plough after
plough, and ruined beast after beast, till the attempt was abandoned in despair. However, it was
made without the most essential ingredient for
success, the superintendence of an English ploughman; and such of the ploughs as were of cast-iron
could not be repaired when once broken, and
therefore ought not to have been adopted; but I
am told, that in several other parts of the island the
plough has been introduced, and completely successful. Another of my farming speculations
answered no better: this was to improve the breed
of cattle in the county, for which purpose Lord
Holland and myself sent over four of the finest
bulls that could be procured in England. One of
them got a trifling hurt in its passage from the
vessel to land; but the remaining three were
deposited in their respective pens without the
least apparent damage. They were taken all possible care of, houses appropriated to shelter them
from the sun and rain, and, in short, no means of
preserving their health was neglected. Yet, shortly

after their arrival in Jamaica, they evidently began to decline; their blood was converted into urine; they paid no sort of attention to the cows, who were confined in the same paddock; and at the end of a fortnight not one was in existence, two having died upon the same day. The injured one, having been bled the most copiously in consequence of its hurt, was that which survived the longest.

### JANUARY 31.

Some days ago, a negro woman, who has lost four children, and has always been a most affectionate mother, brought the fifth, a remarkably fine infant, into the hospital. She complained of its having caught cold, a fever, and so on; but nothing administered was of use, and its manner of breathing made the doctor enquire, whether the child had not had a fall? The mother denied this most positively, and her fondness for the infant admitted no doubt of her veracity. Still the child grew worse and worse; still the question about the fall was repeated, and as constantly denied; until luckily being made in the presence of a new-comer, the latter immediately exclaimed, "that to her certain knowledge the infant had really had a fall, for that the mother having fastened it behind her back, the knot of the handkerchief had slipped, and the baby had fallen upon the floor."—"It is false," answered the mother: "the child did not fall; for when the knot slipped, I had time to catch it by the foot, and so I saved it from falling, just as its head struck against the ground." Fear of being blamed as having occasioned the baby's illness through her own carelessness had induced her to adopt this equivocation, and its life had nearly been the sacrifice of her duplicity. A proper mode of treatment was now adopted without loss of time; their beneficial effect was immediately visible, and the poor little negro is now recovering rapidly. But certainly there is no folly and imprudence like unto negro folly and imprudence. One of my best disposed and most sensible Eboes has had a violent fever lately, but was so nearly well as to be put upon a course of bark. On Wednesday morning a son of his died of dirt-eating, — a practice which neither severity nor indulgence could induce him to discontinue. The boy was buried that night according to African customs, accompanied with dancing, singing, drinking, eating, and riot of all kinds; and the father, although the kindest-hearted negro on my estate, and remarkably fond of his children, danced and drank to such an excess, that I found him on the following morning in a raging fever, and worse than he was when he first entered the hospital. I had warned him against the consequences of the funeral, reminded him of the dangerous malady from which he was but just recovering, and he had promised solemnly to be upon his guard; and such was the manner in which he performed his promise.

FEBRUARY 1. (Sunday.)

During my former visit to Jamaica I had inter-ceded in behalf of a negro belonging to Greenwich estate, named Aberdeen, who had run away re-peatedly, but who attributed his misconduct to the decay of his health, which rendered him unable to work as well as formerly, and to the fear of consequent punishment for not having performed the tasks assigned to him. The fellow while he spoke to me had tears running down his cheeks, looked feeble and ill, and indeed seemed to be quite heart-broken. On my speaking to the attor-ney, he readily promised to enquire into the truth of the man's statement, and to take care that he should be only allotted such labour as his strength might be fully equal to. This morning he came over to see me, and so altered, that I could scarcely believe him to be the same man. He was cleanly dressed, walked with his head erect, and his eyes sparkled, and his mouth grinned from ear to ear, while he told me, that during my absence every thing had gone well with him, nobody had " put upon him ; " he had been tasked no more than suited his strength ; as much as he was able to do, he had done willingly, and had never run away. Even his asthma was better in consequence of the depression being removed from his spirits. So, he said, as soon as he heard of my return, he thought it his duty to come over and show himself to me, and tell me that he was well, and contented, and behaving properly; for that " to be sure, if massa no speak that good word for me to trustee, me no livee now ; me good, massa ! " Gratitude made him absolutely eloquent: his whole manner, and the strong expression of his countenance, put his sincerity out of all doubt, and I never saw a man seem to feel more truly thankful. All negroes, therefore, are not absolutely without some remembrance of kindness shown them; and indeed I ought not in justice to my own people to allow myself to forget, that when I sent a reward to those who had roused themselves to drive the cattle out of my canes the other night, there was considerable difficulty in persuading them to accept the money: they sent me word, " that as they were all well treated on the estate, it was their business to take care that no mischief was done to it, and that they did not deserve to be rewarded for having merely done their duty by me." Nor was it till after they had received repeated orders from me, that their delicacy could be overcome, and themselves persuaded to pocket the affront and the *maccaroni*.

## FEBRUARY 2.

One of the deadliest poisons used by the negroes (and a great variety is perfectly well known to most of them) is prepared from the root of the cassava.

Its juice being expressed and allowed to ferment, a small worm is generated, the substance of which being received into the stomach is of a nature the most pernicious. A small portion of this worm is concealed under one of the thumb-nails, which are suffered to grow long for this purpose; then when the negro has contrived to persuade his intended victim to eat or drink with him, he takes an opportunity, while handing to him a dish or cup, to let the worm fall, which never fails to destroy the person who swallows it. Another means of destruction is to be found (as I am assured) in almost every negro garden throughout the island: it is the arsenic bean, neither useful for food nor ornamental in its appearance; nor can the negroes, when questioned, give any reason for affording it a place in their gardens; yet there it is always to be seen. The alligator's liver also possesses deleterious properties; and the gall is said to be still more dangerous.

## FEBRUARY 3.

On Friday I was made to observe, in the hospital, a remarkably fine young negro, about twenty-two years of age, stout and strong, and whom every one praised for his numerous good qualities, and particularly for his affection for his mother, and the services which he rendered her. He complained of a little fever, and a slight pain in his side. On Saturday he left the hospital, and intended to go to his provision grounds, among the mountains, on Sunday morning; but, as he complained of a pain in his head, his mother prevented his going, and obliged him to return to the hospital in the evening. On Monday he was seized with fainting fits, lost his speech and power of motion, and this morning I was awaked by the shrieks and lamentations of the poor mother, who, on coming to the hospital to enquire for her son, found, that in spite of all possible care and exertions on the part of his medical attendants, he had just expired. Whether it be the climate not agreeing with their African blood (genuine or inherited), or whether it be from some defect in their general formation, certainly negroes seem to hold their lives upon a very precarious tenure. Nicholas, John Fuller, and others of my best and most favoured workmen, the very servants, too, in my own house, are perpetually falling ill with little fevers, or colds, or pains in the head or limbs. However, the season is universally allowed to have been peculiarly unhealthy for negroes; and, indeed, even for white people, the deaths on board the shipping having been unusually numerous this year. As to the barracks, which are scarcely a couple of miles distant from my estate, there the yellow fever has established itself, and, as I hear, is committing terrible ravages, particularly among the wives of the soldiers. — This morning several negro-mothers, belonging to Friendship and Greenwich, came to complain to their attorney (who happened to be at my house) that the overseer obliged them to wean their children too soon. Some of these children were above twenty-two months old, and none under eighteen; but, in order to retain the leisure and other indulgences annexed to the condition of nursing-mothers, the female negroes, by their own good-will, would never wean their offspring at all. Of course their demands were rejected, and they went home in high discontent; one of them, indeed, not scrupling to declare aloud, and with a peculiar emphasis and manner, that if the child should be put into the weaning-house against her will, the attorney would see it dead in less than a week.

FEBRUARY 4.

The violent gale of wind which persecuted us with so much pertinacity on our leaving the English Channel is supposed to have been the tail of a tremendous hurricane, which has utterly laid waste Barbados and several other islands. No less than sixteen of the ships which sailed at the same time with us are reported to have perished upon the passage; so that I ought to consider it at least as a negative piece of good luck to have reached Jamaica myself, " no bones broke, though sore peppered;" but I am still trembling in uncertainty for the fate of the vessel which is bringing out all my Irish supplies, and the non-arrival of which would be a misfortune to me of serious magnitude.

The negroes are so obstinate and so wilful in their general character, that if they do not receive the precise articles to which they have been accustomed, and which they expect as their right, no compensation, however ample, can satisfy them. Thus, at every Christmas it would go near to create a rebellion if they did not receive a certain proportion of salt fish; but if, in the intervening months, accident should prevent their receiving their usual allowance of herrings, the giving them salt fish to the amount of double the value would be considered by them as an act of the grossest injustice.

## FEBRUARY 5.

On Saturday, about eight in the evening, a large centipede dropped from the ceiling upon my dinner-table, and was immediately cut in two exact halves by one of the guests. As it is reported in Jamaica that these reptiles, when thus divided, will re-unite again, or if separated will reproduce their missing members, and continue to live as stoutly as ever, I put both parts into a plate, under a glass cover. On Sunday they continued to move about their prison with considerable agility, although the tail was evidently much more lively and full of motion than the head: perhaps the centipede was a female. On Monday the head was dead, but the tail continued to run about, and evidently endeavoured to to make its escape, although it appeared not to know very well how to set about it, nor to be perfectly determined as to which way it wanted to go: it only seemed to have Cymon's reason for wishing to take a walk, and " would rather go any where, than stay with any body." On Wednesday, at twelve o'clock, its vivacity was a little abated, but only a little ; the wound was skinned over, and I was waiting anxiously to know whether it would subsist without its numskull till a good old age, or would put forth an entirely spick and span new head and shoulders ; when, on going to look at the plate on Thursday morning, lo and behold! the dead head and the living tail had disappeared together. I suppose some of the negro servants had thrown them away through ignorance, but they deny, one and all, having so much as touched the plate, most stoutly ; and as a paper case, pierced in several places, had been substituted for the glass cover, some persons are of opinion that the tail made its escape through one of these air-holes, and carried its head away with it in its forceps. Be this as it may, gone they both are, and I am disappointed beyond measure at being deprived of this opportunity of reading the last volume of " The Life and Adventures of a Centipede's Tail." I have proclaimed a reward for the bringing me another, but I am told that these reptiles are only found by accident ; and that, very possibly, one may not be procured previous to my leaving the island.

## February 6.

Mr. Lutford, the proprietor of a considerable estate in the parish of Clarendon, had frequently accused a particular negro of purloining coffee. About six months ago the slave was sent for, and charged with a fresh offence of the same nature, when he confessed the having taken a small quantity; upon which his master ordered him to fix his eyes on a particular cotton tree, and then, without any further ceremony, shot him through the head. His mistress was the coroner's natural daughter, and the coroner himself was similarly connected with the custos of Clarendon. In consequence of this family compact, no inquest was held, no enquiry was made; the whole business was allowed to be slurred over, and the murder would have remained unpunished if accident had not brought some rumours respecting it to the governor's ear. An investigation was ordered to take place without delay; but Mr. Lutford received sufficient warning to get on shipboard, and escape to America; and the displacing of the custos of Clarendon, for neglecting his official duty, was the only means by which the governor could express his abhorrence of the act.

## February 8. (Sunday.)

My estate is greatly plagued by a negress named Catalina; she is either mad, or has long pretended to be so, never works, and always steals. About a week before my arrival she was found in the trash-house, which she had pitched upon as the very fittest place possible for her kitchen; and there she was sitting, very quietly and comfortably, boiling her pot over an immense fire, and surrounded on all sides by dry canes, inflammable as tinder. This vagary was of too dangerous a nature to allow of her being longer left at liberty, and she was put into the hospital. But her husband was by no means pleased with her detention, as he never failed to appropriate to himself a share of her plunder, and when discovered, the blame of the robbery was laid upon his wife, in a fit of insanity. So, while the general joy at my first arrival drew the hospital attendants from their post, he took the opportunity to carry off his wife, and conceal her. The consequence was, that this morning complaints poured upon me of gardens robbed by Catalina, who had carried off as much as she could, dug up and destroyed the rest, and had shown as little conscience in providing herself with poultry as in helping herself to vegetables. I immediately despatched one of the negro-governors with a party in pursuit of her, who succeeded in lodging her once more in the hospital; where she must remain till I can get her sent to the asylum at Kingston, the only hospital for lunatics in the whole island.

## February 12. (Thursday.)

On my former visit to Jamaica, I found on my estate a poor woman nearly one hundred years old, and stone blind. She was too infirm to walk; but two young negroes brought her on their backs to the steps of my house, in order, as she said, that she might at least touch massa, although she could not see him. When she had kissed my hand, " that was enough," she said; " now me hab once kiss a massa's hand, me willing to die to-morrow, me no care." She had a woman appropriated to her service, and was shown the greatest care and attention; however, she did not live many months after my departure. There was also a mulatto, about thirty years of age, named Bob, who had been almost deprived of the use of his limbs by the horrible cocoa-bay, and had never done the least work since he was fifteen. He was so gentle and humble, and so fearful, from the consciousness of his total inability of soliciting my notice, that I could not help pitying the poor fellow; and whenever he came in my way I always sought to encourage him by little presents, and other trifling marks of favour. His thus unexpectedly meeting with distinguishing kindness, where he expected to be treated as a worthless incumbrance, made a strong impression on his mind. Soon after my departure his malady assumed a more active appearance; but during the last stages of its progress

z

the only fear which he expressed was, that he should not live till last Christmas, when my return was expected to a certainty. In the mean while he endeavoured to find out a means of being of some little use to me, although his weak constitution would not allow of his being of much. Some of his relations being in opulent circumstances, they furnished him with a horse, for he was too weak to walk for more than a few minutes at a time; and, mounted upon this, he passed all his time in traversing the estate, watching the corn that it might not be stolen, warning the pen-keepers if any of the cattle had found their way into the cane-pieces, and doing many other such little pieces of service to the property; so that, as the negroes said, " if he had been a white man he might have been taken for an overseer." At length Christmas arrived; it was known that I was on the sea; Bob, too, was still alive; but still there was nothing to be heard of me. His perpetual question to all who came to visit him was, How was the wind? and he was constantly praying to the wind and the ocean to bring massa's vessel soon to Savanna la Mar, that he might but see him once more, and thank him, before he died. At length I landed; and when, on the day of my arrival on my estate, I expressed my surprise at the non-appearance of several of the negroes, who had appeared to be most attached to me, and I had expected to find most forward in greeting me, I was told that a messenger had been sent to call them, and that their absence was occasioned by their attendance at poor Bob's funeral. Several of his relations, who nursed him on his death-bed, have assured me, that the last audible words which he uttered were — " Are there still no news of massa?"

FEBRUARY 13.

Talk of Lucretia! commend me to a she-turkey! The hawk of Jamaica is an absolute Don Giovanni; and he never loses an opportunity of being extremely rude indeed to these feathered fair ones; not even scrupling to use the last violence, and that without the least ceremony, not so much as saying, " With your leave," or " By your leave," or using any of the forms which common civility expects upon such occasions. The poor timid things are too much frightened by the sudden attack of this Tarquin with a beak and claws, to make any resistance; but they no sooner recover from their flutter sufficiently to be aware of what has happened, than they feel so extremely shocked, that they always make a point of dying; nor was a female turkey ever known to survive the loss of her honour above three days.

FEBRUARY 14.

I think that I really may now venture to hope that my plans for the management of my estate have succeeded beyond even my most sanguine expectations. I have now passed three weeks with my negroes, the doors of my house open all day long, and full liberty allowed to every person to come and speak to me without witnesses or restraint; yet not one man or woman has come to me with a single complaint. On the contrary, all my enquiries have been answered by an assurance, that during the two years of my absence my regulations were adhered to most implicitly, and that, " except for the pleasure of seeing massa," there was no more difference in treatment than if I had remained upon the estate. Many of them have come to tell me instances of kindness which they have received from one or other of their superintendents; others, to describe some severe fit of illness, in which they must have died but for the care taken of them in the hospital; some, who were weakly and low-spirited on my former visit, to show me how much they are improved in health, and tell me " how they keep up heart now, because since massa come upon the property nobody put upon them, and all go well; " and some, who had formerly complained of one trifle or other, to take back their complaints, and say, that they wanted no change, and were willing to be employed in any way that might be thought most for the good of the estate; but although I have now at least *seen* every one of them, and have conversed with numbers, I have not yet been able to find one person who had so much as even an imaginary grievance to lay before me. Yet I find, that it has been found necessary to punish with the lash, although only in a very few instances; but then this only took place on the commission of absolute *crimes*, and in cases where its necessity and justice were so universally felt, not only by others, but by the sufferers themselves, that instead of complaining, they seem only to be afraid of their offence coming to my knowledge; to prevent which, they affect to be more satisfied and happy than all the rest, and now when I see a mouth grinning from ear to ear with a more than ordinary expansion of jaw, I never fail to find, on enquiry, that its proprietor is one of those who have been punished during my absence. I then take care to give them an opportunity of making a complaint, if they should have any to make; but no, not a word comes; "every thing has gone on perfectly well, and just as it ought to have done." Upon this, I drop a slight hint of the offence in question; and instantly away goes the grin, and down falls the negro to kiss my feet, confess his fault, and "beg massa forgib, and them never do so bad thing more to fret massa, and them beg massa pardon, hard, quite hard!" But not one of them has denied the justice of his punishment, or complained of undue severity on the part of his superintendents. On the other hand, although the lash has thus been in a manner utterly abolished, except in cases where a much severer punishment would have been inflicted by the police, and although they are aware of this unwillingness to chastise, my trustee acknowledges that during my absence the negroes have been quiet and tractable, and have not only laboured as well as they used to do, but have done much more work than the negroes on an adjoining property, where there are forty more negroes, and where, moreover, a considerable sum is paid for hired assistance. Having now waited three weeks to see how they would conduct themselves, and found no cause of dissatisfaction since the neglect of the watchman to guard the cattle (and which they one and all attributed to their joy at seeing me again), I thought it time to distribute the presents which I had brought with me for them from England. During my absence I had ordered a new and additional hospital to be built, intended entirely for the use of lying-in women, nursing mothers, and cases of a serious nature, for which purpose it is to be provided with every possible comfort; while the old hospital is to be reserved for those who have little or nothing the matter with them, but who obstinately insist upon their being too ill to work, in defiance of the opinion of all their medical attendants. The new hospital is not quite finished; but wishing to connect it as much as possible with pleasurable associations, I took occasion of the distribution of presents to open it for the first time. Accordingly, the negroes were summoned to the new hospital this morning; the rooms were sprinkled with Madeira for good luck;

and the toast of " Health to the new hospital, and shame to the old lazy house!" was drunk by the trustee, the doctoresses, the governors, &c., and received by the whole congregation of negroes with loud cheering; after which, every man received a blue jacket lined with flannel, every woman a flaming red stuff petticoat, and every child a frock of white cotton. They then fell to dancing and singing, and drinking rum and sugar, which they kept up till a much later hour than would be at all approved of by the bench of bishops; for it is now Sunday morning, and they are still dancing and singing louder than ever.

## February 15. (Sunday.)

To-day divine service was performed at Savanna la Mar for the first time these five weeks. The rector has been indisposed lately with the lumbago: he has no curate; and thus during five whole weeks there was a total cessation of public worship. I had told several of my female acquaintance that it was long since they had been to church; that I was afraid of their forgetting " all about and about it," and that if there should be no service for a week longer I should think it my duty to come and hear them say their Catechism myself. Luckily the rector recovered, and saved me the trouble of hearing them; but the long privation of public prayer did not seem to have created any very great demand for the article, as I have seldom witnessed

a more meagre congregation. It was literally
"two or three gathered together," and it seemed
as if five or six would be too many, and forfeit the
promise. I cannot discover that the negroes have
any external forms of worship, nor any priests in
Jamaica, unless their Obeah men should be considered as such; but still I cannot think that they
ought to be considered as totally devoid of all
natural religion. There is no phrase so common on
their lips as " God bless you!" and "God preserve
you !" and " God will bless you wherever you go!"
Phrases which they pronounce with every appearance of sincerity, and as if they came from the very
bottom of their hearts. " God-A'mity ! God-
A'mity !" is their constant exclamation in pain and
in sorrow; and with this perpetual recurrence to
the Supreme Being, it must be difficult to insist
upon their being atheists. But they have even got
a step further than the belief in a God; they also
allow the existence of an evil principle. One of
them complained to me the other day, that when
he went to the field his companions had told him
" that he might go to hell, for he was not worthy to
work with them ;" and one of his adversaries in
return accused him of being so lazy, " that instead
of being a slave upon Cornwall estate, he was only
fit to be the slave of the devil." Then surely they
could not be afraid of duppies (or ghosts) without
some idea of a future state ; and indeed nothing is
more firmly impressed upon the mind of the Afri-

cans, than that after death they shall go back to Africa, and pass an eternity in revelling and feasting with their ancestors. The proprietor of a neighbouring estate lately used all his influence to persuade his foster-sister to be christened; but it was all in vain: she had imbibed strong African prejudices from her mother, and frankly declared that she found nothing in the Christian system so alluring to her taste as the post-obit balls and banquets promised by the religion of Africa. I confess, that this prejudice appears to me to be so strongly rooted, that in spite of the curates expected from the hands of the bishop of London, I am sadly afraid, that "the pulpit drum ecclesiastic" will find it a hard matter to overpower the gumby; and that the joys of the Christian paradise will be seen to kick the beam, when they are weighed against the pleasures of eating fat hog, drinking raw rum, and dancing for centuries to the jam-jam and kitty-katty. In the negro festivals in this life, the chief point lies in making as much noise as possible, and the Africans and Creoles dispute it with the greatest pertinacity. I am just informed that at the dance last night the Eboes obtained a decided triumph, for they roared and screamed and shouted and thumped their drums with so much effect, that the Creoles were fairly rendered deaf with the noise of their rivals, and dumb with their own, and obliged to leave off singing altogether.

### February 16.

On my arrival I found that idle rogue Nato, as usual, an inmate of the hospital, where he regularly passes at least nine months out of the twelve. He was with infinite difficulty persuaded, at the end of a fortnight, to employ himself about the carriage-horses for a couple of days; but on the third he returned to the hospital, although the medical attendants, one and all, declared nothing to be the matter with him, and the doctors even refused to insert his name in the sick list. Still he persisted in declaring himself to be too ill to do a single stroke of work: so on Thursday I put him into one of the sick rooms by himself, and desired him to get well with the doors locked, which he would find to the full as easy as with the doors open; at the same time assuring him, that he should never come out, till he should be sufficiently recovered to cut canes in the field. He held good all Friday; but Saturday being a holy-day, he declared himself to be in a perfect state of health, and desired to be released. However, I was determined to make him suffer a little for his lying and obstinacy, and would not suffer the doors to be opened for him till this morning, when he quitted the hospital, saluted on all sides by loud huzzas in congratulation of his amended health, and which followed him during his whole progress to the cane-piece. I was informed that a lad, named Epsom, who used to be perpetually running away, had been stationary for the last two years. So on Wednesday last, as he happened to come in my way, I gave him all proper commendation for having got rid of his bad habits; and to make the praise better worth his having, I added a maccarony: he was gratified in the extreme, thanked me a thousand times, promised most solemnly never to behave ill again, and ran away that very night. However, he returned on Saturday morning, and was brought to me all rags, tears, and penitence, wondering " how he could have had such *bad manners* as to make massa fret."

## FEBRUARY 17.

Some of the free people of colour possess slaves, cattle, and other property left them by their fathers, and are in good circumstances; but few of them are industrious enough to increase their possessions by any honest exertions of their own. As to the free blacks, they are almost uniformly lazy and im-provident, most of them half-starved, and only anxious to live from hand to mouth. Some lounge about the highways with pedlar-boxes, stocked with various worthless baubles; others keep miser-able stalls provided with rancid butter, damaged salt-pork, and other such articles: and these they are always willing to exchange for stolen rum and sugar, which they secretly tempt the negroes to pilfer from their proprietors; but few of them ever make the exertion of earning their livelihood creditably. Even those who profess to be tailors, carpenters, or coopers, are for the most part careless, drunken, and dissipated, and never take pains sufficient to attain any dexterity in their trade. As to a free negro hiring himself out for plantation labour, no instance of such a thing was ever known in Jamaica, and probably no price, however great, would be considered by them as a sufficient temptation.

## FEBRUARY 18.

The Africans and Creoles certainly do hate each other with a cordiality which would have appeared highly gratifying to Dr. Johnson in his " Love of Good Haters." Yesterday, in the field, a girl who had taken some slight offence at something said to her by a young boy, immediately struck him with the bill, with which she was cutting canes. Luckily, his loose wrapper saved him from the blow; and, on his running away, she threw the bill after him in his flight with all the fury and malice of a fiend. This same vixen, during my former visit, had been punished for fixing her teeth in the hand of one of the other girls, and nearly biting her thumb off; and on hearing of this fresh instance of devilism, I asked her mother, " how she came to have so bad a daughter, when all her sons were so mild and good ?" — "Oh, massa," answered she, " the girl's father was a Guinea-man."

## February 19.

Neptune came this morning to request that the name of his son, Oscar, might be changed for that of Julius, which (it seems) had been that of his own father. The child, he said, had always been weakly, and he was persuaded, that its ill-health proceeded from his deceased grandfather's being displeased, because it had not been called after him. The other day, too, a woman, who had a child sick in the hospital, begged me to change its name for any other which might please me best: she cared not what; but she was sure that it would never do well, so long as it should be called Lucia. Perhaps this prejudice respecting the power of names produces in some measure their unwillingness to be christened. They find no change produced in them, except the alteration of their name, and hence they conclude that this name contains in it some secret power; while, on the other hand, they conceive that the ghosts of their ancestors cannot fail to be offended at their abandoning an appellation, either hereditary in the family, or given by themselves. It is another negro-prejudice that the eructation of the breath of a sucking child has something in it venomous; and frequently nursing mothers, on showing the doctor a swelled breast, will very gravely and positively attribute it to the infant's having broken wind while hanging at the nipple.

## February 20.

I asked one of my negro servants this morning whether old Luke was a relation of his. " Yes," he said.—" Is he your uncle, or your cousin?" —" No, massa."—" What then? "—" He and my father were shipmates, massa."

## February 23.

The law-charges in Jamaica have lately been regulated by the House of Assembly; and by all accounts (except that of the lawyers) it was full time that something should be done on the subject. A case was mentioned to me this morning of an estate litigated between several parties. At length a decision was given: the estate was sold for 16,000*l.*; but the lawyer's claim must always be the first discharged, and as this amounted to more than 16,000*l.* the lawyer found himself in possession of the estate. This was the fable of Æsop's oyster put in action with a vengeance.

## February 25.

A negro, named Adam, has long been the terror of my whole estate. He was accused of being an Obeah-man, and persons notorious for the practice of Obeah had been found concealed from justice in his house, who were afterwards convicted and transported. He was strongly suspected of having poisoned more than twelve negroes, men and women; and having been displaced by my former trustee from being principal governor, in revenge he put poison into his water jar. Luckily he was observed by one of the house servants, who impeached him, and prevented the intended mischief. For this offence he ought to have been given up to justice; but being brother of the trustee's mistress she found means to get him off, after undergoing a long confinement in the stocks. I found him, on my arrival, living in a state of utter excommunication; I tried what reasoning with him could effect, reconciled him to his companions, treated him with marked kindness, and he promised solemnly to behave well during my absence. However, instead of attributing my lenity to a wish to reform him, his pride and confidence in his own talents and powers of deception made him attribute the indulgence shown him to his having obtained an influence over my mind. This he determined to employ to his own purposes upon my return; so he set about forming a conspiracy against Sully, the present chief governor, and boasted on various estates in the neighbourhood that on my arrival he would take care to get Sully broke, and himself substituted in his place. In the mean while he quarrelled and fought to the right and to the left; and on my arrival I found the whole estate in an uproar about Adam. No less than three charges of assault, with intent to kill, were preferred against him. In a fit of jealousy he had endeavoured to strangle Marlborough with the thong of a whip, and had nearly effected his purpose before he could be dragged away: he had knocked Nato down in some trifling dispute, and while the man was senseless had thrown him into the river to drown him; and having taken offence at a poor weak creature called Old Rachael, on meeting her by accident he struck her to the ground, beat her with a supplejack, stamped upon her belly, and begged her to be assured of his intention (as he eloquently worded it) "to kick her guts out." The breeding mothers also accused him of having been the cause of the poisoning a particular spring, from which they were in the habit of fetching water for their children, as Adam on that morning had been seen near the spring without having any business there, and he had been heard to caution his little daughter against drinking water from it that day, although he stoutly denied both circumstances. Into the bargain, my head blacksmith being perfectly well at five o'clock, was found by his son dead in his bed at eight; and it was known that he had lately had a dispute with Adam, who on that day had made it up with him, and had invited him to drink, although it was not certain that his offer had been accepted. He had, moreover, threatened the lives of many of the best negroes. Two of the cooks declared, that he had severally directed them to dress Sully's food apart, and had given them powders to mix with it. The first to whom he applied refused positively; the second he treated with liquor, and when she had drunk, he gave her the poison, with instructions how to use it. Being a timid creature, she did not dare to object, so threw away the powder privately, and pretended that it had been administered; but finding no effect produced by it, Adam gave her a second powder, at the same time bidding her remember the liquor which she had swallowed, and which he assured her would effect her own destruction through the force of Obeah, unless she prevented it by sacrificing his enemy in her stead. The poor creature still threw away the powder, but the strength of imagination brought upon her a serious malady, and it was not till after several weeks that she recovered from the effects of her fears. The terror thus produced was universal throughout the estate, and Sully and several other principal negroes requested me to remove them to my property in St. Thomas's, as their lives were not safe while breathing the same air with Adam. However, it appeared a more salutary measure to remove Adam himself; but all the poisoning charges either went no further than strong suspicion, or (any more than the assaults) were not liable by the laws of Jamaica to be punished, except by flogging or temporary imprisonment, which would only have returned him to the estate with increased resentment against those to whom he should ascribe his sufferings, however deserved.

However, on searching his house, a musket with a plentiful accompaniment of powder and ball was found concealed, as also a considerable quantity of materials for the practice of Obeah : the possession of either of the above articles (if the musket is without the consent of the proprietor) authorises the magistrates to pronounce a sentence of transportation. In consequence of this discovery, Adam was immediately committed to gaol ; a slave court was summoned, and to-day a sentence of transportation from the island was pronounced, after a trial of three hours. As to the man's guilt, of that the jury entertained no doubt after the first half hour's evidence; and the only difficulty was to restrain the verdict to transportation. We produced nothing which could possibly affect the man's life ; for although perhaps no offender ever better deserved hanging ; yet I confess my being weak-minded enough to entertain doubts whether hanging or other capital punishment ought to be inflicted for any offence whatever : I am at least certain, that if offenders waited till they were hanged by me, they would remain unhanged till they were all so many old Parrs. However, although I did my best to prevent Adam from being hanged, it was no easy matter to prevent his hanging himself. The Obeah ceremonies always commence with what is called, by the negroes, "the Myal dance." This is intended to remove any doubt of the chief Obeah-man's supernatural powers; and in the course of it, he undertakes to show his art by killing one of the persons present, whom he pitches upon for that purpose. He sprinkles various powders over the devoted victim, blows upon him, and dances round him, obliges him to drink a liquor prepared for the occasion, and finally the sorcerer and his assistants seize him and whirl him rapidly round and round till the man loses his senses, and falls on the ground to all appearance and the belief of the spectators a perfect corpse. The chief Myal-man then utters loud shrieks, rushes out of the house with wild and frantic gestures, and conceals himself in some neighbouring wood. At the end of two or three hours he returns with a large bundle of herbs, from some of which he squeezes the juice into the mouth of the dead person; with others he anoints his eyes and stains the tips of his fingers, accompanying the ceremony with a great variety of grotesque actions, and chanting all the while some_thing between a song and a howl, while the assistants hand in hand dance slowly round them in a circle, stamping the ground loudly with their feet to keep time with his chant. A considerable time elapses before the desired effect is produced, but at lengt.. the corpse gradually recovers animation, rises from the ground perfectly recovered, and the Myal dance concludes. After this proof of his power, those who wish to be revenged upon their enemies apply to the sorcerer for some of the same powder, which produced apparent death upon their companion, and as they never employ the means used for his recovery, of course the powder once administered never fails to be lastingly fatal. It must be superfluous to mention that the Myal-man on this second occasion substitutes a poison for a narcotic. Now, among other suspicious articles found in Adam's hut, there was a string of beads of various sizes, shapes, and colours, arranged in a form peculiar to the performance of the Obeah-man in the Myal dance. Their use was so well known, that Adam on his trial did not even attempt to deny that they could serve for no purpose but the practice of Obeah; but he endeavoured to refute their being his own property, and with this view he began to narrate the means by which he had become possessed of them. He said that they belonged to Fox (a negro who was lately trans-ported), from whom he had taken them at a Myal dance held on the estate of Dean's Valley; but as the assistants at one of these dances are by law condemned to death equally with the principal performer, the court had the humanity to interrupt his confession of having been present on such an occasion, and thus saved him from criminating himself so deeply as to render a capital punishment inevitable. I understand that he was quite una-bashed and at his ease the whole time; upon hearing his sentence, he only said very coolly, " Well! I ca'n't help it!" turned himself round, and walked out of court. That nothing might be wanting, this fellow had even a decided talent for hypocrisy. When on my arrival he gave me a letter filled with the grossest lies respecting the trustee, and every creditable negro on the estate, he took care to sign it by the name which he had lately received in baptism; and in his defence at the bar to prove his probity of character and purity of manners, he informed the court that for some time past he had been learning to read, for the sole purpose of learning the Lord's Prayer. The nick-name by which he was generally known among the negroes in this part of the country, was Buonaparte, and he always appeared to exult in the appellation. Once condemned, the marshal is bound under a heavy penalty to see him shipped from off the island before the expiration of six weeks, and probably he will be sent to Cuba. He is a fine-looking man between thirty and forty, square built, and of great bodily strength, and his countenance equally expresses intelligence and malignity. The sum allowed me for him is one hundred pounds currency, which is scarcely a third of his worth as a labourer, but which is the highest value which a jury is permitted to mention.

### March 1. (Sunday.)

Last night the negroes of Friendship took it into their ingenious heads to pay me a compliment of an extremely inconvenient nature. They thought, that it would be highly proper to treat me with a nightly serenade just by way of showing their *enjoyment* on my return; and accordingly a large body of them arrived at my doors about midnight, dressed out in their best clothes, and accompanied with drums, rattles, and their whole orchestra of abominable instruments, determined to pass the whole night in singing and dancing under my windows. Luckily, my negro-governors heard what was going forwards, and knowing my taste a little better than my visiters, they hastened to assure them of my being in bed and asleep, and with much difficulty persuaded them to remove into my village. Here they contented themselves with making a noise for the greatest part of the night; and the next morning, after coming up to see me at breakfast, they went away quietly. One of them only remained to enquire particularly after Lady H———, as her mother had been her nurse, and she was very particular in. her enquiries as to her health, her children, their ages and names. When she went away, I gave her a plentiful provision of bread, butter, plantains, and cold ham from the breakfast table; part of which she sat down to eat, intending, as she said, to carry the rest to her piccaninny at home. But in half an hour after she made her appearance again, saying she was come to take leave of me, and hoped I would give her a *bit* to buy tobacco. I gave her a maccaroni, which occasioned a great squall of delight. Oh!

since I had given her so much, she would not buy tobacco but a fowl; and then, when I returned, she would bring me a chicken from it for my dinner; that is, if she could keep the other negroes from stealing it from her, a piece of extraordinary good luck of which she seemed to entertain but slender hopes. At length off she set; but she had scarcely gone above ten yards from the house, when she turned back, and was soon at my writing-table once more, with a " Well! here me come to massa again!" So then she said, that she had meant to eat part of the provisions which I had given her, and carry home the rest to her boy; but that really it was so good, she could not help going on eating and eating, till she had eaten the whole, and now she wanted another bit of cold ham to carry home to her child, and then she should go away perfectly contented. I ordered Cubina to give her a great hunch of it, and Mrs. Phillis at length took her departure for good and all.

### MARCH 4. (Wednesday.)

I set out to visit my estate in St. Thomas's in the East, called Hordley. It is at the very furthest extremity of the island, and never was there a journey like unto my journey. Something disagreeable happened at every step; my accidents commenced before I had accomplished ten miles from my own house; for in passing along a narrow shelf of rock, which overhangs the sea near Blue-fields, a pair of young blood-horses in my carriage took fright at the roaring of the waves which dashed violently against them, and twice nearly overturned me. On the second occasion one of them actually fell down into the water, while the off-wheel of the curricle flew up into the air, and thus it remained suspended, balancing backwards and forwards, like Mahomet's coffin. Luckily, time was allowed the horse to recover his legs, down came the wheel once more on terra firma, and on we went again. We slept at Cashew (an estate near Lacovia), and the next morning at daylight proceeded to climb the Bogr, a mountain so difficult, that every one had pronounced the attempt to be hopeless with horses so young as mine; but those horses were my only ones, and therefore I was obliged to make the trial. The road is bordered by tremendous precipices for about twelve miles; the path is so narrow, that a servant must always be sent on before to make any carts which may be descending stop in recesses hollowed out for this express purpose; and the cartmen are obliged to sound their shells repeatedly, in order to give each other timely warning. The chief danger, however, proceeds from the steepness of the road, which in some places will not permit the waggons to stop, however well their conductors may be inclined; then down they come drawn by twelve or fourteen, or sometimes sixteen oxen, sweeping every thing before them, and any carriage unlucky enough to find itself in their course must infallibly be dashed over the precipice. To-day, it really appeared as if all the estates in the island had agreed to send their produce by this particular road; the shells formed a complete chorus, and sounded incessantly during our whole passage of the mountain; and at one time there was a very numerous accumulation of carts and oxen in consequence of my carriage coming to a complete stop. As we were ascending,—"It is very well," said a gentleman who was travelling with me, (Mr. Hill) "that we did not come by this road three months sooner. I remember about that time travelling it on horseback, and an enormous tree had fallen over the path, which made me say to myself as I passed under it, 'Now, how would a chaise with a canopy get along here? The tree hangs so low that the carriage never could pass, and it would certainly have to go all the way home again.' Of course, the obstacle must now be removed; but if I remember right, this must have been the very spot.... and as I hope to live, yonder is the very tree still!"—And so it proved; although three months had elapsed, the impediment had been suffered to remain in unmolested possession of the road, and to pass my carriage under it proved an absolute impossibility. After much discussion, and many fruitless attempts, we at length succeeded in unscrewing the wheels, lifting off the body, which we carried along, and then built the curricle up again on the opposite side of the tree. However, by one means or other (after leaving a knocked-up saddle-horse at a coffee plantation, to the owner of which I was a perfect stranger, but who very obligingly offered to take charge of the animal) we found ourselves at the bottom of the mountain; but the fatal tree, and the delay occasioned by taking unavoidable shelter from tremendous storms of rain, had lost us so much time, that night surprised us when we were still eight miles distant from our destined inn. The night was dark as night could be; no moon, no stars, nor any light except the flashing of myriads of fire-flies, which, flapping in the faces of the young horses, frightened them, and made them rear. The road, too, was full of water-trenches, precipices, and deep and dangerous holes. As to the ground, it was quite invisible, and we had no means of proceeding with any chance of safety except by making some of the servants lead the horses, while others went before us to explore the way, while they cried out at every moment,—" Take care ; a little to the left, or you will slip into that water-trench—a little to the right, or you will tumble over that precipice."—Into the bargain there was neither inn nor gentleman's house within reach; and thus we proceeded crawling along at a foot's pace for five eternal miles, when we at length stopped to beg a shelter for the night at a small estate called Porous. By this time it was midnight; all the family was gone to bed; the gates were all locked;

and before we could obtain admittance a full hour elapsed, during which I sat in an open carriage, perspiration streaming down from my head to my feet through vexation, impatience and fatigue, while the night-dew fell heavy and the night-breeze blew keen; which (as I had frequently been assured) was the very best recipe possible for getting a Jamaica fever. On such I counted both for myself and my white servant, when I at length laid myself down in a bed at Porous; but to my equal surprise and satisfaction we both rose the next morning without feeling the slightest inconvenience from our risks of the preceding day, and in the evening of Friday, the 5th, I reached Miss Cole's hotel at the Spanish Town. One of my young horses, however, was so completely knocked up by the fatigue of crossing the mountain, that I could get no further than Kingston (only fourteen miles) this next day. In consequence of the delay, I was enabled to visit the Kingston theatre; the exterior is rather picturesque; within it has no particular recommendations; the scenery and dresses were shabby, the actors wretched, and the stage ill lighted; the performance was for the benefit of the chief actress, who had but little reason to be satisfied with the number of her audience; and I may reckon it among my other misfortunes on this ill-starred expedition, that it was my destiny to sit out the tragedy of " Adelgitha," whom the author meant only to be killed in the last act, but whom the actors murdered in all five. The heroine was the only one who spoke tolerably, but she was old enough and fat enough for the Widow Cheshire; Guiscard did not know ten words of his part; the tyrant was really comical enough; and Lothair was played by a young Jamaica Jew about fifteen years of age, and who is dignified here with the name of " the Creole Roscius." His voice was just breaking, which made him " pipe and whistle in the sound," his action was awkward, and altogether he was but a sorry specimen of theatrical talent: however, his *forte* is said to lie in broad farce, which perhaps may account for his being no better in tragedy. On Sunday, the 8th, I resumed my journey, but my horses were so completely knocked up, that I was obliged to hire an additional pair to convey me to Miss Hetley's inn on the other side of the Yallacks River, which is nineteen miles from Kingston. This river, as well as that of Morant (which I passed about ten miles further) both in breadth and strength sets all bridges at defiance, and in the rainy season it is sometimes impassable for several weeks. On this occasion there was but little water in either, and I arrived without difficulty at Port Morant, where I found horses sent by my trustee to convey me to Hordley. The road led up to the mountains, and was one of the steepest, roughest, and most fatiguing that I ever travelled, in spite of its pic-

turesque beauties. At length I reached my estate,
jaded and wearied to death; here I expected to
find a perfect paradise, and I found a perfect hell.
Report had assured me, that Hordley was the
best managed estate in the island, and as far as
the soil was concerned, report appeared to have
said true; but my trustee had also assured me,
that my negroes were the most contented and
best disposed, and here there was a lamentable
incorrectness in the account. I found them in a
perfect uproar; complaints of all kinds stunned
me from all quarters: all the blacks accused all
the whites, and all the whites accused all the
blacks, and as far as I could make out, both parties
were extremely in the right. There was no attachment to the soil to be found *here ;* the negroes
declared, one and all, that if I went away and left
them to groan under the same system of oppression without appeal or hope of redress, they would
follow my carriage and establish themselves at
Cornwall. I had soon discovered enough to be
certain, that although they told me plenty of
falsehoods, many of their complaints were but too
well founded; and yet how to protect them for
the future or satisfy them for the present was no
easy matter to decide. Trusting to these fallacious
reports of the Arcadian state of happiness upon
Hordley, I supposed, that I should have nothing
to do there but grant a few indulgences, and
establish the regulations already adopted with

success on Cornwall; distribute a little money, and allow a couple of play-days for dancing; and under this persuasion I had made it quite impossible for me to remain above a week at Hordley, which I conceived to be fully sufficient for the above purpose. As to grievances to be redressed, I was totally unprepared for any such necessity; yet now they poured in upon me incessantly, each more serious than the former; and before twenty-four hours were elapsed I had been assured, that in order to produce any sort of tranquillity upon the estate, I must begin by displacing the trustee, the physician, the four white book-keepers, and the four black governors, all of whom I was modestly required to remove and provide better substitutes in the space of five days and a morning. What with the general clamour, the assertions and denials, the tears and the passion, the odious falsehoods, and the still more odious truths, and (worst of all to me) my own vexation and disappointment at finding things so different from my expectations, at first nearly turned my brain; and I felt strongly tempted to set off as fast as I could, and leave all these black devils and white ones to tear one another to pieces, an amusement in which they appeared to be perfectly ready to indulge themselves. It was, however, considerable relief to me to find, upon examination, that no act of personal ill-treatment was alleged against the trustee himself, who was allowed to be sufficiently humane in his own nature, and was only complained of for allowing the negroes to be maltreated by the book-keepers, and other inferior agents, with absolute impunity. Being an excellent planter, he confined his attention entirely to the cultivation of the soil, and when the negroes came to complain of some act of cruelty or oppression committed by the book-keepers or the black governors, he refused to listen to them, and left their complaints unenquired into, and consequently unredressed. The result was, that the negroes were worse off, than if he had been a cruel man himself; for his cruelty would have given them only one tyrant, whereas his indolence left them at the mercy of eight. Still they said, that they would be well contented to have him continue their trustee, provided that I would appoint some protector, to whom they might appeal in cases of injustice and ill-usage. The trustee declaring himself well satisfied that some such appointment should take place, a neighbouring gentleman (whose humanity to his own negroes had established him in high favour with mine) was selected for this purpose. I next ordered one of the book-keepers (of the atrocious brutality of whose conduct the trustee himself upon examination allowed that there could be no doubt) to quit the estate in two hours under pain of prosecution; away went the man, and when I arose the next morning, another book-keeper had taken himself off of his own accord, and that in so much haste that he left all his clothes behind him. My next step was to displace the chief black governor, a man deservedly odious to the negroes, and whom a gross and insolent lie told to myself enabled me to punish without seeming to displace him in compliance with their complaints against him; and these sources of discontent being removed, I read to them my regulations for allowing them new holidays, additional allowances of salt-fish, rum, and sugar, with a variety of other indulgences and measures taken for protection, &c. All which, assisted by a couple of dances and distribution of money on the day of my departure had so good an effect upon their tempers, that I left them in as good humour apparently, as I found them in bad. But to leave them was no such easy matter; the weather had been bad from the moment of my commencing my journey, but from the moment of my reaching Hordley, it became abominable. The rain poured down in cataracts incessantly; the old crazy house stands on the top of a hill, and the north wind howled round it night and day, shaking it from top to bottom, and threatening to become a hurricane. The storm was provided with a very suitable accompaniment of thunder and lightning; and to complete the business, down came the mountain torrents, and swelled Plantain Garden River to such a degree, that it broke down the dam-head, stopped the mill, and all work was at a stand-still for two days and nights. But the worst of all was that this same river lay between me and Kingston; bridge there was none, and it soon became utterly impassable. Thus it continued for four days; on the fifth (the day which I had appointed for my departure, and on which I gave the negroes a parting holiday) the water appeared to be somewhat abated at a ford about four miles distant; for as to crossing at my own, that was quite out of the question for a week at least. A negro was despatched on horseback to ascertain the height of the water; his report was very unfavourable. However, as at worst I could but return, and had no better means of employing my time, I resolved to make the experiment. About forty of the youngest and strongest negroes left their dancing and drinking, and ran on foot to see me safe over the water. The few hours which had elapsed since my messenger's examination, had operated very favourably towards the reduction of the water, although it was still very high. But a servant going before to ascertain the least dangerous passage, and the negroes rushing all into the river to break the force of the stream, and support the carriage on both sides, we were enabled to struggle to the opposite bank, and were landed in safety with loud cheering from my sable attendants, who then left me, many with tears running down their cheeks, and all with thanks for the protection which

I had shown them, and earnest entreaties that I would come to visit them another time. Whether my visit will have been productive of essential service to them must remain a doubt; the trustee at least promised me most solemnly that my regulations for their happiness and security should be obeyed, and that the slave-laws (of which I had detected beyond a doubt some very flagrant violations) should be carried into effect for the future with the most scrupulous exactness. If he breaks his promise, and I discover it, I have pledged myself most solemnly to remove him, however great may be his merits as a planter; if he contrives to keep me in ignorance of his proceedings (which, however, from the precautions which I have now taken, I trust, will be no easy matter), and the state of the negroes should continue after my departure to be what it was before my arrival, then I can only console myself with thinking, that the guilt is his, not mine; and that it is on *his* head that the curse of the sufferers and the vengeance of heaven will fall, not on my own. I have been told that this estate of mine is one of the most beautiful in the island. It may be so for anything that I can tell of the matter. The badness of the weather and the disquietude of my mind during the whole of my short stay, made every thing look gloomy and hideous; and when I once found myself again beyond my own limits, I felt my spirits lighter by a hundred weight. Of all the points which had displeased me at Hordley, none had made me more angry for the time, than the lie told me by the chief governor, which occasioned my displacing him. This fellow, who for the credit of our family (no doubt) had got himself christened by the name of John Lewis, had the impudence to walk into my parlour just as I was preparing to go to bed, and inform me, that he could not get the business of the estate done. Why not? He could get nobody to come to the night-work at the mill, which he supposed was the consequence of my indulging the negroes so much. Indeed! and where were the people who ought to come to their night-work? in the negro village? No; they were in the hospital, and refused to come out to work. Upon which I blazed up like a barrel of gunpowder, and volleying out in a breath all the curses that I ever heard in my life, I asked him, whether any person really had been insolent enough to select a whole night party from the sick people in the hospital, not one of whom ought to stir out of it till well? There stood the fellow, trembling and stammering, and unable to get out an answer, while I stamped up and down the piazza, storming and swearing, banging all the doors till the house seemed ready to tumble about our ears, and doing my best to out-herod Herod, till at last I ordered the man to begone that instant, and get the work done properly. He did not wait to be told twice, and was off in a twinkling. In a quarter of an hour

I sent for him again, and enquired whether he had succeeded in getting the proper people to work at the mill? Upon which he had the assurance to answer, that all the people were there, and that it was not of their not being at the mill that he had meant to complain. Of what was it then? "Of their not being in the field." When? "Yesterday. He could not get the negroes to come to work, and so there had been none done all day." And who refused to come? " All the people." But who? "All." But who, who, who?—their names, their names, their names? " He could not remember them all." Name one—well?—speak then, speak! " There was Beck." And who else? " There was Sally, who used to be called Whanica." And who else? " There was .... there was Beck." But who else? " Beck ... and Sally" ... But who else? who else? " Little Edward had gone out of the hospital, and had not come to work." Well! Beck and Sally, and little Edward; who else? " Beck, and little Edward, and Sally." But who else: I say, who else? " He could not remember any body else." Then to be sure I was in such an imperial passion, as would have done honour to " her majesty the queen Dolallolla." Why, you most impudent of all impudent fellows that ever told a lie, have you really presumed to disturb me at this time of night, prevent my going to bed, tell me that you can't get the business done, and that none of the people would come to work, and make such a disturbance, and all because two old women and a little boy missed coming into the field yesterday! Down dropped the fellow in a moment upon his marrow bones: "Oh, me good massa," cried he (and out came the truth, which I knew well enough before he told me), "me no come of my own head; me *ordered* to come; but me never tell massa lie more, so me pray him forgib me!" But his obeying any person on my own estate in preference to me, and suffering himself to be converted into an instrument of my annoyance, was not to be easily overlooked; so I turned him out of the house with a flea in his ear as big as a camel; and the next morning degraded him to the rank of a common field negro. The trustee pleaded hard for his being permitted to return to the waggons, from whence he had been taken, and where he would be useful. But I was obdurate. Then came his wife to beg for him, and then his mother, and then his cousin, and then his cousin's cousin: still I was firm; till on the day of my departure, the new chief governor came to me in the name of the whole estate, and begged me to allow John Lewis to return to the command of the waggons, "for that all the negroes said, that it would be *too sad a thing* for them to see a man who had held the highest place among them, degraded quite to be a common field negro." There was something in this appeal which argued so good a feeling, that I did not think it right to

resist any longer; so I hinted that if the trustee
should ask it again as a favour to himself, I might
perhaps relent; and the proper application being
thus made, John Lewis was allowed to quit the
field, but with a positive injunction against his
ever being employed again in any office of authority over the negroes. I found baptism in high
vogue upon Hordley, but I am sorry to say, that
I could not discover much effect produced upon
their minds by having been made Christians, except
in one particular : whenever one of them told me a
monstrous lie (and they told me whole dozens), he
never failed to conclude his story by saying —
" And now, massa, you know, I've been christened; and if you do not believe what I say, I'm
ready to *buss the book* to the truth of it." The
whole advantages to be derived by negroes from
becoming Christians, seemed to consist with them
in two points; being a superior species of magic
itself, it preserved them from black Obeah; and
by enabling them to take an oath upon the Bible
to the truth of any lie which it might suit them
to tell, they believed that it would give them the
power of humbugging the white people with perfect ease and convenience. They had observed the
importance attached by the whites to such an attest-
ation, and the conviction which it always appeared
to carry with it ; as to the crime or penalty of per-
jury, of that they were totally ignorant, or at least
indifferent; therefore they were perfectly ready to

" buss the book," which they considered as a piece of buckra superstition, mighty useful to the negroes, and valued taking their oath upon the Bible to a lie, no more than Mrs. Mincing did the oath which she took in the Blue Garret " upon an odd volume of Messalina's Poems." Although I set out from Hordley at two o'clock, it was past seven before I reached an estate called " The Retreat," which was only twelve miles off, so abominable was the road. Here I stopped for the night, which I passed at supper with the musquitoes,— " not where I ate, but where I was eaten." Morant River had been swelled by the late heavy rains to a tremendous height, and its numerous quicksands render the passage in such a state extremely dangerous. However, a negro having been sent early to explore it, and having returned with a favourable report, we proceeded to encounter it. A Hordley negro, well acquainted with these perilous rivers, had accompanied me for the express purpose of pointing out the most practicable fords; but for some time his efforts to find a safe one were unavailing, his horse at the end of a minute or two plunging into a quicksand or some deep hole, among the waters thrown up from which he totally disappeared for a moment, and then was seen to struggle out again with such an effort and leap, as were quite beyond the capability of any carriage's attempting. However, at the end of half an hour he was fortunate to find a place, where he could cross (up to his horse's belly in the water, to be sure), but at least without tumbling into holes and quicksands; and here we set out, conscious that our whole chance of reaching the opposite shore consisted in keeping precisely the path which he had gone already, and determined to stick as close as possible to his horse's tail.   But no sooner were we fairly in the water, than my young horses found themselves unable to resist the strength and rapidity of the torrent, which was rolling down huge stones as big as rocks from the mountain; and to my utter consternation, I perceived the curricle carried down the stream, and the distance from my guide (who, by swimming his horse. had reached the destined landing-place in safety) growing wider and wider with every moment.   We were now driving at all hazards; every moment I expected to see a horse or a wheel sink down into some deep hole, the chaise overturned, and ourselves either swal- lowed up in a quicksand, or dashed to pieces against the stones, which were rolling around us. I never remember to have felt myself so com- pletely convinced of approaching destruction, and I roared out with all my might and main :—" We are carried away! all is over!" although, to be sure, I might as well have held my tongue, seeing that all my roaring could not do the least possible good.   However, my horses, although too weak to resist the current, were fortunately strong enough to keep their legs; while they drifted down the stream, they struggled along in an oblique direction, which gradually (though but slowly) brought us nearer to the opposite shore; and after several minutes passed in most painful anxiety, a desperate plunge out of the water enabled them to *jump* the carriage upon terra firma on the same side with my guide, although at a considerable distance from the spot where he had landed. The Yallack's River was less dangerous; but even this too had been sufficiently swelled to make the crossing it no easy matter; so that what with one obstacle and another, when I reached Kingston at six o'clock with my bones and my vehicle unbroken, I was almost as much surprised as satisfied. I dined with the curate of Kingston (Rev. G. Hill), where I met the admiral upon this station, Sir Home Popham, and a large party. At Kingston I was obliged to send back a horse, which had been lent me in aid of my own; another had been dropped at " the Retreat;" a third could get no farther than the mountains; and my companion's three horses had found themselves unable even to reach Spanish Town, and I had thus been obliged to leave them and theirs behind upon the road. On the morning of our departure from Cornwall, when my Italian servant saw the quantity of horses, mules, servants, and carriages collected for the journey, he clapped his hands together in exultation, and exclaimed,—" They will certainly take us for the king of England!" But now when after leaving one horse in one place and another horse in another, on the morning of Monday the 16th, he beheld my whole caravan reduced to one pair of chaise horses and a couple of miserable mules, he cast a rueful look upon my diminished cavalry and sighed to himself,—" I verily believe, we shall return home on foot after all!" I reached Spanish Town in time to dine with the chief justice (Mr. Jackson), and intended to remain two or three days longer; but the fatality, which had persecuted me from the very commencement of this abominable journey, was not exhausted yet. On Tuesday morning, my landlady just hinted, that " she thought it right to let me know, that to be sure there *was* a gentleman unwell in the house; but she supposed, that I should not care about it: however, if I particularly disliked the neighbourhood of a sick person, she would procure me lodgings." I asked, " What was the complaint?" " Oh! he was a little sick, that was all." To which I only could answer, that, " in that case I hoped he would get better;" and thought no more about it. However, when I went to visit the governor, I found, that this " little sickness" of my landlady's was neither more nor less than the yellow fever; of which the gentleman in question was now dying, of which a lady had died only two days before, and of which another European, newly arrived, had fallen ill in this very same hotel only a fortnight before, and had died, after throwing himself out of an upper window in a fit of delirium. Under all these circumstances, I thought it to the full as prudent not to prolong my residence in Spanish Town; and accordingly, on Wednesday the 18th, I resumed my journey homewards. I travelled the north side of the island, which was the road used by me on my return two years ago. I have nothing to add to my former account of it, except that there need not be better inns anywhere than the Wellington hotel at Rio Bueno, and Judy James's at Montego Bay, which latter is now, in my opinion, by far the prettiest town in Jamaica. Indeed, all the inns upon this road are excellent, with the solitary exception of the Blackheath Tavern, which I stopped at by a mistake instead of that of Montague. At this most miserable of all inns that ever entrapped an unwary traveller, there was literally nothing to be procured for love or money : no corn for the horses; no wine without sending six miles for a bottle; no food but a miserable starved fowl, so tough that the very negroes could not eat it; and a couple of eggs, one of which was addled: there was but one pair of sheets in the whole house, and neither candles, nor oranges, nor pepper, nor vinegar, nor bread, nor even so much as sugar, white or brown. Yams there were, which prevented my servants from going to bed quite empty, and I contented myself with the far-fetched bottle of wine and the solitary egg, which I eat by the light of a lamp filled with stinking oil. The one pair of sheets I seized upon to my own share, and my servants made themselves as good beds as they could upon the floor with great coats and travelling mantles. It was on Wednesday night, that after the fatigue of crossing Mount Diablo, "myself I unfatigued" in this delectable retreat, which seemed to have been established upon principles diametrically opposite to those of Shenstone's. On Thursday I slept at Rio Bueno, on Friday at Montego Bay, passed Saturday at Anchovy estate (Mr. Plummer's), and was very glad, on Sunday the 22d, to find myself once more quietly established at Cornwall, fully determined to leave it no more, till I leave it on my return to England. The lady, who had died so lately at Kingston, had arrived not long before in a vessel, both the crew and passengers of which landed (to all appearance) in perfect health after a favourable passage from England. Of course, they soon dispersed in different directions; yet almost all of them were attacked nearly at the same period by the fever, which seemed to have a particular commission to search out such persons as had arrived by that particular ship, at however remote a distance they might be from each other.

## March 29. (Sunday.)

This morning (without either fault or accident) a young, strong, healthy woman miscarried of an eight months' child; and this is the third time that she has met with a similar misfortune. No other symptom of child-bearing has been given in the course of this year, nor are there above eight women upon the breeding list out of more than one hundred and fifty females. Yet they are all well clothed and well fed, contented in mind, even by their own account, over-worked at no time, and when upon the breeding list are exempted from labour of every kind. In spite of all this, and their being treated with all possible care and indulgence, rewarded for bringing children, and therefore anxious themselves to have them, how they manage it so ill I know not, but somehow or other certainly the children do not come.

## MARCH 31.

During the whole three weeks of my absence, only two negroes have been complained of for committing fault. The first was a domestic quarrel between two Africans; Hazard stole Frank's calabash of sugar, which Frank had previously stolen out of my boiling-house. So Frank broke Hazard's head, which in my opinion settled the matter so properly, that I declined spoiling it by any interference of my own. The other complaint was more serious. Toby, being ordered to load the cart with canes, answered "I wo'nt"—and Toby was as good as his word; in consequence of which the mill stopped for want of canes, and the boiling-house stopped for want of liquor. I found on my return that for this offence Toby had received six lashes, which Toby did not mind three straws. But as his fault amounted to an act of downright rebellion, I thought that it ought not by any means to be passed over so lightly, and that Toby ought to be *made* to mind. I took no notice for some days; but the Easter holidays had been deferred till my return, and only began here on Friday last. On that day, as soon as the head governor had blown the shell, and dismissed the negroes till Monday morning, he requested the pleasure of Mr. Toby's company to the hospital, where he locked him up in a room by himself. All Saturday and Sunday the estate rang with laughing, dancing, singing, and huzzaing. Salt-fish was given away in the morning; the children played at ninepins for jackets and petticoats in the evening; rum and sugar was denied to no one. The gumbys thundered; the kitty-katties clattered; all was noise and festivity; and all this while, " qualis mœrens Philomela," sat solitary Toby gazing at his four white walls! Toby had not minded the lashes; but the loss of his amusement, and the disgrace of his exclusion from the fête operated on his mind so forcibly, that when on the Monday morning his door was unlocked, and the chief governor called him to his work, not a word would he deign to utter; let who would speak, there he sat motionless, silent, and sulky. However, upon my going down to him myself, his voice thought proper to return, and he began at once to complain of his seclusion and justify his conduct. But he no sooner opened his lips than the whole hospital opened theirs to censure his folly, asking him how he could presume to justify himself when he knew that he had done wrong? and advising him to humble himself and beg my pardon; and their clamours were so loud and so general (Mrs. Sappho, his wife, being one of the loudest, who not only "gave it him on both sides of his ears," but enforced her arguments by a knock on the pate now and then), that they fairly drove the evil spirit out of him; he confessed his fault with great penitence, engaged solemnly never to commit such another, and set off to his work full of gratitude for my granting him forgiveness. I am more and more convinced every day, that the best and easiest mode of governing negroes (and governed by some mode or other they must be) is not by the detestable lash, but by confinement, solitary or otherwise; they cannot bear it, and the memory of it seems to make a lasting impression upon their minds; while the lash makes none but upon their skins, and lasts no longer than the mark. The order at my hospital is, that no negro should be denied admittance; even if no symptoms of illness appear, he is allowed one day to rest, and take physic, if he choose it. On the second morning, if the physician declares the man to be shamming, and 'the plea of illness is still alleged against going to work, then the negro is locked up in a room with others similarly circumstanced, where care is taken to supply him with food, water, physic, &c., and no restraint is imposed except that of not going out. Here he is suffered to remain unmolested as long as he pleases, and he is only allowed to leave the hospital upon his own declaration that he is well enough to go to work; when the door is opened, and he walks away unreproached and unpunished, however evident his deception may have been. Before I adopted this regulation, the number of patients used to vary from thirty to forty-five, not more than a dozen of whom perhaps had anything the matter with them: the number at this moment is but fourteen, and all are sores, burns, or complaints the reality of which speaks for itself. Some few persevering tricksters will still submit to be locked up for a day or two; but their patience never fails to be wearied out by the fourth morning, and I have not yet met with an instance of a patient who had once been locked up with a fictitious illness, returning to the hospital except with a real one. In general, they offer to take a day's rest and physic, promising to go out to work the next day, and on these occasions they have uniformly kept their word. Indeed, my hospital is now in such good order, that the physician told the trustee the other day that " mine gave him less trouble than any hospital in the parish."

My boilers, too, who used to make sugar the colour of mahogany, are now making excellent; and certainly, if appearances may be trusted, and things will but last, I may flatter myself with the complete success of my system of management, as far as the time elapsed is sufficient to warrant an opinion. I only wish from my soul that I were but half as certain of the good treatment and good behaviour of the negroes at Hordley.

## April 1. (Wednesday.)

Jug-Betty having had two leathern purses full of silver coin stolen out of her trunk, her cousin Punch told her to have patience till Sunday, and he thought that by that time he should be able to find it for her. Upon which she very naturally suspected her cousin Punch of having stolen the money himself, and brought him to-day to make her charge against him. However, he stuck firmly to a denial, and as several days had been suffered to elapse since the theft, there could be no doubt of his having concealed the money, and therefore no utility in searching his person or his house. I found great fault with the persons in authority for not having taken such a measure without a moment's delay; but the trustee informed me that it frequently produced very serious consequences, many instances having occurred of the disgrace of their house being searched having offended negroes so much to the heart, as to occasion their committing

c c

suicide: so that it was a proceeding which was seldom ventured upon without urgent necessity. It was now too late to take it, at all events; the man confessed, indeed, that he had quitted his work, and gone down to the negro-village on the day of the robbery, which rendered his guilt highly probable, but he could be brought to confess no more; and as to his saying that he thought he could find the money by Sunday, he explained *that* into an intention of "going to consult a brown woman at the bay, who was a fortune-teller, and who when any thing was stolen, could always point out the thief by *cutting the cards.*" This was all that we could extract from him, and we were obliged to dismiss him. However, the fright of his examination was not without good consequences: one of the stolen purses had belonged to a sister of Jug-Betty's, not long deceased; and on her return home, *this* purse (with its contents untouched) was found lying on the sister's grave in her garden. Perhaps, the thief had taken it without knowing the owner; and on finding that it had belonged to a dead person, he had surrendered it through apprehension of being haunted by her *duppy*.

### April 5. (Sunday.)

Clearing their grounds by fire is a very expeditious proceeding, consequently in much practice among the negroes; but in this tindery country it is extremely dangerous, and forbidden by the law. As I returned home to-day from church, I observed a large smoke at no great distance, and Cubina told me, he supposed that the negroes of the neighbouring estate of Amity were clearing their grounds. " Then they are doing a very wrong thing," said I ; " I hope they will fire nothing else but their grounds, for with so strong a breeze a great deal of mischief might be done." However, in half an hour it proved that the smoke in question arose from my own negro-grounds, that the fire had spread itself, and I could see from my window the flames and smoke pouring themselves upwards in large volumes, while the crackling of the dry bushes and brush-wood was something perfectly terrific. The alarm was instantly given, and whites and blacks all hurried to the scene of action. Luckily, the breeze set the contrary way from the plantations; a morass interposed itself between the blazing ground and one of my best cane-pieces: the flames were suffered to burn till they reached the brink of the water, and then the negroes managed to extinguish them without much difficulty. Thus we escaped without injury, but I own I was heartily frightened.

### April 8.

This morning I was awaked by a violent coughing in the hospital; and as soon as I heard any of the servants moving, I despatched a negro to ask,

" whether any body was bad in the hospital ?" He returned and told me, "No, massá; nobody bad there; for Alick is better, and Nelson is dead." Nelson was one of my best labourers, and had come into the hospital for a glandular swelling. Early this morning he was seized with a violent fit of coughing, burst a large artery, and was immediately suffocated in his blood! This is the sixth death in the course of the first three months of the year, and we have not as yet a single birth for a set-off. Say what one will to the negroes, and treat them as well as one can, obstinate devils, they will die!

APRIL 9.

I had mentioned to Mr. Shand my having found a woman at Hordley, who had been crippled for life, in consequence of her having been kicked in the womb by one of the book-keepers. He writes to me on this subject: — " I trust that conduct so savage occurs rarely in *any* country. I can only say, that in my long experience nothing of the kind has ever fallen under my observation." Mr. S. then ought to consider *me* as having been in high luck. I have not passed six months in Jamaica, and I have already found on one of my estates a woman who had been kicked in the womb by a white book-keeper, by which she was crippled herself, and on another of my estates another woman who had been kicked in the womb by another white book-keeper, by which he had crippled the child. The name of the first man and woman were Lory and Jeannette; those of the second were Fullwood and Martia: and thus, as my two estates are at the two extremities of the island, I am entitled to say, from my own knowledge (*i.e.* speaking *literally*, observe), that " white book-keepers kick black women in the belly *from one end of Jamaica to the other.*"

APRIL 15. (Wednesday.)

About noon to-day a well-disposed healthy lad of seventeen years of age was employed in unhaltering the first pair of oxen of one of the waggons, in doing which he entangled his right leg in the rope. At that moment the oxen set off full gallop, and dragged the boy along with them round the whole inclosure, before the other negroes could succeed in stopping them. However, when the prisoner was extricated, although his flesh appeared to have been terribly lacerated, no bones were broken, and he was even able to walk to the hospital without support. He was blooded instantly, and two physicians were sent for by express. At two o'clock he was still in perfect possession of his senses, and only complained of the soreness of his wounds: but in half an hour after he became apoplectic; sank into a state of utter insensibility, during which a dreadful rattling in his throat was the only sign of still existing life, and before six in the evening all was over with him!

### April 17.

Pickle had accused his brother-in-law, Edward the Eboe, of having given him a pleurisy by the practice of Obeah. During my last visit I had convinced him that the charge was unjust (or at least he had declared himself to be convinced), and about six weeks ago they came together to assure me, that ever since they had lived upon the best terms possible. Unluckily, Pickle's wife miscarried lately, and for the third time; previously to which Edward had said, that his wife would remain sole heiress of the father's property. This was enough to set the suspicious brains of these foolish people at work; and to-day Pickle and his father-in-law, old Damon, came to assure me, that in order to prevent a child coming to claim its share of the grandfather's property, Edward had practised Obeah to make his sister-in-law miscarry; the only proof of which adduced was the above expression, and the woman's having miscarried "just according to Edward's very words!" To reason with such very absurd persons was out of the case. I found too, that the two sisters were quarrelling perpetually, and always on the point of tearing each other's eyes out. Therefore, as domestic peace " in a house so disunited" was out of the question, I ordered the two families to separate instantly, and to live at the two extremities of the negro village; at the same time forbidding all intercourse between them whatsoever: a plan, which was received with approbation by all parties; and Edward moved his property out of the old man's house into another without loss of time. Among other charges of Obeah, Pickle declared, that his house having been robbed, Edward had told him that Nato was the offender; and in order to prove it beyond the power of doubt, he had made him look at something round, " just like massa's watch," out of which he had taken a sentee (a something) which looked like an egg; this he gave to Pickle, at the same time instructing him to throw it at night against the door of Nato's house; which he had no sooner done and broken the egg, than the very next day Nato's wife Philippa " began to bawl, and halloo, and went mad."   Now that Philippa had bawled and hallooed enough was certainly true; but it was also true that she had confessed her madness to have been a trick for the purpose of exciting my compassion, and inducing me to feed her from my own table.   Yet was this simple fellow persuaded that he had made her go mad by the help of his broken egg, and his old fool of a father-in-law was goose enough to encourage him in the persuasion.

### April 19. (Sunday.)

" And massa," said Bridget, the doctoress, this morning, " my old mother a lilly *so-so* to-day; and him tank massa much for the good supper massa

send last night; and him like it so well.—Laud!
massa, the old lady was just thinking what him
could yam (eat) and him no fancy nothing; and
him could no yam salt, and him just wishing for
something fresh, when at that very moment Cubina come to him from massa with a stewed pig's
head so fresh: it seemed just as if massa had got
it from the Almighty's hands himself."

## APRIL 22.

Naturalists and physicians, philosophers and
philanthropists, may argue and decide as they
please; but certainly, as far as mere observation
admits of my judging, there does seem to be a very
great difference between the brain of a black
person and a white one. I should think that
Voltaire would call a negro's reason "une raison
très particulière." Somehow or other, they never
can manage to do anything *quite* as it should be
done. If they correct themselves in one respect
to-day they are sure of making a blunder in some
other manner to-morrow. Cubina is now twenty-
five, and has all his life been employed about the
stable; he goes out with my carriage twice every
day; yet he has never yet been able to succeed in
putting on the harness properly. Before we get to
one of the plantation gates we are certain of being
obliged to stop, and put something or other to
rights: and I once remember having laboured for
more than half an hour to make him understand

that the Christmas holidays came at Christmas; when asked the question, he always hesitated, and answered, at hap-hazard, "July," or " October." Yet, Cubina is far superior in intellect to most of the negroes who have fallen under my observation. The girl too, whose business it is to open the house each morning, has in vain been desired to unclose all the jalousies : she never fails to leave three or four closed, and when she is scolded for doing so, she takes care to open those three the next morning, and leaves three shut on the opposite side. Indeed, the attempt to make them correct a fault is quite fruitless : they never can do the same thing a second time in the same manner; and if the cook having succeeded in dressing a dish well is desired to dress just such another, she is certain of doing something which makes it quite different. One day I desired, that there might be always a piece of salt meat at dinner, in order that I might be certain of always having enough to send to the sick in the hospital. In consequence, there was nothing at dinner but salt meat. I complained that there was not a single fresh dish, and the next day, there was nothing but fresh. Sometimes there is scarcely anything served up, and the cook seems to have forgotten the dinner altogether : she is told of it ; and the next day she slaughters without mercy pigs, sheep, fowls, ducks, turkeys, and everything that she can lay her murderous hands upon, till the table absolutely groans under the

load of her labours. For above a month Cubina
and I had perpetual quarrels about the cats being
shut into the gallery at nights, where they threw
down plates, glasses, and crockery of all kinds,
and made such a clatter that to get a wink of sleep
was quite out of the question. Cubina, before he
went to rest, hunted under all the beds and sofas,
and laid about him with a long whip for half an
hour together; but in half an hour after his
departure the cats were at work again. He was
then told, that although he had turned them out,
he must certainly have left some window open:
he promised to pay particular attention to this
point, but that night the uproar was worse than
ever; yet he protested that he had carefully
turned out all the cats, locked all the doors, and
shut all the windows. He was told, that if he had
really turned out all the cats, the cats must have
got in again, and therefore that he must have left
some one window open at least. " No," he said,
" he had not left one; but a pane in one of the
windows had been broken two months before, and
it was there that the cats got in whenever they
pleased." Yet he had continued to turn the cats
out of the door with the greatest care, although he
was perfectly conscious that they could always
walk in again at the window in five minutes after.
But the most curious of Cubina's modes of proceeding is, when it is necessary for him to attack
the pigeon-house. He steals up the ladder as slily

and as softly as foot can fall; he opens the door, and steals in his head with the utmost caution; on which, to his never-failing surprise and disappointment, all the pigeons make their escape through the open holes; he has now no resource but entering the dove-cot, and remaining there with unwearied patience for the accidental return of the birds, which nine times out of ten does not take place till too late for dinner, and Cubina returns empty-handed. Having observed this proceeding constantly repeated during a fortnight, I took pity upon his embarrassment, and ordered two wooden sliders to be fitted to the holes. Cubina was delighted with this exquisite invention, and failed not the next morning to close all the holes on the right with one of the sliders; he then stepped boldly into the dove-cot, when to his utter confusion the pigeons flew away through the holes on the left. Here then he discovered where the fault lay, so he lost no time in closing the remaining aperture with the second slider, and the pigeons were thus prevented from returning at all. Cubina waited long with exemplary patience, but without success, so he abandoned the new invention in despair, made no farther use of the sliders, and continues to steal up the ladder as he did before. A few days ago, Nicholas, a mulatto carpenter, was ordered to make a box for the conveyance of four jars of sweetmeats, of which he took previous measure; yet first he made a box so small that it would scarcely hold a single jar, and then another so large that it would have held twenty; and when at length he produced one of a proper size, he brought it nailed up for travelling (although it was completely empty), and nailed up so effectually too, that on being directed to open it that the jars might be packed, he split the cover to pieces in the attempt to take it off. Yet, among all my negroes, Nicholas and Cubina are not equalled for adroitness and intelligence by more than twenty. Judge then what must be the remaining three hundred!

APRIL 23.

In my medical capacity, like a true quack I sometimes perform cures so unexpected, that I stand like Katterfelto, "with my hair standing on end at my own wonders." Last night, Alexander, the second governor, who has been seriously ill for some days, sent me word, that he was suffering cruelly from a pain in his head, and could get no sleep. I knew not how to relieve him; but having frequently observed a violent passion for perfumes in the house negroes, for want of something else I gave the doctoress some oil of lavender, and told her to rub two or three drops upon his nostrils. This morning, he told me that "to be sure what I had sent him was a grand medicine indeed," for it had no sooner touched his nose than he felt something cold run up to his forehead, over his head, and all the way down his neck, to the back-bone; instantly, the headach left him, he fell fast asleep, nor had the pain returned in the morning. But I am afraid, that even this wonderful oil would fail of curing a complaint which was made to me a few days ago. A poor old creature, named Quasheba, made her appearance at my breakfast table, and told me, "that she was almost eighty, had been rather weakly for some time past, and somehow she did not feel as she was by any means right." "Had she seen the doctor? Did she want physic?" "No, she had taken too much physic already, and the doctor would do her no good; she did not want to see the doctor." "But what then was her complaint?" "Oh! she had no particular complaint; only she was old and weakly, and did not find herself by any means so well as she used to be, and so she came just to tell massa, and see what he could do to make her quite right again, that was all." In short, she *only* wanted me to make her young again!

### APRIL 24.

Mr. Forbes is dead. When I was last in Jamaica, he had just been poisoned with corrosive sublimate by a female slave, who was executed in consequence. He never was well afterwards; but as he lived intemperately, the whole blame of his death must not be laid upon the poison.

## April 30.

A free mulatto of the name of Rolph had frequently been mentioned to me by different magistrates, as remarkable for the numerous complaints
brought against him for cruel treatment of his
negroes. He was described to me as the son of a
white ploughman, who at his death left his son six
or seven slaves, with whom he resides in the heart
of the mountains, where the remoteness of the
situation secures him from observation or control.
His slaves, indeed, every now and then contrive
to escape, and come down to Savannah la Mar to
lodge their complaints; but the magistrates, hitherto, had never been able to get a legal hold upon
him. However, a few days ago, he entered the
house of a Mrs. Edgins, when she was from home,
and behaving in an outrageous manner to her
slaves, he was desired by the head-man to go
away. Highly incensed, he answered, " that if
the fellow dared to speak another word, it should
be the last that he should ever utter." The negro
dared to make a rejoinder; upon which Rolph
aimed a blow at him with a stick, which missed
his intended victim, but struck another slave who
was interposing to prevent a scuffle, and killed him
upon the spot. The murder was committed in
the presence of several negroes; but negroes are
not allowed to give evidence, and as no free person was present, there are not only doubts whether

the murderer will be punished, but whether he can even be put upon his trial.

## MAY 1. (Friday.)

This morning I signed the manumission of Nicholas Cameron, the best of my mulatto carpenters. He had been so often on the very point of getting his liberty, and still the cup was dashed from his lips, that I had promised to set him free, whenever he could procure an able negro as his substitute; although being a good workman, a single negro was by no means an adequate price in exchange. On my arrival this year I found that he had agreed to pay 150*l.* for a female negro, and the woman was approved of by my trustee. But on enquiry it appeared that she had a child, from which she was unwilling to separate, and that her owner refused to sell the child, except at a most unreasonable price. Here then was an insurmountable objection to my accepting her, and Nicholas was told to his great mortification, that he must look out for another substitute. The woman, on her part, was determined to belong to Cornwall estate and no other: so she told her owner, that if he attempted to sell her elsewhere she would make away with herself, and on his ordering her to prepare for a removal to a neighbouring proprietor's, she disappeared, and concealed herself so well, that for some time she was believed to have put her threats of suicide into execution. The idea of losing his 150*l.* frightened

her master so completely, that he declared himself
ready to let me have the child at a fair price, as
well as the mother, if she ever should be found;
and her friends having conveyed this assurance to
her, she thought proper to emerge from her hiding-place, and the bargain was arranged finally.
The titles, however, were not yet made out, and
as the time of my departure for Hordley was
arrived, these were ordered to be got ready against
my return, when the negroes were to be delivered
over to me, and Nicholas was to be set free. In
the meanwhile, the child was sent by her mistress
(a free mulatto) to hide some stolen ducks upon a
distant property, and on her return blabbed out
the errand: in consequence the mistress was committed to prison for theft; and no sooner was she
released, than she revenged herself upon the poor
girl by giving her thirty lashes with the cattle-
whip, inflicted with all the severity of vindictive
malice. This treatment of a child of such tender
years reduced her to such a state, as made the
magistrates think it right to send her for protection
to the workhouse, until the conduct of the mistress
should have been enquired into. In the meanwhile, as the result of the enquiry might be the
setting the girl at liberty, the joint title for her
and her mother could not be made out, and thus
poor Nicholas's manumission was at a stand-still
again. The magistrates at length decided, that
although the chastisement had been severe, yet

(according to the medical report) it was not such as to authorise the sending the mistress to be tried at the assizes. She was accordingly dismissed from farther investigation, and the girl was once more considered as belonging to me, as soon as the title could be made out. But the fatality which had so often prevented Nicholas from obtaining his freedom, was not weary yet. On the very morning, when he was to sign the title, a person whose signature was indispensable, was thrown out of his chaise, the wheel of which passed over his head, and he was rendered incapable of transacting business for several weeks. Yesterday, the titles were at length brought to me complete, and this morning put Nicholas in possession of the object, in the pursuit of which he has experienced such repeated disappointments. The conduct of the poor child's mulatto mistress in this case was most unpardonable, and is only one of numerous instances of a similar description, which have been mentioned to me. Indeed, I have every reason to believe, that nothing can be uniformly more wretched, than the life of the slaves of free people of colour in Jamaica; nor would any thing contribute more to the relief of the black population, than the prohibiting by law any mulatto to become the owner of a slave for the future. Why should not rich people of colour be served by poor people of colour, hiring them as domestics? It seldom happens that mulattoes are in possession of plantations; but when a white man dies, who happens to possess twenty negroes, he will divide them among his brown family, leaving (we may say) five to each of his four children. These are too few to be employed in plantation work; they are, therefore, ordered to maintain their owner by some means or other, and which means are frequently not the most honest, the most frequent being the travelling about as higglers, and exchanging the trumpery contents of their packs and boxes with plantation negroes for stolen rum and sugar. I confess I cannot see why, on such bequest being made, the law should not order the negroes to be sold, and the produce of the sale paid to the mulatto heirs, but absolutely prohibiting the mulattoes from becoming proprietors of the negroes themselves. Every man of humanity must wish that slavery, even in its best and most mitigated form, had never found a legal sanction, and must regret that its system is now so incorporated with the welfare of Great Britain as well as of Jamaica, as to make its extirpation an absolute impossibility, without the certainty of producing worse mischiefs than the one which we annihilate. But certainly there can be no sort of occasion for continuing in the colonies the existence of *domestic slavery*, which neither contributes to the security of the colonies themselves, nor to the opulence of the mother-country, the revenue of which derived from colonial duties would suffer no defalcation whatever, even if neither whites nor blacks in the West Indies were suffered to employ slaves, except in plantation labour.

## MAY 2.

I gave my negroes a farewell holiday, on which occasion each grown person received a present of half-a-dollar, and every child a maccaroni. In return, they endeavoured to express their sorrow for my departure, by eating and drinking, dancing and singing, with more vehemence and perseverance than on any former occasion. As in all probability many years will elapse without my making them another visit, if indeed I should ever return at all, I have at least exerted myself while here to do everything which appeared likely to contribute to their welfare and security during my absence. In particular, my attorney has made out a list of all such offences as are most usually committed on plantations, to which proportionate punishments have been affixed by myself. From this code of internal regulations the overseer is not to be allowed to deviate, and the attorney has pledged himself in the most solemn manner to adhere strictly to the system laid down for him. By this scheme, the negroes will no longer be punished according to the momentary caprice of their superintendent, but by known and fixed laws, the one no more than the other, and without respect to partiality or prejudice. Hitherto, in everything which had not been previously determined by the public law, with a penalty attached to the breach of it, the negro has been left entirely at the mercy of the overseer, who if he was a humane man punished him slightly, and if a tyrant, heavily; nay, very often the quantity of punishment depended upon the time of day when the offence was made known. If accused in the morning, when the overseer was in cold blood and in good humour, a night's confinement in the stocks might be deemed sufficient; whereas if the charge was brought when the superior had taken his full proportion of grog or sangaree, the very same offence would be visited with thirty-nine lashes. I have, moreover, taken care to settle all disputes respecting property, having caused all negroes having claims upon others to bring them before my tribunal previous to my departure, and determined that from that time forth no such claims should be enquired into, but considered as definitively settled by my authority. It would have done the Lord Chancellor's heart good to see how many suits I determined in the course of a week, and with what expedition I made a clear court of chancery. But perhaps the most astonishing part of the whole business was, that after judgment was pronounced, the losers as well as the gainers declared themselves perfectly satisfied with the justice of the sentence. I must acknowledge, however, that the negro principle that "massa can do no wrong," was of some little assistance to me on this occasion. " Oh! quite just, me good, massa! what massa say, quite just! me no say nothing more; me good, massa!" Then they thanked me "for massa's goodness in giving them so long talk!" and went away to tell all the others "how just massa had been in taking away what they wanted to keep, or not giving them what they asked for." It must be owned that this is not the usual mode of proceeding after the loss of a chancery suit in England. But to do the negroes mere justice, I must say, that I could not have wished to find a more tractable set of people on almost every occasion. Some lazy and obstinate persons, of course, there must inevitably be in so great a number; but in general I found them excellently disposed, and being once thoroughly convinced of my real good-will towards them, they were willing to take it for granted, that my regulations must be right and beneficial, even in cases where they were in opposition to individual interests and popular prejudices. My attorney had mentioned to me several points, which he thought it advisable to have altered, but which he had vainly endeavoured to accomplish. Thus the negroes were in the practice of bequeathing their houses and grounds, by which means some of them were become owners of several houses and numerous gardens in the village, while others with large families were either inadequately provided for, or not provided for at all. I made it public, that from henceforth no negro should possess more than one house, with a sufficient portion of ground for his family, and on the following Sunday the over-seer by my order looked over the village, took from those who had too much to give to those who had too little, and made an entire new distribution according to the most strict Agrarian law. Those who lost by this measure, came the next day to complain to me; when I avowed its having been done by my order, and explained the propriety of the proceeding; after which they declared them-selves contented, and I never heard another mur-mur on the subject. Again, mothers being allowed certain indulgences while suckling, persist in it for two years and upwards, to the great detri-ment both of themselves and their children: com-plaint of this being made to me, I sent for the mothers, and told them that every child must be sent to the weaning-house on the first day of the fifteenth month, but that their indulgences should be continued to the mothers for two months longer, although the children would be no longer with them. All who had children of that age immediately gave them up; the rest promised to do so, when they should be old enough; and they all thanked me for the continuance of their indulgences, which they considered as a boon newly granted them. On my return from Hordley, I was told that the negroes suffered their pigs to infest the works and grounds in the immediate vicinity of the house in such numbers, that they were become a perfect nuisance; nor could any remonstrance prevail on them to confine the animals within the village. An order was in consequence issued on a Saturday, that the first four pigs found rambling at large after two days should be put to death without mercy; and accordingly on Monday morning, at the negro breakfast hour, the head governor made his appearance before the house, armed cap-a-pee, with a lance in his hand, and an enormous cutlass by his side. The news of this tremendous apparition spread through the estate like wildfire. Instantly all was in an uproar; the negroes came pouring down from all quarters; in an instant the whole air was rent with noises of all kinds and creatures; men, women, and children shouting and bellowing, geese cackling, dogs barking, turkeys gobbling; and, look where you would, there was a negro running along as fast as he could, and dragging a pig along with him by one of the hind legs, while the pigs were all astonishment at this sudden attack, and called upon heaven and earth for commiseration and protection, —

" With many a doleful grunt and piteous squeak,
　Poor pigs! as if their pretty hearts would break!"

From thenceforth not a pig except my own was to be seen about the place; yet instead of complaining of this restraint, several of the negroes came to assure me, that I might depend on the animals not being suffered to stray beyond the village for the future, and to thank me for having given them the warning two days before. What other negroes may be, I will not pretend to guess; but I am certain that there cannot be more tractable or better disposed persons (take them for all in all) than my negroes of Cornwall. I only wish, that in my future dealings with white persons, whether *in* Jamaica or out of it, I could but meet with half so much gratitude, affection, and good-will.

THE END.

LONDON:
Printed by A. SPOTTISWOODE,
New-Street-Square.

CPSIA information can be obtained at www.ICGtesting.com
Printed in the USA
BVOW06s0122050813

327732BV00004B/55/P